Culture, Political Economy and Civilisation in a Multipolar World Order

This book demonstrates how Russia's multifaceted rejection of American unipolarity and de-territorialised neo-liberal capitalism has contributed to the gestation of the present multipolar moment in the global political economy. Analysing Western world order precepts via the actions of a powerful, albeit precarious, national political economy and state structure situated on the periphery of Western world order, Silvius explores the manner in which culture and ideas are mobilised for the purposes of national, regional and international political and economic projects in a post-global age.

The book:

- Explains and analyses the tensions of post-Soviet Russia's integration into, and simultaneous partial rejection of, the capitalist global political economy.
- Provides an overview of the social, political and historical origins of Russian *samobytnost'* (uniqueness) after the fall of the Soviet Union and demonstrates their significance to contemporary understandings of world order.
- Explores how structures of cultural difference and practices of cultural differentiation interact with the normative legacies of American hegemonic aspirations in contemporary world order structures.
- Evaluates how cultural and civilisational representations are mobilised for state-projects and their corresponding regional and international dimensions within the global political economy.

This book will be of great interest to students and scholars of Russian Foreign Policy, IPE and comparative political economy.

Ray Silvius is an Assistant Professor in the Department of Political Science at the University of Winnipeg, Canada. He writes on international political economy, Russia, the emerging multipolar world order, and the political economy of refugees.

RIPE Series in Global Political Economy

Series Editors: James Brassett (University of Warwick, UK), Eleni Tsingou (*Copenhagen Business School, Denmark*), Susanne Soederberg (*Queen's University, Canada*) and Jacqueline Best (*University of Ottawa, Canada*)

The RIPE Series published by Routledge is an essential forum for cutting-edge scholarship in International Political Economy. The series brings together new and established scholars working in critical, cultural and constructivist political economy. Books in the RIPE Series typically combine an innovative contribution to theoretical debates with rigorous empirical analysis.

The RIPE Series seeks to cultivate:

- Field-defining theoretical advances in International Political Economy.
- Novel treatments of key issue areas, both historical and contemporary, such as global finance, trade, and production.
- Analyses that explore the political economic dimensions of relatively neglected topics, such as the environment, gender relations, and migration.
- Accessible work that will inspire advanced undergraduates and graduate students in International Political Economy.

The *RIPE Series in Global Political Economy* aims to address the needs of students and teachers. Titles include:

Asymmetric Crisis in Europe and Possible Futures
Critical political economy and post-Keynesian perspectives
Edited by Johannes Jäger and Elisabeth Springler

Hybrid Rule and State Formation
Public–private power in the 21st century
Edited by Shelley L. Hurt and Ronnie D. Lipschutz

Global Economic Governance and the Development Practices of the Multilateral Development Banks
Edited by Susan Park and Jonathan R. Strand

Ethics and Economic Governance
Using Adam Smith to understand the global financial crisis
Chris Clarke

Susan Strange and the Future of Global Political Economy
Power, control and transformation
Randall Germain

Culture, Political Economy and Civilisation in a Multipolar World Order
The case of Russia
Ray Silvius

Culture, Political Economy and Civilisation in a Multipolar World Order

The case of Russia

Ray Silvius

Routledge
Taylor & Francis Group
LONDON AND NEW YORK

First published 2017
by Routledge

2 Park Square, Milton Park, Abingdon, Oxfordshire OX14 4RN
52 Vanderbilt Avenue, New York, NY 10017

Routledge is an imprint of the Taylor & Francis Group, an informa business

First issued in paperback 2018

British Library Cataloguing in Publication Data
A catalogue record for this book is available from the British Library

Library of Congress Cataloging in Publication Data
A catalog record for this book has been requested

ISBN: 978-1-138-95604-9 (hbk)
ISBN: 978-0-367-08569-8 (pbk)

Typeset in Times New Roman
by Taylor & Francis Books

Contents

List of tables vi
Acknowledgements vii

1 Introduction and methodology 1

2 A critical historicism for post-Soviet Russia within international political economy 21

3 Examining Russia's post-communist transitional political economy 52

4 The embedding of Russian state-sanctioned multipolarity in the post-Soviet conjuncture 80

5 The Russian state, Eurasianism and civilisations in the contemporary global political economy 100

6 Aleksandr Dugin's Eurasianism: co-opting or co-opted in Russia's Putin-era civilisational project? 122

7 The legacy of Vladislav Surkov: regime-sanctioned culture in the service of national political economy 148

8 Conclusion 171

Appendix 180
Index 184

Tables

A.1 Russian GDP growth (percentage) 180
A.2 Russian central government debt, as percentage of GDP 180
A.3 Russian current account surplus and reserves, in current US dollars (billions) 180
A.4 Gross domestic product per capita, in current US Dollars, select years 181
A.5 Gini Index (0 = perfect equality; 100 = perfect inequality); select years 181
A.6 Outward foreign direct investment, percentage of world total, select years 181
A.7 Inward foreign direct investment, percentage of world total, select years 181
A.8 Commodity structure of exports of the Russian Federation, percentage of total 182
A.9 Ease of doing business rankings 182
A.10 Number of people employed in the Russian economy by ownership type (measured by the thousands) 182
A.11 Percentage of people employed in the Russian economy by ownership type 183

Acknowledgements

As an 'intellectual' project, this book began during my Ph.D. studies at Carleton University. I feel fortunate to have done my doctoral studies in an environment that was to my mind equal parts critical, permissive and heterogeneous.

My utmost appreciation is extended to my doctoral supervisor, Randall Germain, whose good humour, constant encouragement, and sage wisdom helped guide me first to a completed Ph.D., and subsequently to this completed project. There is no better mentor in the world of International Political Economy that I am aware of. Randall recognised some virtue in my initially clumsy formulations, perhaps thinking in his historical mode of thought that there was an important question worth broaching in all of this. I also thank Rianne Mahon and Piotr Dutkiewicz for their guidance and immensely helpful comments on early versions of my dissertation. Additional gratitude is extended to Piotr for helping to facilitate a number of crucial experiences in Moscow and Warsaw. Such experiences were indispensable, not necessarily for any 'data' collected during them, but for giving me a further sense of the historical and geographical markers that shape one's thinking.

Likewise, I am grateful to Anastasia Nesvetailova, who, since serving as the external reviewer during my Ph.D. defense, has been a consistent supporter. My deepest appreciation also extends to my Russian language instructor at Carleton, Marina Sabanadze, for her patience and intelligence in assisting me with my Russian language studies at Carleton University.

This project has come to fruition while I have taught at the University of Winnipeg. During this period, I have enjoyed the immense fortune of having supportive friends and colleagues, as well as inquisitive students. The unflinching collegiality of Peter Ives must be acknowledged in particular. Peter might be known to most in academic spheres as a peerless scholar of Gramsci and language. He is equally capable at helping a young colleague learn the ropes in a department, in a university and in the academic publishing world. My thanks as well to Carlos Colorado, whose friendship and deep commitment to scholarly dialogue and interdisciplinary collaboration have made the day to day more enjoyable. Moreover, I extend my sincere appreciation to invaluable research support provided by my former University of Winnipeg Political

Science students, Jessica Praznik, Mitchell Sherren and Dana Tucker. Similarly, thank you to another student, Terra Poole, for assisting with some of the final pesky formatting work on this manuscript.

I also acknowledge the Social Sciences and Research Council of Canada (SSHRC), the Ontario Graduate Scholarship (OGS), and Carleton University for providing doctoral funding, which enabled the original research upon which this work is based. The author also acknowledges the University of Winnipeg for providing funding for additional research supports.

So goes the academic side. I have had the immense fortune to have experienced slivers of post-communism from the ground up. The existential engagement with the book's subject matter began when I lived in Jõhvi, Estonia, while on a Canadian government funded exchange programme called Canada World Youth. Ostensibly, we Canadians were there to talk about 'civil society' with our Estonian counterparts. In actuality, we had thorough and complicated encounters in post-communism, nationalism, history, language and empires in apartments, on rock beaches, on buses, in what might be described as disco bars. This experience has conditioned a certain caution that I take into my work on geographical and historical spheres whose complex realities I have not had to negotiate for extended periods but which intrigue me nonetheless. My firm wish in such situations is a dignified and progressive outcome for all involved, but I hesitate to name exactly what this might look like.

On the personal side, I have an unpayable debt to my mother, who raised me in such a way as to always first give the other person the benefit of the doubt and instilled in me her own distinctive sense of intrigue about the world. Growing up in a single parent household in semi-rural Manitoba, Canada, I should never have been able to experience global politics in far-off interstitial zones, but perhaps that was somehow a fate that she helped facilitate.

Finally, all of the other sentiments and more go to Jill. I apologise for dragging you into post-communist geographies when all you wanted was to travel to warm waters.

Chapter 4 is derived in part from an article, 'The Embedding of Russian State-Sanctioned Multipolarity in the Post-Soviet Conjuncture' published in *Globalizations* on 29 October 2015, available online: http://www.tandfonline.com/doi/full/10.1080/14747731.2015.1102944.

Chapter 5 is derived in part from an article, 'The Russian State, Eurasianism, and Civilisations in the Contemporary Global Political Economy' published in *Journal of Global Faultlines* in April 2014, available online: https://www.keele.ac.uk/journal-globalfaultlines/issues/volume2number1.

1 Introduction and methodology

The introductory chapter proceeds as follows. Section 1 consists of an introduction, during which I situate the book thematically. In Section 2, I state my research problem and questions. Section 3 is comprised of the methodology. Section 4 contains key concepts of this work and a rationale for their use. The chapter concludes with Section 5, in which I outline the structure of the work.

1 Introduction

In this book, I explore the limits to liberal democratic universalism and US hegemony at both the material and ideational level by way of the example of contemporary Russia, and how select Russian officials, state bodies, and 'political technologists', a term I describe below, represent the contemporary global political economy. As the Russian political economy becomes selectively integrated into the global capitalist political economy, it would appear that there is little discursive space for articulating Russia's *samobytnost'* or uniqueness. However, such integration involves considerable state involvement, which is reflected in Russian state attempts to articulate a response to liberal democratic universalism and American hegemony in an environment of geoeconomic and geopolitical contestation. In this response, select Russian officials seek to reject Western triumphalism by appealing to 'home grown', but 'polysemic', ideas and cultural frames that valorise Russian conduct and question the moral and practical legitimacy of American hegemonic precepts. Collectively, these efforts provide the basis for what may be considered Russian alternative 'state-sanctioned' understandings of world order.

This book is about the emergence of such understandings during the post-Soviet conjuncture, with a particular emphasis on the 'Putin era' (2000–present) and the unevenly 'resurgent' Russia of this era. It is a work that accentuates the 'semiotic' (symbolic) and 'extra-semiotic' (material) dimensions of state projects amid the prolonged 'transitional' Russian political economy. In suggesting here that beliefs are *produced* by the state, my contribution gauges the role of key state officials and state organs in both opening and circumscribing political imaginations in accordance with projects of 'world order' significance.

As it engages with historical materialist and historicist modes of analysis, this book reflects an interest with the state's role vis-à-vis social forces and its attempts to articulate a hegemonic consensus about Russia's place in, and nature of, world order. The Russian state strives to produce a relatively coherent set of concepts about world order, which it attempts to establish as a new normal, common-sense thinking about global affairs to rival liberal internationalism. It then attempts to convince the Russian citizenry and the external world of the veracity of such concepts. Thus I conceive of the Russian state as a multitudinous agent which, in addition to its authoritative, bureaucratic and coercive role in administering the Russian economic base, articulates a particular vision of national, international, and 'civilisational' political and economic life. In addition to its role of organising the Russian economy along a combination of statist and market principles, official Russia develops concepts and ideas that render these moves intelligible according to longer Russian intellectual and cultural legacies. It does so by developing and utilising 'cultural' terminology – understood as collective intelligibility, purported tendencies, shared intersubjective meanings and familiar frames – as a means of rendering political decisions intelligible and fostering legitimacy and consent.

This book also reflects my view of the state's coercive and consensual role as being embedded within certain cultural and historical understandings while the state works to cultivate such understandings. Situated within the field of International Political Economy (IPE), the work embodies a concern with the relationship between the domestic and international and upholds the argument that the two may only be understood dialectically. Moreover, it develops out of reflections upon a specific body of literature found in IPE – that which focuses on the phenomenon of world order, global capitalism and the internationalisation/transnationalisation of the state – and a questioning of some of its theoretical and practical implications when it comes to investigating developments beyond the mature capitalist core. As such, this book grows out of discussions within the field of IPE and is particularly concerned with examining national-cultural contexts in which large-scale historical shifts occur. Central to the concern is the manner by which national representations – how the nation and its members have been imagined – have accompanied shifting social and economic orders whereby members of Russian society have negotiated, accepted, or rejected new forms of capitalist sociability.

I develop a synopsis and critique of the materialist precepts of world order thinking in critical IPE in Chapter 2. For the purposes of locating the project here, it is sufficient to allude to the strengths and insights as well as the shortcomings of this literature. This literature, which develops the thinking of Robert Cox in various ways, is implicitly concerned with the extension of American hegemony over the global periphery in transforming statist developmental regimes to (neo)liberal-capitalist models (and in some cases the role of European capital in transforming its sphere of influence). The transnational variant of this literature, represented by scholars such as William Robinson and those of the Amsterdam School, conceives of social relations across national borders as the primary motor for global political and economic change, particularly by way of transforming and disciplining national units within the global periphery. In doing so this literature is able to perceive the constitution of social classes across borders and escape narrow methodological nationalism to tell us much about the nature of contemporary transformations in the global political economy.

Nonetheless, these insights warrant further reflection. Where does Russia fit in the context of understanding America's ambitions towards global systems management? Historically, where does the Soviet Union's attempt at forging a state-socialist alternative world order fit amid theorising on the American world order? And if in fact post-socialist Russia is in the process of adopting a liberal-capitalist, or state-capitalist, or quasi-capitalist order, what does this look like and how has it been accomplished? As it pertains to Russia, what does the disassembling of the Soviet empire, a prolonged transition to a market economy and the reconstitution of political authority look like? Rendering comparable those national political economies and societies deemed peripheral, or semi-peripheral, to the global capitalist core comes at the cost of specificity and overlooks emerging fault lines within the US-led global liberal democratic project. Furthermore, broad comparative sweeps mask the manner by which historicised ideas become activated in the present amidst emerging geopolitical and geoeconomic tensions. On the one hand, only on a most generic level was Russia's emergence from the Soviet period comparable to fellow post-Soviet states and other 'transitioning' economies, due to its size, geopolitical position, imperial history and aspirations to global prominence. On the other, Russia faces broad systemic pressures and resulting political struggles while selectively integrating into the global political economy. This book, therefore, takes as its starting point Russia's distancing from Soviet economic practices in becoming a 'state capitalist' political economy, while official Russia has nonetheless made selective appeals to Russian difference, particularity and identity on the terrain of 'culture' and 'civilisation'. Collectively, such appeals constitute Russian state-sanctioned alternative understandings of world order.

My entry into the question of world order comes through an analysis of the 'ideational' limits of liberal internationalism as represented by Putin-era Russia, which provides us with a case which manifests the failure of any easy transmission of the ideas associated with a Western-inspired liberal democracy or global capitalist 'sociability'. Components of world order as articulated by official Russia result from a perceived need to offer a vision of Russia in the world which captures Russia's reputed uniqueness and reflects a wealthier, more assertive and 'sovereign' Russia than was evident in the immediate post-Soviet period. This is by no means a straightforward process: for example, ideas about a modern, democratising and market-friendly Russia, which is increasingly integrated into global economic structures, have also figured prominently in Putin's readings of world order, particularly during his first term as president. However, the uncontested adoption of Western liberal thought deemed to correspond with American liberal hegemony did not occur, as a particularly Russian 'filter' was tacitly or overtly employed to shape understandings of global political life and Russia's place within it. In addition to reflecting material conflicts arising out of economic competition and military threats, Russian state-sanctioned alternative understandings of world order display a thoroughly intersubjective or ideational component, whereby global political life is translated through shared understandings of moral appropriateness, legitimacy and manageability. An investigation of these understandings forms the basis of this work. The result is a series of ideational and material practices which are temporally conjoined but whose logical relationships reflect the messy world of political volition.

My intention with this book is to add to the discussion about world order as found in the IPE tradition the extent to which semiotic and extra-semiotic, ideational and material elements of state projects need not directly coincide. In addition to being constituted by material practices, national political economies are consolidated through mediating devices in the form of intersubjectively held or produced beliefs, representations of national social orders whereby the limits of the possible are understood and circumscribed. To declare that such things matter is hardly controversial. But it has important ramifications for how the international/transnational is conceived in an era in which the concepts associated with American hegemony and global capitalism – those which are intended to provide the consensual basis for extended American leadership – are met by 'rising' non-Western political economies seeking their own 'ideational stamp' on world order. Do corresponding representations constitute a threat to global capitalist sociability? Do they contain counterhegemonic potential? Are they better thought as comprising an ideological veneer with which market practices are consolidated, albeit in new national or regional forms? Such questions animate this work.

2 Problem statement, research question and temporal parameters

In this work I examine Putin-era Russia by way of conceptions of Russian state, society and nation amid contemporary world order, as well as the nature of this world order itself. It is therefore designed to understand the creation, existence or perpetuation of national, if not 'civilisational', intersubjective ideas amid concrete transformations in Russia's social, economic and political order and the production of new and reinvented concepts which accompany that order. The Russian case demonstrates that significant fault lines within contemporary world order exist at the material and ideational level. In the process, it provides clues as to what a post-hegemonic world order may look like according to prominent tendencies within official Russia's self-representations.

The research questions I pose are situated with one eye on the manner by which Russian leadership interprets Russia's collective place within world order and the other on how it understands and represents this order itself. How are we to understand state-sanctioned representations of Russia in the

Putin era, and how do these representations stand in relation to the advent of a capitalist economy and social order? How has political authority cultivated particular intersubjective understandings to legitimize both its role within society and Russia's place in the world? What does the terrain of national representation tell us about contemporary Russian state projects and how do we conceive of contemporary world order in light of this terrain?

This book has been developed to meet the following objectives. First, my intent is to bring critical scrutiny and a larger cultural component to the critical IPE literature through a specific case, Russia. In doing so, my objective is to assist in incorporating the phenomenon of Russian post-communist transitions into contemporary IPE thinking through granting attention to the Russian case. Specifically, I examine representations of state and society amid a transition to some form of capitalist society, and the state's role in developing the imagery, concepts and ideas deemed suitable for the purposes of this order. Second, this book is a contribution to the emerging sub-discipline of Cultural Political Economy by developing an understanding of cultural representations in the case of post-Soviet and Putin-era Russia.

At the time of writing (Fall 2015), amidst open geopolitical and geoeconomic competition between Russia and the West over Ukraine and Syria, as well as Russian state efforts to further consolidate the Eurasian Economic Union, Russian 'revisionism' is a matter for much speculation in English language scholarship and popular commentary. However, my intention is to demonstrate official Russia's longer run disarticulation of American hegemony and 'concepts of control'. Such a disarticulation unevenly spans the longer post-Soviet moment, takes new shapes during Putin's first two presidential terms (2000–2008) and that of Dmitri Medvedev (2008–2012), before manifesting itself more decisively in Putin's third presidential term (2012–present). This book is an extended and updated version of my dissertation, which focused primarily on the period corresponding with Putin's first two terms as president, and in which an earlier, but similar, case was made. There is a need to consider the longer trajectory of ideas and tendencies which predate, yet figure prominently in, the present geopolitical and geoeconomic conflicts between Russia and the West, in general, and Russia and the United States, more specifically.

I acknowledge that powerful arguments can be made about the long-run historical antecedents to Russia's contemporary global position, including relative 'backwardness' and the late development of capitalist, and then socialist, projects of national modernisation amid prevailing world orders.[1] There is no good reason to avoid incorporating this into a purportedly historical analysis other than to cite the limits dictated by feasibility and my desire to focus on the post-communist period and contemporary questions. Moreover, by concentrating on Putin's first two presidential terms, insofar as ideas and practices associated with Russian difference became concrete during this time, this work serves as an 'empirical corrective'[2] to disciplinary trends of forecasting globalised or multipolar political economies. This matter is taken up throughout the book.

3 Methodology

Rationales for employing particular methodologies in the social sciences range from informed to the dogmatic. The debate concerning the appropriateness of focusing solely on Russia, the former members of the Soviet Union, or assimilating both into wider comparative/positivist accounts of 'democratic transition' is not new and scarcely resolvable here (see Schmitter & Karl, 1994; Bunce, 1995 and 1999). The legitimacy of single cases is also firmly established within the universe of social science research. Single cases are indeed warranted as phenomena in their own right, as *intrinsic case studies* that are interesting for their own unique qualities (Berg, 2001). For the field of IPE, *national* cases are far from obsolete, as they serve as prisms through which broader global forces are refracted. They are therefore helpful in extending discussions on particular theoretical orientations. My critical historicist approach straddles what Eckstein (1975; see also Blaikie, 2000, pp. 219–225) refers to as the *configurative-ideographic* and *heuristic* case studies. In the former, a descriptive account is given to provide understanding of a phenomenon under examination. In the latter, a case is examined to provide tentative understandings towards the development of theory. A certain caveat applies here, though, with a rejection of strictly positivist methodologies: generalizable knowledge is not sought here nor understood as the appropriate standard for this project, yet appropriate attempts are made to provide tentative explanations within the case studied. Therefore, it is erroneous to view this as a purely descriptive exercise, and I am uncertain as to whether typologies within the social sciences consulted thus far aptly capture the logic of historical research.

An appropriate methodological strategy is required to understand complex and far reaching transformations. A critical historicist conception of the macro-historical transformation of society and economy is sensitive to historical change, contingency and social agency. It contains insights into the shared ideational and cultural frames through which political, economic and social orders are mediated, consolidated, or rejected. Furthermore, it views historically specific, particular social formations as the broader configurations in which human action is patterned. Sensitive to shared cognitive frameworks, this approach eschews economism and determinism and defends a non-reductionist reading of the relationship between economic base and political superstructure while redirecting attention to shared representations in understanding the prospects for collective social action.

Aspects of the historicist IPE approach bear a certain resemblance to the configurative approach as outlined by Katznelson (1997) with important distinctions. The configurative approach suggests that 'variables' are complicatedly conjoined in specific historical instances. Therefore, it rejects the positivist inclination to seek universal hypotheses. Furthermore, direct univariate causation is impossible to determine; variables are co-extensive and reciprocal. Actors are not atomistic, unfettered and rational in the abstract; they are embedded in a shared temporal milieu. An approach to historical inquiry within the configurative tradition therefore similarly emphasises the shared frameworks within which actors imagine and act. Historicist IPE similarly acknowledges historical complexity, with the important added condition of consciousness, perception and agency. In its critical variant, historicist IPE asks how political, economic and social institutions come about by way of the balance of social forces, but it remains sensitive to how ideas about collective social life endure *despite* radical political and economic transformations.

In developing configurative and contextual accounts of social action and meaning, a critical historicist approach demonstrates one's scepticism of isolating individual variables for cause-effect analysis. Interpretive actions are required both on the part of the scholar and social actors to comprehend the generation of intersubjective human meanings while offering a limited and weaker, non-determinative form of the cause-effect mechanisms of social change. Critical historicism scrutinises the subject/object divide, which posits that external reality discloses itself fully to a rational mind capable of deploying objective categories in the process of measuring and distilling social reality.

The 'case' of Russia warrants particular attention for a number of reasons: 1) as the primary inheritor of Soviet institutions; 2) as a self-declared global power, wherein ideas of Russia's international prestige and significance are causally efficacious; 3) as a site where alternative ideas about world order are produced; 4) as nonetheless representing a lacuna in conceptions of global change in much IPE speculation. A single case is warranted here, particularly given the size, complexity, and 'world historical significance' of the case!

How does one study intersubjective ideas? The task is daunting to the researcher in the uncertainty and opportunity such a study presents. Cultural representations, symbols and understandings are shared, produced, rejected and challenged by all members of a national political community, to varying degrees. As such, the terrain of cultural production is vast and, for all practical purposes, limitless. The contours of my investigation necessitate that I focus upon and thoroughly analyse a bounded range of concrete instances deemed emblematic or most powerful in expressing the phenomenon of national intersubjective ideas, while linking these to a theoretical understanding and empirical display of the contemporary nature of the Russian political state. While this could legitimately come in the form of, for example, artistic production, literature and developments in popular culture, such aspects are not given a predominant place here. These forms are relevant to the current study insofar as shared normative and ideational frameworks are crucial for understanding political orders. Indeed, investigating non-state-sanctioned cultural production guards against reducing nationalism to instrumental attempts by state authorities to produce the nation by instead seeking the substance of nationalist understandings in society itself. Nonetheless, I am specifically concerned with the 'positive' role of state authority in fashioning worlds amid social, economic and political complexity (Poulantzas, 2000). As such, I have largely focused my attention on 'speech acts' of representatives of various iterations of 'official Russia': select Russian officials, governing bodies, or 'political technologists' deemed to consolidate or represent existing political authority. The research strategy employed, therefore, is to analyse the content of Russian government documents, reports and initiatives and presidential speeches to detect 'official' understandings of the nation and/or world order.

A note on terminology is warranted here. As it pertains to questions of foreign policy and corresponding understandings of world order, I use the terms Putin's regime, Russian officials, the Russian state and the executive somewhat interchangeably. I am operating under the assumption that while the production of foreign policy concepts and ideas invariably involves a complex of actors and institutions, the president bears an overwhelming amount of responsibility for the formulation of foreign policy in Russia (see Trenin and Lo, 2005). While the Russian state is characterised formally by a dual executive structure comprised of the presidential administration, on the one hand, and prime minister and ministries on the other, the precise relationship between the two remains murky (Sakwa, 2008). While foreign and domestic policy ideas may come from a variety of sources during the period in question, they are invariably given the presidential stamp of approval by Putin. Thus, when representatives of the Russian state spoke about foreign or domestic policy during Putin's presidency, it may be assumed that there was either tacit or explicit approval from Putin.

I examine documents, speeches and commentary produced by the Putin regime to determine what components constitute the administration's conceptions of Russia in world order and how this state of affairs is represented to Russian and non-Russian population. Given this intention, I have focused primarily on that material expressing Russia's 'positive' role in fashioning world order processes, and its 'negative' role in resisting the extension of American ideational and material influence. That is to say, I am purposefully seeking concepts that serve to frame the nature of contemporary world order, Russia's status in this order and the legitimacy of this order.

Seeking understandings of world order in the vast array of documents and speeches presented by the Russian state as well as synopses of these documents and speeches may be misleading: these do not have as their primary intent a demonstration of a Kremlin position on world order alone. Rather, they are, on the one hand, comprehensive statements on multiple aspects of Russian political economy and society, as well as both the internal and external challenges to Russia's governability. The comprehensive aspect is most evident in the case of the annual Addresses to the Federal Assembly. On the other hand they are also very specific statements and positions offered by Russian officials for very specific purposes and to very specific audiences.

It is not always clear, perhaps, how an individual statement or document contributes to an alternative conception of world order. By alternative conceptions of world order, I mean those which are purposefully given with the intention of creating a contradistinction to the 'concepts of control' that frequently accompany American aspirations to global leadership: polyarchic democracy, human rights, and capital mobility, for example. In doing so, official Russia cultivates political and practical legitimacy amongst social forces and actors that are, at best, lukewarm, and worst, hostile to liberal postulates and American geopolitical and geoeconomic power. In conceiving of 'official Russia', I clearly do not mean to suggest that a monolithic entity has imposed a consistent vision of world order during the period under question. Certainly, during the Putin era, Russian state discourse is a complex and multifaceted phenomenon that resists easy classification and binary oppositions. Rather, I wish to demonstrate that flexible and polysemic ideas cultivated at different times by dispersed actors cohere into a relatively stable understanding of contemporary world order that serves as a counterpoint to liberal universalism and American hegemony.

My decision to impose such an analytical framework – that is, searching for understandings of world order in the statements, speeches and documents produced by official Russia – was made on the assumption that we can find important regularities and ambiguities within these statements and that these tell us something about the strategic positioning of the Russian state. When deemed appropriate, I have included longer quotations so as to present ideas in greater context. In so doing, I hope to preserve the integrity of the statements without reducing the words to a simplified code. That is to say, I do not wish to simply count up the number of times Russian officials speak about, for example, Eurasianism or multipolarity without postulating some significance of these terms. To involve Clifford Geertz (1973), one simply does not go to the trouble of accumulating considerable amounts of material from the Russian government only to count particular words. One could employ a strictly quantitative methodology to determine the prevalence of certain 'buzzwords' in Putin's discourse (see Godzimirski, 2008, for example), however, my analysis proceeds from the judgement that much energy has been expended to reconciling Russian particularity with the nature of contemporary world order. Proceeding from this assumption permits some degree of abstraction from particular documents, which enables tentative conclusions about common prevalent themes, while the particularity of much of the work is retained.

While I engage with neo-Gramscian scholarship in this book, I depart somewhat from the understanding of state as political plus civil society. When I employ the term official Russia, I refer to its political authority, headed by the president and comprised of those supportive of state apparatuses. I do this out of methodological necessity as I investigate the role that such a group plays as a socialising force in offering state-sanctioned visions of world order. I would have preferred to explore in greater detail the link between this Russian political state and the vast complex of civil society institutions, economic actors, the Russian Orthodox Church, think tanks, technocratic experts, bureaucratic fractions and the media, but such a project is overly ambitious. Indeed, in confining myself largely to the Putin regime, I was ensured of a relatively accessible stock of information which demonstrated state views on the matter of contemporary world order.

If one may see Putin's regime as increasingly fusing political and economic power in Russia (Stent, 2008),[3] ideas produced by the regime become explicitly attached to political–economic imperatives. In a period of the continued large-scale transformation of the Russian political economy, what are the recurring ideas and conceptual frameworks utilised by the Russian state? This question follows from my conception of representations, which has a threefold purpose. First, how has official Russia interpreted prevailing trends in the global political economy and Russia's place within it? Second, how does it appeal to Russian particularities when representing material 'facts'? Third, how can we understand world order and the corresponding domestic component in Russia as a normative vision on the part of the Russian state and a project that it seeks to implement amid contemporary constraints and opportunities?

The inner workings of Russian elite circles and political negotiations stemming therefrom remain beyond the scope of my analysis. Indeed, this is a perennial problem of 'Kremlinology': how does one make plausible inferences about Russian elite negotiations based on scattered clues? Avoiding such speculation on the inner workings of Kremlin power and the extent to which Putin represents a particular faction may lead to an incomplete theorisation of the problem of Russian (political) state power. Nonetheless, it remains beyond the scope of my analysis. Indeed, it reflects a genuine problem about how such information is made available, particularly to an English speaking public. Ascribing coherence in foreign policy to a comprehensive Putin plan is also partly due to the somewhat mythical insistence upon the cohesion of such a plan, whether it pertains to foreign or domestic policy. Such an insistence is somewhat misleading. For example, Russian thinking on multipolarity and Eurasianism unquestionably predates Putin's presidency. Furthermore, no single political figure can determine the intersubjective ideas used to understand political phenomena. Yet Putin has been thought of as being capable of such an undertaking, which is part of the very power of Putinism itself.

I decided upon prevalent themes after an initial reading of major speeches and documents, including the annual speeches to the federal assembly, which represent a significant component of the Russian government's vision of itself and its priorities and are meant for consumption by Russian society, Russian politicians and anyone who cares to access them. I came to such a decision after engaging with various secondary sources and attending numerous conferences in my early scholarly life in which advocates and detractors made ostensibly objective and disinterested assessments of the state of affairs in Russia. Given that the Putin era has been much commented upon, and of intense interest to scholarly audiences in both Russia and beyond, it is difficult to conceive of an analytical and conceptual framework completely from scratch, as it were. Cox's dictum that theory is always for someone and some purpose often appears in the practice of Russian studies and the intellectual production accompanying it. Indeed, given the highly politicised nature of scholarly or popular work on Russia, where research interests and conceptual frameworks appear to be influenced by the very question of whether one is a

Russophile or Russophobe, any purported objectivity in one's conceptual apparatus is often a pretence that evaporates quickly during discussion sessions.

The nature of social research suggests that there is no clean abstraction away from one's preconceptions and the social, cultural and professional environment in which he or she acts. Any *a priori* move to determine what is important prior to engaging in the source material leaves an indelible mark on the research process itself. Inducing categories from a strict reading of empirical sources prevents one from situating such sources in a broader environment and hypothesising as to their significance. While both of these approaches might tell us something, they lack a sense of reflexivity on the part of the scholar. In other words, the analysis undertaken here involves a threefold negotiation between source material, secondary material, and personal judgements on my part. I find it difficult to conceive of historicised and admittedly reflexive research in any other fashion than to acknowledge this from the onset of my engagement with source materials.

I have attempted to capture both continuity and context in the themes. On the one hand, the themes of the chapters recur across different time frames. On the other, the themes are what may be called permissive signifiers – malleable concepts that vary in substance according to how they have been employed to explain a variety of phenomena. I capture this notion through an exploration of the 'polysemic' and 'commonsensical' qualities of world order concepts. The durability of certain aspects of state thinking is revealed despite what we can assume to be a need to respond to Russia's shifting position in contemporary world order. Drawing out the multiple strands of Putin-era conceptions of world order enables one to highlight the ambiguities inherent in state views while avoiding oversimplification. Indeed, we may both seek out prevalent themes and question the internal coherence and stability of Putin's vision as it pertains to Russia's international position and domestic transformation.[4]

With this method in mind, it is important to consider historicist precepts of knowledge production, which I speak to further in the following chapter. It was only possible to search a variety of databases by imposing certain limitations. My methodological choice was to seek out certain concepts that I deemed important after an initial engagement with both empirical and theoretical material. To my judgement, concepts such as Eurasianism and civilisation, multipolarity, and sovereign democracy are significant within the production of knowledge about Russian state and society in a manner that eclipses a mere frequency count of 'buzzwords'. An objective content analysis may in fact tell us what Putin spoke about the most in his speeches, press releases and so on. However, this alone does not tell us the significance of these concepts.

It is my intent to demonstrate both the frequent occurrence of certain key concepts while surmising that these contribute to particular Russian state understandings of world order that depart from American liberal precepts. The selection of these concepts also reflects a limitation to the academic writing process, namely the need to categorise and extract themes from an immense volume of literature and data, material which primarily came to be known to me through key words searches. In the production of one's book there can be no entirely objective process which is not conditioned by pre-selection mechanisms and the exercise of judgement to determine what is significant and what is not. A second book could be written by accumulating, standardising and coding the marginal notes and material excised from the current work.

The work was further conditioned by my abilities to work in the Russian language. My ability to translate from Russian to English is limited. I believe that I successfully did this (while also consulting with native speakers, nonetheless) for the section on 'Concept 2020' in Chapter 7. Furthermore, I have translated some shorter selections. I acknowledge that having an even greater number of original Russian language sources would be optimal, and yet the project is not compromised absent this. First, the project is located within the fields of IPE and International Relations (IR) as opposed to Russian Studies; IPE and IR necessitate a less intensive engagement with Russian language sources. My primary theoretical engagement is with English language scholarship on world order and global capitalism.

Second, I have consulted a substantial range of Russian authors, political figures, and experts who have either written in, or have been translated into English. I examine in detail sources from four databases.[5] Two – the World News Connection and the Current Digest of the Russian Press – consist of articles that have been pre-selected by an editorial team for their perceived significance and subsequently translated. Multiple articles that appear on these are segments of the original. The same can be said for a third database – that of Kremlin.ru. I chose a fourth – Radio Free Europe and Radio Liberty's (RFERL) Russian content – for its accessibility and depth, despite it being fairly consistent in its overt disdain for Putin and Russian state power. If theory is always for some person and some purpose, as Robert Cox would suggest, so too is the production of knowledge on Russia.

Third, I have consulted numerous works produced and translated by the Russian state itself. By heavily utilising work that has been both *produced* and *translated* by the Russian state, I have relied on material that is consciously selected and scrutinised by state organs and presumably embody the result of a vetting process in which political authorities are sensitive to political messaging. I therefore take as axiomatic the notion that the Russian state wishes audiences to see this particular representation of itself in the English language to an audience beyond Russia. Nonetheless, I do not have the ability to undertake a comparative analysis of the Russian and English sections of the Kremlin.ru website and others from which official statements and documents are taken. Such an analysis may reveal a considerable difference between the two both in volume of material available and meaning conveyed.

4 Concepts and justifying their use

The central concept of this work is world order. I follow Cox in conceiving of world order as a configuration of global political and economic life characterised by a particular constellation of material forces that can be apprehended at any particular moment; however, the forces comprising a world order are diachronic in nature, changing over time. Cox (1986) advocates examining global politics within three spheres of activity: 1) *social forces* (reflecting the organisation of production); 2) *forms of state* (reflecting state–society complexes); and 3) *world orders* (the configuration of forces bearing upon states) (pp. 218–221; Cox, 1987; Bieler & Morton, 2004). World orders may be understood historically and investigated according to the extent to which they stabilise, are contested, and dissipate. There is no straightforward way to detect the durability of world orders, as they are more confidently approached retrospectively after massive transitions. World orders, such as the *pax Britannica* (mid-nineteenth century until World War II) and *pax Americana* (post-World War II until the contemporary period), will exhibit periods of greater, lesser, or no hegemonic leadership according to the particular constellation of material capabilities, ideas and institutions (Cox, 1996b). While I sketch Russia's material position in world order, for the purposes of this book I am explicitly concerned with the production of ideas by Russian political authority. These ideas contribute to official Russian alternative understandings of world order. It is my contention that the actions of the Russian state in the Putin era suggest new fault lines that may potentially signify the emergence of a post-hegemonic era, or at least an era in which American hegemony is contested in new ways.

My approach to the main concepts in this work acknowledges the centrality of polysemic concepts and ideas to political discourse (Jenson, 2010; Best, 2012). A polysemic idea is that which has multiple meanings and possible interpretations. Polysemic ideas can be helpful for the purposes of fostering consensus in that they may be utilised to bring together numerous and disparate people and groups who are nonetheless positively oriented towards the idea. While a polysemic idea may have both scientific and common-sense meanings, its strength is found precisely in its ambiguity and capacity to be somehow relevant or meaningful to multiple groups with multiple positions. Polysemic ideas are therefore useful in attempts to construct ideological cohesion, consensus and legitimacy. That a concept may be polysemic is not dissimilar to Gramsci's notion of common sense, whereby common sense shapes and constrains perception. It must be recognised and overcome in order to see the broader field of political possibilities. A philosophy of common sense comprises the following:

> the conception of the world which is uncritically absorbed by the various social and cultural environments in which the moral individuality of the average man is in development. Common sense is not a single unique conception, identical in time and space. It is the 'folklore' of philosophy, and, like folklore, it takes countless different forms. Its most fundamental characteristic is that it is a conception which, even in the brain of one individual, is fragmentary, incoherent and inconsequential,

> in conformity with the social and cultural position of those masses whose philosophy it is.
>
> (Gramsci, 1971, p. 419)

I suggest that Putin has attempted to forge a new common sense about Russia's place in world affairs. A Putin-era understanding of world order may be said to be comprised of a number of polysemic ideas derived from Russian cultural and political practices and thinking. As I demonstrate, these are sufficiently ambiguous to assist those who deploy them in order to fashion a broad consensus while being sufficiently specific to enable them to coalesce around a post-American-hegemonic understanding of global affairs. Moreover, often referenced to explain objective criteria and moral/ethical considerations, these concepts are filled with content with the intention of demonstrating that a post-hegemonic world order is both in formation and morally defensible. Finally, these concepts are deployed with the intention of valorising Russian interests and Russia's return to global significance. This may be seen as an attempt to redress the concerns of a sufficient enough number of Russian elites and officials who deemed Russian national interests and great power status to have been compromised during the tumultuous 1990s (see Mankoff, 2009).

The concepts I have chosen constitute neither a timeless essence of some putative Russian imperial character (see Pipes, 2004), nor abstract phenomena independent of time and space. I have attempted to locate them in the context of Russia's Putin-era state project, a time during which the Russian national political economy witnessed considerable growth and recovery after the moribund state of the 1990s. It is also a time characterised by the recentralisation of authority in the Russian political system and revalorisation of the role of the Russian state in political, social and economic development. The main concepts under investigation constitute a form of common sense of the Putin era insofar as they offer a form of reasoning and accessible ontology to uphold these ends. Furthermore, as I demonstrate, these concepts are sufficiently ambiguous so as to speak to the broad sentiments of Putin-era state building and resurgence while also covering specific policy decisions, announcements, etc. Also, I have chosen these concepts because they have been the subject of considerable academic and intellectual scrutiny and/or are representative of longer trends of Russian political and intellectual production. Furthermore, the concepts were chosen according to methodological limitations outlined above.

The chosen concepts can also be found in statements offered and material produced by the Russian state. The 2008 Foreign Policy Concept of the Russian Federation, for example, uses these concepts and their analogues to express Russia's improved position in international affairs and contemporary state priorities. The Concept states, for instance, that 'It is for the first time in the contemporary history that global competition is acquiring a civilisational dimension which suggests competition between different value systems and development models within the framework of universal democratic and market economy principles'. Moreover, 'As the constraints of the bipolar confrontation are being overcome, the cultural and civilisational diversity of the modern world is increasingly in evidence. A religious factor in shaping the system of contemporary international relations is growing, inter alia, as regards its moral foundation'. The concept defends the right of a number of rising states (the 'Troika' – Russia, India and China; BRIC – troika + Brazil) to manage world development; the common civilisational heritage of the Commonwealth of Independent States (CIS) and its member states; the creation of a polycentric (multipolar) world order, which is the result of a more equitable distribution of development resources across multiple power centres; a strengthened Russian state, economically strong, transitioning away from resource dependence towards an innovative economy and resolving 'social problems' (see also Putin, 2000); and a re-enacting of the role of the sovereign state, which is to be defended against the 'arbitrary interference' of others. It is significant to note for the purposes of this work that the Foreign Policy Concept also signals Russia's intentions to influence how others view it:

> In public diplomacy, Russia will seek its objective perception in the world, develop its own effective means of information influence on public opinion abroad, strengthen the role of the Russian mass media in the international information environment providing them with essential state support, as well as actively participate in international information cooperation, and take necessary measures to repel information threats to its sovereignty and security.

This work should be taken as a demonstration of how the Russian state has proceeded to do this very thing throughout the Putin era.

I have imparted unity on these concepts largely out of analytical feasibility. As a form of common sense cultivated by Russian officials, understandings of world order are at times fragmentary and disjointed, in that particular words and concepts crop up in official documents, unofficial documents, specially selected works which the Kremlin elects to place on its website for the purposes of public consumption, seemingly rehearsed speeches and off-the-cuff remarks by Putin and other Russian officials. Whether or not they are inconsequential, as Gramsci suggests, is a matter for debate. I suggest that they are consequential precisely because they offer a conception of world order in line with Russian aspirations for renewed significance and authority in global affairs. They represent an official Kremlin-sanctioned line of thinking meant to increase social solidarity, stability and cohesiveness under the aegis of the mighty state, all elements which the Putin regime deemed as underpinning its legitimacy in the Putin era.

5 Structure of this work

There are six substantive chapters (Chapters 2 through 7) and a conclusion (Chapter 8). The six substantive chapters are organised into two broad sections. Chapters 2 and 3 are comprised of the theoretical and substantive fields within which the book is situated: critical IPE and the material dimensions of Russia's position with the contemporary global political economy. Chapters 4, 5, 6 and 7 contain the specific concepts under investigation and are comprised of both scholarly reflections on each chapter's central concept and an empirical demonstration of how these concepts have been employed by the Putin regime.

In Chapter 2, I set the book in the context of IPE scholarship on globalisation, world order, and the cultural, material and ideational aspects of contemporary state projects. I develop a methodology grounded in critical historicist analysis of world orders and state projects, which I employ to understand how intersubjective ideas derived from previous epochs are mobilised, appropriated and transformed by social, political and economic actors for contemporary national hegemonic projects. In this chapter I also develop a framework for understanding the positions of such actors in the context of Russia's post-Soviet transition towards state-directed capitalism. Such a transition has been accompanied by efforts on the part of Russian state officials, 'organic intellectuals' and 'political technologists' to articulate Russian difference while interrogating the postulates of neo-liberal globalisation and American hegemony.

In Chapter 3, I consider Russia's transitional political economy in the 1990s – its uneven but considerable adoption of free market principles, institutions and normative order – as well as Russia's Putin-era 'resurgence'. While at the level of national political economy, Putin-era Russia has undoubtedly witnessed an improvement in its overall material conditions, it remains imperfectly integrated into the global political economy. It remains challenged by a semi-peripheral status whereby resource extraction plays a dominant role in the material well-being of state, economy and society, the persistence of geoeconomic/geopolitical struggle against the core, and a centralised political structure to manage the economic and political contradictions attending Russia's prolonged transition to a market economy. It is in this context that Putin has cultivated the political economy of 'defensive regionalism' – state-directed attempts to reconstitute Soviet-era trade and production networks across ostensibly sovereign national political economies. In this context, the Kremlin presides over a complicated state-capital configuration that includes bureaucratic and private, domestic and international capital, not all of which can be easily disciplined into serving national development imperatives.

Chapter 4 demonstrates the manner in which key Russian officials engaged with and propagated the notion of multipolarity in the wider post-Soviet conjuncture – first in the 1990s, intensively during Russia's 'resurgence' coinciding with Vladimir Putin's first two presidential terms, and finally as the establishment of a global 'common sense' following the 2007–2008 financial crises and the concomitant rise of the BRICS formation. Here I demonstrate an earlier, and, potentially, deeper unsettling of neo-liberal globalisation and American unipolarity and hegemony than that offered in the nascent 'multipolar turn' in the sub-disciplines of IPE and International Relations. Embedding common-sense understandings of multipolarity that cohere to state strategy, key Russian officials invite us to efface the divide between academic and political practice when understanding how world order concepts are propagated and normalised. A multifaceted treatment of multipolarity does not render it analytically dubious; rather, it cements its importance as a common-sense understanding of global political affairs serving an explicit political function.

Chapter 5 demonstrates the activation of concepts pertaining to culture and civilisation in imagining the GPE through the prism of Russian state-led regionalisation initiatives. It focuses on how certain Russian thinkers and officials employ such concepts to critique American hegemony, to consolidate and defend Russia's political apparatus, to obtain legitimacy for Russian state conduct both at home and abroad, and to consolidate Eurasian economic space under Russian hegemony. Russian debates over Eurasianism, civilisational difference and geopolitical identity were common in the 1990s and have filtered into Putin-era Russian state discourse about Eurasian political and economic integration initiatives. Eurasianist thinking has been activated in the Putin-era civilisational project, which I refer to as 'embedded civilisationalism' and which combines elements of neo-liberal and state-directed capitalism, regional (Eurasian) consolidation, and the revalorisation/naturalisation of Russian/Slavic/Eurasian cultural and civilisational norms.

In Chapter 6, I examine the relationship between Aleksandr Dugin's Eurasianism, conceived by its author as a post-Soviet *weltanschauung* for Russia's resurgence and predicated on a mix of geopolitical, esoteric, cultural and civilisational logics, and the Russian state-led discursive and material project of 'embedded civilisationalism'. While some commentators have been quick to declare Dugin as an ideologist with deep ties to Russia's political elite, if not the Kremlin itself, this chapter demonstrates that the selective endorsement of his and other strands of Eurasianist thinking by Russia's political establishment serves largely a strategic purpose for the latter's aspirations to integrate Eurasian space under Russian leadership. Architects of Russia's regional hegemonic project therefore co-opt strands of Russian society for the purposes of state-directed capitalism.

In Chapter 7, I investigate the work of Vladislav Surkov, still a prominent representative of the Putin regime and one-time ambitious self-declared Russian public philosopher, in the wider context of Kremlin-affiliated 'political technologists' – para-political professionals who espouse the Kremlin line for elite and broader public consumption. For such figures, the consolidation of state-directed capitalism in Russia necessitated a domestic and geopolitical identity to replace that of the Soviet Union and to attenuate the profound polarisation of Russian society between those seeking Russia's integration into Western liberal institutions and those advocating for the reconstitution of a neo-imperial Russia from a variety of nationalist, communist and conservative positions. Russian political technologists have borrowed selectively from broader Russian political, cultural and philosophical debates in order to assert the historical and ethical basis for the Russian state's domestic and international involvement: Russia could be capitalist provided that it was also a great power, sovereign in its conduct vis-à-vis the USA, and able to demonstrate to its public the compatibility of a market economy with Russian cultural and political traditions. The centrality of such figures as producers and mobilisers of world order concepts invites us to critique academic positions and popular commentary that suggest that Russian state practices are born of invariant Russian cultural traits. Chapter 8 concludes the work.

Notes

1 For an explanation of the Soviet Union's development of 'real socialism' amid a hostile world order, see Cox (1996a). For interesting attempts to assimilate the Soviet experience into World Systems Theory, see Luke (1985) and Boswell & Chase-Dunn (2000). For a useful comparison between nineteenth-century and late twentieth-century Russian/Soviet reforms as domestic responses to improve/- shore up international standing, see Bunce (1993).

2 I thank an anonymous reviewer of a previous work for articulating my contribution in such a manner.

3 Stent (2008) suggests that this process be understood as creating 'Russian Inc.'. 'In this system, political and economic elites are symbiotically connected, and the Kremlin officials who manage the affairs of state also manage and largely control the state's major economic assets. The chairmen of the boards of most of Russia's strategic industries, including energy companies, are either members of the presidential administration or holders of high government office, often making it difficult for an outsider to discern how much ostensibly commercial decisions are driven by political interests. Moreover in this system it is difficult to differentiate national from personal interests' (p. 1092).

For Mankoff (2008) the state's growing hold on economy will limit the development of factions. The Kremlin inner circle has become thoroughly cross-fertilised with the boards of Gazprom (which has included Dmitry Medvedev and German Gref), Rosneft (Igor Sechin), Transneft (Viktor Khristenko, Minister of Industry and Arkady Dyorkovich, Presidential Administration Official).

4 Evans (2008), however, argues that Putin's actions have been guided by core values and principles which were delineated even prior to his taking the Office of President; among these are that Russia is fundamentally oriented to Europe, insofar as it is essential for Russia's national interests; that economic growth and modernisation in a paradigm of state dominant development are essential to Russia's survival in a 'Hobbesian' world; that Russia upholds the universal values of democracy though through the prism of particular values, namely an emphasis on state sovereignty; and that Russian society requires a 'fundamental unity of values' by all sub-groups so as to avoid internal disintegration.

5 Following APA style convention, I have not indicated when these articles were retrieved, as the databases are stable and unlikely to change.

References

Berg, B. (2001). *Qualitative research methods of the social sciences.* Boston: Allyn and Bacon.

Best, J. (2012). Bureaucratic ambiguity. *Economy and Society*, 41(1), 84–106.

Bieler, A., & Morton, A. D. (2004). A critical theory route to hegemony, world order and historical change: Neo-Gramscian perspectives in international relations. *Capital and Class*, 28(1), 85–113.

Blaikie, N. (2000). *Designing social research*. Cambridge: Polity Press.

Boswell, T., & Chase-Dunn, C. (2000). *The spiral of capitalism and socialism: Toward global democracy*. Boulder: Lynne Rienner Publishers.

Bunce, V. (1993). Domestic reform and international change: The Gorbachev reforms in historical perspective. *International Organization*, 47(1), 107–138.

Bunce, V. (1995). Should Transitologists be grounded? *Slavic Review*, 54(1), 111–127.

Bunce, V. (1999). The political economy of postsocialism. *Slavic Review*, 58(44), 756–793.

Cox, R. (1986). Social forces, states and world orders: Beyond International Relations theory. In R. Keohane (Ed.), *Neorealism and its critics* (pp. 204–254). New York: Columbia University Press.

Cox, R. (1987). *Production, power and world order: Social forces in the making of history*. New York: Columbia University Press.

Cox, R. (1996a). 'Real socialism' in historical perspective. *Approaches to world order* (pp. 209–236). Cambridge: Cambridge University Press.

Cox, R. (1996b). Social forces, states, and world orders: Beyond international relations theory. *Approaches to world order* (pp. 85–123). Cambridge: Cambridge University Press.

Eckstein, H. (1975). Case study and theory in Political Science. In F.E. Greenstein and N.W. Polsby (Eds.), *Handbook of Political Science*, vol. 7: Strategies of inquiry (pp. 79–137). Reading, MA: Addison-Wesley.

Evans, A. (2008). Putin's legacy and Russia's identity. *Europe-Asia Studies*, 60(6), 899–912.

Geertz, C. (1973). *The interpretation of cultures: Selected essays*. New York: Basic.

Godzimirski, J. (2008). Putin and post-Soviet identity: Building blocks and buzzwords. *Problems of Post-Communism*, 55(5), 14–27.

Gramsci, A. (1971). *Selections from the prison notebooks*. London: Lawrence & Wishart.

Jenson, J. (2010). Diffusing ideas for after neoliberalism: The social investment perspective in Europe and Latin America. *Global Social Policy*, 10(1), 59–84.

Katznelson, I. (1997). Structure and Configuration in Comparative Politics. In M. Lichbach and A. Zuckerman (Eds.). *Comparative politics: Rationality, culture, and structure* (pp. 40–58). Cambridge: Cambridge University Press.

Luke, T. (1985). Technology and Soviet foreign trade: On the political economy of an underdeveloped superpower. *International Studies Quarterly*, 29(3), 327–353.

Mankoff, J. (2008). Russian foreign policy and the United States after Putin. *Problems of Post-Communism*, 55(4), 42–51.

Mankoff, J. (2009). *Russian foreign policy: The return of great power politics*. New York: Rowman and Littlefield Publishers.

Pipes, R. (2004). Flight from Freedom: What Russians think and want. *Foreign Affairs*, 83(3), 9–15.

Poulantzas, N. (2000). *State, power, socialism*. London: Verso.

Putin, V. (2000). The modern Russia: Economic and social problems. *Vital Speeches of the Day*, 66(8), 231–236.

Sakwa, R. (2008). *Russian politics and society*. 4th. London: Routledge.

Schmitter, P., & Karl, T. (1994). The conceptual travels of Transitologists and Consolidologists: how far to the East should they go? *Slavic Review*, 54(1), 173–185.
Stent, A. (2008). Restoration and revolution in Putin's foreign policy. *Europe-Asia Studies*, 60(6), 1089–1106.
Trenin, D., & Lo, B. (2005). *The landscape of Russian foreign policy decision making*. Moscow: Carnegie Center.

2 A critical historicism for post-Soviet Russia within international political economy

1 Introduction

The first goal of this chapter is to formulate a historicised approach for incorporating intersubjective meaning into International Political Economy (IPE) analyses of political and economic transitions of 'world order' significance. The second goal of this chapter is to consider whether the main methodological tenets of world order literature are sufficient to understand the Russian post-communist transition, the consolidation of capitalism in Russia, and Russia's place within a multipolar global political economy. The third goal is to establish a framework for understanding how official Russia mobilises cultural content for the purpose of articulating its political economy projects at international, regional and domestic levels. The Russian case demonstrates that significant fault lines within contemporary world order exist at the material and ideational level, and it provides clues as to what the semiotic and extra-semiotic dimensions of a post-hegemonic world order may look like according to official Russia.

This chapter lays the foundation for my theoretical framework via an engagement with critical IPE. Much of this literature can be referred to as 'Gramsci-inspired', a reflection of Robert Cox's influence that acknowledges that a range of debates within the corpus prevents one from simply declaring a neo-Gramscian school.[1] To acknowledge a broad stream of work that is in a variety of ways sympathetic to the Coxian research project in IPE, the term world order literature may even be used. I engage with this work to formulate a critical historicist framework for understanding the emerging multipolar global political economy, a framework that is best conceived of as considering how intersubjective ideas unevenly co-evolve with material parameters and how present day subjectivities are informed by the mobilised ideational content of previous epochs.

In this chapter I place particular emphasis on the notion of historical structures and insights from the field of Cultural Political Economy (CPE). I seek to develop an analytical place for the production of intersubjective ideas – understood as meanings shared by a particular social group and conditioned by shared cultural and historical experience – while still maintaining the significance of the material base to inform the limits of the possible. I do this by exploring concepts within Coxian historicism and CPE and advocate for an approach to the investigation of intersubjective meaning that takes into consideration both the semiotic (intersubjective) and extra-semiotic (social and material) factors without reducing meaning to either exclusively. Taking semiotic and extra-semiotic factors into consideration here necessitates examining the ways in which Russian officials employ ideas from Russian culture and history in efforts to represent the parameters of contemporary world order and Russia's place in it.

A critical historicist approach takes cues from historical materialism in its attention to the place of social forces in the process of production, distribution and knowledge creation. However, here I also seek to understand how Russian state organs and officials produce concepts and ideas corresponding to their real or desired place within that order. In the post-Soviet period, various iterations of the Russian state have sought to organise both a particular type of peripheral capitalism (see Chapter 3), as well as a relatively coherent set of concepts about world order. Such a political economy and such corresponding ideas then function as a form of Russian state-sanctioned, 'common-sense' thinking about global affairs that directly engages, and seeks to rival, various strains of liberal internationalism, exceptionalism and exemptionalism in the American hegemonic project. This is in spite of the fact that post-Soviet Russia has become integrated into global capitalist structures at a rate perhaps once deemed unimaginable in the immediate aftermath of Soviet counter-hegemonic practices. Critical historicism acknowledges the potential incongruities between, and complexities amongst, the real and imagined, and the (inter)subjective and objective, incongruities and complexities that are the hallmark of the Putin-era ontology of world order.

The chapter proceeds as follows. In Section 2, I consult critical IPE, CPE and related literature to situate my approach to understanding intersubjective ideas. In Section 3, I consider polysemic ideas and common sense as they relate to Russian state projects. In Section 4, I interrogate some of the assumptions of globalising capitalism stemming from critical IPE world order literature and build the case to consider what a contemporary plural world order may look like. Section 5 serves as a conclusion to the chapter.

2 Critical historicism and cultural political economy: locating ideas in the historical process

The approach offered here seeks an historicised account of large-scale social, political and ideational structures and their interactions within the global political economy.[2] The materialism is reflected in an account of politics based on the material necessities of life, the production and obtainment of such necessities, and the social relations that result from this process, be they domestically, internationally or transnationally situated. Historical materialist scholarship proceeds from the understanding that the history of capitalism, its encounter with other modes of production, and the manner in which it is constitutive of broader political relationships can tell us important things about social reality and the conflict that inheres within and across social spaces.[3] Furthermore, asserting the primacy of the *historical* in historical materialism requires us to examine the historical specificity of particular social formations, the factors surrounding their genesis, and the contradictions contributing to their potential dissolution or transformation. Such an account of historical specificities must always accompany any discussion as to the nature of purportedly 'global' capitalism (van der Pijl, 2005; Meiksins Wood, 2002; Sutcliffe, 2002).

Robert Cox's work has been of particular importance in the development of a critical orientation to historical IPE and IR more generally. Critical theory in IR/IPE is given its name because, as Cox (1986) explains 'it stands apart from the prevailing order of the world and asks how that order came about' in order to transform it. This is in contrast to problem-solving theory, which 'takes the world as it finds it, with the prevailing social and power relationships and institutions into which they are organised, as the given framework for action' (p. 208). This is not uncharacteristic of the early reception of Cox in mainstream IR, which emphasises that neo-Gramscian scholarship challenges orthodox IR precisely on the basis of its proponents' commitment to examining the role of intellectuals in knowledge production (Tooze, 1990). For Cox, neo-realism is the quintessential problem-solving theory in that it understands (then) contemporary world order in ahistorical fashion and offers a static mode of analysis that precludes any investigations into its origins (Cox, 1986).

This broadly conceived conception of critical theory is to be distinguished from the Habermasian Critical Theory strain in IR, of which Andrew Linklater is perhaps the most prolific contributor. For many, however, critical theory suggests a wider movement within the field, encompassing Marxist, hermeneutic, post-structural, post-modern, scientific realist and feminist approaches (Mittleman, 1998; Smith, 1996). While critical/post-positivist scholarship has somewhat fuzzy boundaries, it is frequently situated as a protest movement against dominant strains of scholarship within the discipline, developing in large part as a reaction to the scientific-positivist aspirations of mainstream IR/IPE. The reception and categorisation of critical and post-positivist scholarship has been influenced by the somewhat imprecise and misleading divide within IR/IPE scholarship in the late 1980s and throughout the 1990s, whose pace was set by Robert Keohane in his seminal 1988 article, 'International Institutions: Two Approaches'. Here, Keohane makes the distinction between 'rationalists' – who employed positivist methodologies and adhered largely to assumptions of states as unitary, rational actors – and 'reflectivists' – whose binding force is found in their commitment to understanding intersubjectivity and the mutual-constitutiveness of actors and institutions, as well as the impact of cultural norms and practices (pp. 381–382). This characterisation of the discipline primarily reflects developments within American IR and, arguably, obscures the various origins, trajectories and divisions within 'reflectivist' orientations. This is especially clear when it comes to the grouping of Marxist-inspired scholarship with disparate academic orientations that focus differently, if at all, on questions of political economy.

In order to escape the uncertain terrain from which critical scholarship in IR/IPE emerged and where, in many cases, it still rests, I use the term 'critical historicist'. This suggests an emphasis on viewing macro historical transformations in the global political economy. It seeks to avoid some ambiguous terminology, as 'historicist' in the Coxian sense differs somewhat from the more self-consciously reflexive historicism as detailed below. Historical inquiry in IPE deploys a methodology predicated on viewing the 'diachronic' aspects of international and domestic structures, that is their evolution, dissipation and transformation over time, as well as (but not exclusively) a 'synchronic understanding' that involves 'contemplating the coherence of a social relationship within its own [static] terms' (Sinclair, 1996, p. 8). Social/political totalities are therefore understood both in terms of their long-term transformations, which can only be grasped through macro-historical inquiry, and in terms of the practices which govern their operations at any particular point in time.

This critical historicist method of inquiry seeks to bridge the understanding/explaining divide in IR (see Hollis and Smith, 1990), offering an analysis that examines the regularities of human conduct in historical limitation, while also seeking to ascertain both the generation of intersubjective human meanings (understanding) and a limited and weaker form of the cause-effect mechanisms of global change (explanation).[4] Cast in historical terms, any explanation that may be offered is imperfect, conditional and susceptible to change, thereby rejecting the precepts of positivist knowledge formation.[5] Positivist approaches stand in direct contrast to historical modes of inquiry, with the latter's insistence upon historical specificity, the changing nature of social reality over time, and a particular relationship between the researcher and the historical record that obviates any clean subject/object distinction. Historical knowledge contrasts with that generated by empiricism and positivism insofar as its practitioners: 1) reject the subject/object divide (on this point see also Gill, 1993); 2) reject the fact/value distinction; 3) reject both methodological and ontological individualism; 4) reject causation between events in favour of an understanding of the meaning of historical change; 5) reject universal laws; 6) adopt a comparative historical method – comparing past and present to guide present social action (Langley, 2002, p. 19; see also Thompson, 1978). Proponents of an historical approach to IPE openly acknowledge the need to understand both the consciousness of and conditions facing historical actors and the place of the analyst in the reconstruction of history through chosen forms of analysis (see Amoore et al., 2000; Germain, 1997). If the first aspect of a critical historicist method as I have outlined is its attempt to understand macro historical transformation, the second is a reflexive positioning whose holders are cognizant of the historical limitations to thought in both historical actors and the researcher her or himself.

Historical inquiry, therefore, presupposes a meaningful question posed with latent or manifest intent on the part of the inquirer and the deployment of methodological and theoretical devices to help capture the phenomenon under question. This follows from E. H. Carr's (1961/1983) suggestion that the mind of the historian enters into a relationship with the historical record, thus obviating a strict subject/object dualism. Against charges of idealism, whereby historical interpretation remains arbitrary and premised *entirely* upon the discretion of the inquiring scholar, Carr suggests that history is not wholly created from the historian's mind and that all interpretations are not equally valid by way of this dialogue between the historian and the historical record. Though a strict objective history remains impossible so long as the historian decides which questions to ask and filters information through a mind that is itself located amidst discrete historical processes, a deep engagement with, and reconstruction of, historical evidence enables the analyst to eschew a purely subjective position.

Lawson (2010) questions the once prominent conventional wisdom of an 'eternal divide' within the discipline that firmly demarcated 'classical' (viz. *historical*) approaches from those aspiring to the status of a positivist social science. Instead, history and international relations are necessarily co-implicated, even in approaches that have different aims: a positivist 'history as scripture' approach, through which historical episodes are selected to confirm theory and a post-positivist 'butterfly' approach, which sees history as pure contingency and chance. Lawson borrows from both E. H. Carr and the Cambridge School of Historians, the latter of which is exemplified by Quentin Skinner, so as to reaffirm the significance of context in historical research, which includes the social processes by which a scholar engages with a particular body of material whereby historical materials become social facts. This at once serves as a corrective against the tendency manifested in the 'history as scripture' school, whereby the scholar ignores the multiple contexts in which historical knowledge is produced and adheres to a 'mythology of coherence' that enables theory testers to find in history the facts and patterns they require to validate a hypothesis. Lawson states, 'If scholars have a particular view to peddle, they will find evidence to support it' (p. 14). Moreover, events are theorisable 'in that certain "happenings" have outcomes that can be studied via the ways in which social formations emerge, become institutionalized, and change' (p. 15). In such a way may events escape pure contingency: they may be placed in analytical categories which are derived from social meaningfulness and purposive action. In such a reading, both scholar and the finished scholarly product are implicated in social processes that are more than the result of an individual's volition.

The position of Carr and Lawson has important affinities with historical materialist scholarship that focuses on the historicity of capitalism. If the historicist position articulated by Carr is defined by a rejection of completely arbitrary accounts of history by way of insisting upon the veracity of the historical record (through its relationship with the historian), historical materialism insists upon both the unity of capitalism (in that, such as it exists, it remains a coherent system) and the specificity (in terms of its historical contingency) of capitalist processes against post-modern assertions of the singular primacy of discourse, text and plurality (Meiksins Wood, 1995). In both cases, *both* historical interpretation *and* historical action are constrained and informed by the material parameters of human existence.

As it pertains to examining contemporary world order structures, such a reflexive and material positioning necessitates that a thinker triangulates: 1) how her/his subjectivity bears upon the content under analysis; with 2) the self-representations of the subject(s) under study; and 3) the wider social structures within which knowledge about the subject(s) is created.[6] This positioning might suggest the following for an IPE analysis of how social, political and economic actors articulate aspirates to hegemony, and such actors' relationship with knowledge production in and about Putin-era Russia.

First, one should be sensitive about the extent to which liberal hegemonic discourses in English language scholarship and commentary on Russia frequently reduce the Putin era to one of authoritarianism and Soviet restorationism while holding Russian political and economic developments to standards that correspond with Anglo-American experiences of polyarchy and capitalism (see, for example, Aslund, 2013). In a corresponding manner, contemporary literature on Russian state 'de-politicising' discourses developed during the Putin era fail to appreciate the extent to which Russian state representatives have engaged in such practices in wider material and ideational contexts of geopolitical and geoeconomic competition (Casula, 2013). Liberal hegemonic discourses depicting Russian foreign policy as antiquated revanchism render Western practices the standard bearers for appropriate global conduct and in the process foreclose a more finely tuned, dialectical analysis of a post-Soviet space that is now subject to intense competition among those with regional hegemonic aspirations (Russia, China) or non-contiguous, extra-territorial 'global' projects (the United States).

Second, it emphasises that Russian state organs and key social forces have considerable power for producing hegemonic knowledge about Russia's place in the global political economy for *Russian* public consumption. Furthermore, such knowledge is produced, often times in English and through means accessible by non-Russian speakers (see Chapter 1), with the intention of fostering consent for Russian state projects vis-à-vis American aspirations at the level of world order. In the first instance we should therefore acknowledge the central role of Russian state organs in mobilising Russian cultural motifs for the sake of legitimating, substantiating and explaining contemporary state-led economic and political projects. One result is, for example, a mixture of contemporary geoeconomic and geopolitical projects on Eurasian space that are articulated on the basis of Russia's stated historical cultural affinities with its neighbours. In the second instance, we should be sensitive to the manner by which actors create a generic cultural logic for an emerging multipolar global political economy to which non-Russian states and peoples can contribute.

Third, it argues that the Russian state inserts itself as the guarantor of social and cultural harmony for the Russian populace as a means to attenuate social, cultural and class conflict within Russia and increasingly as the guarantor of Slavic/Eurasian unity across various dimensions of the post-Soviet sphere. Such a position is well distanced from regional and international visions articulated by the Soviet state, insofar as it de-emphasises class-based difference as an explanation for both domestic and international discord. In other words, the logic given by the Russian state for its contemporary regional and international projects is often of a cultural/civilisation nature, as opposed to that which is overtly class conscious. As I demonstrate in this work, the cultural shell to accompany the material multipolar global political economy has been some time in the making.

The idea of historical structures and the semiotic/extra-semiotic model found in Cultural Political Economy demonstrate how meaning and interpretation are constrained by material parameters. Within the sub-discipline of IPE, the analytical category of historical structures is best articulated in the work of Robert Cox and related 'neo-Gramscian' scholarship (see also Gill, 1993). For Cox (1987), historical structures 'mean persistent social practices, made by collective human activity, and transformed through collective human activity' (p. 4). Structures are to be understood as produced by human agents and meaningful primarily insofar as they reflect collective human understanding in particular epochs. Structures are therefore repeated social practices which acquire a certain human objectivity, shaping human activity though not determining it in any mechanistic or straightforward sense. What begin as subjective practices become intersubjectively held beliefs among a group of people, acquiring in the process a certain human objectivity insofar as they represent consensus positions on matters of social significance (Bieler & Morton, 2001; Ives, 2006). Some critical IPE scholars emphasise the salience of Gramsci's philosophy of praxis when advocating for the adoption of transformative political projects. Such projects are to be realised through particular agents and their situated knowledge (Rupert, 2000; 2003; 2005; Cox, 2002). This precludes an abstract individualism that stands outside of the historical process and particular social and cultural formations.

With its deep engagement with material social, political and economic structures, critical historicism does not accord 'ideas' foundational analytical or ontological importance in historical analysis. While a prominent constructivist approach to IR might wonder whether international political reality is in fact 'ideas all the way down' (Wendt, 1999), historicist analysis is better conceived as retaining a commitment to understanding the correspondence between prevailing ideas that govern political orders and the material structures and interests which lie behind them. Such structures are nonetheless imperfectly and obliquely translated through symbolic, cultural and emotive representations. Ideas are not sought as the metaphysical or ontological origins of political and social life, but rather as the cultural realm of understanding and contestation, through which such political and social life is rendered meaningful and intelligible. Nor are analyses predicated on the discursive practices behind the production of identities themselves sufficient for understanding the actions of social and political actors (Laffey, 2000). Nonetheless, for historicist scholarship, investigating shared social understandings, or intersubjective ideas, is a crucial facet to understanding the potentialities for historical change, as shared cognition is as important to the material order of social relations which it defends or challenges.

The negotiation between intersubjective ideas and material forces figures prominently in Cox's particular reading of historical materialism, one that refuses to view material circumstances as completely *determinative* of social forms and social action. Structures in this reading are therefore not taken as part of a general ontology that is insensitive to human agency, consciousness and historical change. This is in contrast to other historical materialist readings in which structures are little more than capital's attempts to subordinate labour and discipline labour in the production process (Bonefeld, 1992; see also Burnham, 2002). Such readings neglect the cognitive and institutional structures that mediate historical change (Bieler & Morton, 2003).

For an historical, international and broader cultural reading this is insufficient, for it refuses to posit the existence of historical structures outside of class struggle, or the various institutional and intersubjective orders which mediate, if not constitute, economic relationships. Yet such recognition is crucial when seeking to understand resistance to economic globalisation, as this resistance is always culturally embedded (see Chin & Mittleman, 1997). This work thus defends a notion of structure which emphasises that behaviour is structured according to rules and tendencies, but not automatically caused by such structures. This is similar to Amin and Palan's (1996) concept of historicised political economy, which:

> forces an understanding, simultaneously, of how continuities are maintained and how societies evolve and change, with both aspects drawing upon subtle interactions between 'agents in institutions' and 'institutions in agents.' The latter metaphor draws attention to the structured influences on individual behaviour (from class, race and status to schooling, collective memory and ideology). The former metaphor highlights the dual aspect of institutions as products of collective rationalities (from laws and hard associational rules to conventions and tacit codes of conduct) and conscious actor interaction (from leaders and elites to groups in opposition and conflict). Thus, a historicised international political economy, at its best, moulds a broadly based institutionalist perspective that assimilates the distinction between structure and agency, to account for the fixity and flow of social evolution.
>
> (pp. 211–212)

Loosely situated within a wider historical-materialist camp, critical historicism is premised upon an understanding that limitations to transformation are to be found in the existing 'objective' material order, referring both to material relations between states and the material conditions of the production which give rise to social relations and condition political forms.[7] It is the very parameters of material life, domestically and internationally, as well as the power relations these entail and entrench through ideology, that warrant careful attention in analysis. Furthermore, recognising a role for 'ideas' in historical analysis permits that analytical weight be given to the manner in which the various material aspects of production and inter-state relations are mediated and asserted through intersubjective understandings.[8] How such material phenomena are represented and accepted is of equal importance – that is, the representation of historical change is as crucial as the material parameters themselves.[9]

CPE attempts to bridge the material/ideational divide in political economy without reducing emergent social phenomena to either. CPE scholars go beyond discourse analysis to examine the semiotic-material nexus of political economy. According to Jessop & Sum (2001), the intellectual leadership behind the Lancaster School of Political Economy, CPE may be considered as involving the following:

> a critical, self-reflexive approach to the definition and methods of political economy and to the inevitable contextuality and historicity of its claims to knowledge. It rejects any universalistic, positivist account of reality, denies the subject-object duality, allows for the co-constitution of subjects and objects and eschews reductionist approaches to the discipline. However, in taking the 'cultural turn,' political economy should continue to emphasise the materiality of social relations and the constraints involved in processes that also operate 'behind the backs' of the relevant agents. It can thereby escape the sociological imperialism of pure social constructionism and the voluntarist vacuity of certain lines of discourse analysis, which seem to imply that one can will anything into existence in and through an appropriately articulated discourse. 'Cultural political economy' should recognise the emergent extra-discursive features of social relations and their impact on capacities for action and transformation.
>
> (p. 94; see also Jessop & Oosterlynck, 2008)

The contribution of the CPE approach is found in its rejection of transhistorical analysis and insistence upon the significance of path-dependency, history and institutions in shaping social outcomes; its acknowledgment of the significance of the 'cultural turn' and the centrality of the production of intersubjectivity; and its emphasis on the co-evolution of semiotic and extra-semiotic (material) processes on social formations (Jessop, 2004; Jessop & Oosterlynck, 2008; Jones, 2008; Sum & Jessop, 2013). Textual/discourse analysis alone is insufficient to understand social totalities; rather, the semiotic aspects – intersubjective meaning – must be understood with the extra-semiotic (material) elements of the natural and social world (Jessop, 2004). This approach builds on critical semiotic analysis to determine the manner by which mechanisms of selection 'select and consolidate radically new practices and … stabilise routine practices'. Social reproduction is ensured through the variation, selection, retention and reinforcement of particular discourses and practices, which are then selectively recruited, inculcated and retained through particular social organisations and institutions (Jessop & Oosterlynck, 2008, p. 1159). Cautioning us to resist the temptation of siding with either the 'structuralist Scylla' or the 'constructivist Charybdis', Sum and Jessop (2013) instead emphasise the complex interaction, co-evolution and co-constitution of the semiotic and extra-semiotic realms of the social world (see pp. 147–195).

Best and Paterson (2010) have opened up the field of cultural political economy by demonstrating a number of ways in which 'culture' may be considered as constitutive of material economic existence. Seeking to avoid a reduction to culture as 'ideas and norms' as does constructivism or reducible to class, as does neo-Gramscian scholarship, Best and Paterson outline a multitude of manners by which culture can be conceptualised for the purposes of GPE research.[10] For Best and Paterson, the creation of free market economies on a global scale necessitates 'cultural work to produce the sorts of people and institutions that can sustain such economies' (p. 14). Such a suggestion finds an analogue in this work in my investigating the manner by which market logic has been legitimised in post-Soviet Russia through 'official' discourse that bends Russia's historical (national or civilisational) character to more utilitarian purposes (see Chapter 7) or expresses contemporary economic and political projects as those that are distinctly civilisational in nature (Chapters 5 and 7).

However, Best and Paterson's analysis of three broad shifts in the 'global' political economy – to consumption, to financialisation, and to neo-liberalism – is only partly helpful in the context of the (post)Soviet experience. So, too, is their insistence that 'We may no longer be experiencing the kind of dramatic cultural change that accompanied the invention of the modern market economy' (p. 15). The Russian post-Soviet social formation and corresponding state project are the products of the Soviet legacy on both an ideational and material plane. They are the collective entities within which intersubjective ideas derived from an 'alternative globality' in the form of the Soviet Union, as well as a pre-Soviet Russian engagement with Eurocentric modernity have been articulated, activated and contested. They are the site for what have been, following Soviet counterhegemonic internationalism and *homo sovieticus*, the profound reconstitution of geopolitical, geoeconomic, cultural, and civilisational, identities, discourses and practices.

Nonetheless, CPE is well situated to demonstrate how current economic and political phenomena are mediated, diagnosed and remedied through deploying the historical imagination. Samman (2015) distinguishes between the function a past crisis performs from the practices of historical imagination. Building on the insights of new crisis theorists, Samman suggests that crises are invariably overdetermined (innumerable factors contribute to a crisis 'objectively') and indeterminate (it is unclear how or which diagnosis can be 'path shaping' in the context of narrative competition). Once historicised, each 'crisis' provides an unlimited range of interpretive options. In such a moment, historical representation occurs through three distinct but interrelated practices: 1) *analogical reasoning* ('which consists of drawing analogies between crises' [p. 16]); 2) *narrativisation* ('which imposes a story order on history through the selection, sequencing, and configuration of more than one of its events' [p. 17]); 3) *lesson drawing*, which involves transposing the causal chain created through *narrativisation* into the present (p. 17; see also Samman, 2014).

CPE seeks to avoid 'soft cultural economics' and 'hard political economy'. The latter is found in deterministic Marxism, neo-classical economics, and approaches that reify and naturalise the economy without considering how it is constituted through practices at different scales at a given point in time. The production of intersubjective meaning helps ensure institutional stability and enables state intervention (see Jones, 2008). When addressing the significance of culture in political economy, a critical CPE approach must not overlook the disruptive aspects of economic systems. Furthermore, it must reject an 'imperialist culturism' which sees actors' positions being comprised entirely of cultural meaning and negates the constitutive and restraining effects of social, economic and political systems (Sayer, 2001).

CPE builds on Jessop's strategic relational approach to state theory, which rejects any general theory of the state in favour of historically and temporally situated processes and struggles associated with complex institutional ensembles.[11] In this reading, the state is a social relation, whose unity and coherence is always in a state of flux and subject to both structural impediments and competitive dynamics. While the state is not an abstract entity, it structures outcomes of the struggle of competing factions (Jessop, 1990; Glassman, 1999). The notion of a stable state entity is subordinated to a process-based account of political struggle and strategy whereby actors offer leadership in moments of material and discursive overdetermination and indeterminacy (see also Samman, 2015). Jessop's related concept of 'state project' is best understood not by referring to what the state is as such, but rather what its proponents do to impart a form of unity upon complex social formations.[12] Jessop (1990, p. 9) argues that the concept of state project is intended to acknowledge that disunity of a state and hence the need to (and difficulty of) imposing a functional unity upon state organs. Such a process-account of the state sees state concepts as prone to fits of unity and disunity and thus constantly reformulated according to various directives.[13] The state thereby imparts a degree of cohesion over fractious class and class relevant forces (see Poulantzas, 1973) and is inconceivable without an eye to the social struggles that undergird, and, in a sense, produce it. 'State effects' – the processes and practices by which the state is demarcated from society – are integral to this process; an investigation of such denaturalises the states and instead asks how the state is constantly produced and reproduced through material and discursive distinctions. The abstract appearance of the 'state idea' cannot be dissociated from the material practices of the state (see Mitchell, 1999).

A CPE approach directs us to examine the intersubjective element of state-produced ideas without disavowing the coercive and consensual role of the state. CPE elaborates on the notion of the state as a social relation by examining in greater detail the extent to which discursive practices couple with institutional practices to factor into the shaping of identities and subjectivities of the state system itself (Jessop & Oosterlynck, 2008). CPE informs my attempts to outline the contours of Putin-era state building and detail the manner in which both state and society have been *represented* and acted upon emerging from the disintegrative social and political entity of the 1990s. In investigating the activities of the Putin regime, I wish to examine how the Russian state has sought to impart unity and consensus on matters pertaining to Russia's position within world order.

A critical historicist examination of the extension of capitalist market and production relations would proceed in the space between an un-mediated view of class struggle and an overtly formal view of global and national institutions that elides questions of power, distribution and representation. An analysis cast in critical historical terms permits an examination of such relationships as instantiated in concrete historical forms across Western and non-Western contexts. Furthermore, on the terrain of IR and IPE scholarship, this might mean analysing the determinative aspects of the international state system without reducing historical transformations to either the economic base or political superstructure. An historicist approach to examining the global political economy would point towards the political, social and cognitive 'structures' through which global capitalism is mediated without rendering it a static, ahistorical entity or the unfolding of a singular economic, political, or cultural logic.

3 Common sense and polysemicity

Historical structures and intersubjective ideas yield content used to substantiate and articulate shared historical experiences. However, they may also serve as the means through which political 'reality' is distilled and articulated as a means to generate legitimacy. Shared intersubjective understandings may be captured and utilised by political authority to circumscribe the field in which debate occurs and in which political life is to be apprehended. They may be the means by which new forms of domination, inequality and hierarchy are rendered 'common-sensical'. The strength of officially sanctioned discourse is that it demonstrates both considerable regularity, in that it deploys concepts consistently enough to preclude alternative political horizons and possibilities, and ambiguity, in that diverse and seemingly unrelated phenomena may be said to confirm the legitimacy of the discourse itself. Jenson's (2010) notion of polysemic concepts and ideas is relevant in this regard (see also Best, 2012). A polysemic idea is that which has multiple meanings and possible interpretations. In the present work, I stress that polysemic ideas may be helpful to fashion consensus by organising political reality into a flexible, but circumscribed, picture meant to appeal to numerous and disparate people within defined political communities. Polysemic ideas contain both scientific and common-sense meanings; however, I suggest that they are most interesting to us here as containing enough ambiguity and capacity to be somehow relevant and meaningful to multiple groups with multiple positions.

That a concept may be polysemic is consistent with Gramsci's notion of common sense. As I suggested in the introductory chapter, for Gramsci, common sense shapes and constrains perception. As a 'chaotic aggregate of disparate conceptions' (Gramsci, 1971, p. 422), common sense lacks scientific legitimacy or consistency, yet its contents are frequently invoked by political authority to confirm our suspicions about political and social life. A large vein within neo-Gramscian scholarship concerns itself with the relationship between alter-/anti-globalisation movements and hegemonic consciousness (see Rupert, 2000; Eschle & Maiguashca, 2005; Gill, 2000). 'Global civil society' or some variant thereof is analytically and politically central to such studies, serving as the collective actor striving to create counter-hegemonic 'common sense' at the global level vis-à-vis neo-liberal globalising forces (Rupert, 2003). Common sense that valorises neo-liberal economics at the global level is frequently intertwined with what might be referred to as 'imperial common sense', which according to Gill (2012) signifies 'the strategic, international, or global dimensions of the wider creed of Americanism' (p. 510). It consists of 'key elements of American common sense – beliefs in the self-evident virtues of capitalism, individualism, religion, patriotism and the dominant global role of the USA' (p. 511).

Significant to this study, new forms of imperial common have developed since the Cold War. During the Cold War, American organic intellectuals such as George Kennan and Polish-born Zbigniew Brzezinski (the latter an important contemporary figure) cultivated a rationale for American geopolitical and geoeconomic interests vis-à-vis the Soviet Union, whereby left political conduct and Soviet geopolitical and geoeconomic interests became intertwined to the extent that imagining left politics without invoking the specter of the 'Soviet menace' was difficult in English language scholarship or within the Anglo-American universe. Such neo-liberal common sense mixed with cultural nationalism, served an important legitimising function in the immediate aftermath of the USSR (see Shields, 2014, for the Polish case).

Russia's prolonged and multifaceted transition from state socialism to state-directed capitalism has been accompanied by the resurgence of great power rhetoric and attempts by Russian officials to combat any positive connotations associated with the USA's global hegemonic project. The consolidation of state-directed capitalism necessitated a domestic and geopolitical identity to replace that of the Soviet Union and to attenuate the profound polarisation of Russian society between those seeking Russia's integration into Western global liberal institutions and those advocating for the reconstitution of a neo-imperial Russia from a variety of nationalist, communist and conservative positions. Russian political technologists – para-political professionals who espouse the Kremlin line in a variety of highly visible venues – have borrowed selectively from broader Russian political, cultural and philosophical debates to assert the historical and ethical basis for the Russian state's domestic and international conduct (Etkind & Shcherbak, 2008). During Russia's seemingly interminable post-Soviet transition, such figures have insisted that Russia could be capitalist provided that it was also a great power, 'sovereign' in its conduct vis-à-vis the USA, and able to demonstrate to its public the compatibility of a market economy with Russian cultural and political traditions while raising national living standards.

To promote a *domestically* hegemonic view with intrinsic class content, Kremlin-affiliated organic intellectuals – the so-called political technologists – emerged, constituting the social and material basis for information production and leadership on politically and economically sensitive questions associated with Russian political and economic transitions. This group served more than a straightforward political function of insulating the Kremlin from internal and external criticism, rejecting both Soviet-style state socialism and capitalism organised by a politically autonomous and counter-regime capitalist class. They were charged with the task of normalising the Russian state's 'modernizing imperative' ('Rossiya 2020' 2008; 'Konsepsiya dolgosrochnovo' 2008) and cementing Russian society's transition to a market economy under the aegis of the Russian state. This was done by synthesising notions about Russia's culture, the practice of Russian state craft, and political economy in pronouncements of domestic and international political reality.

For official Russia, class relations are largely purged from the analysis of a holistic and integrative state mechanism that ensures social solidarity and oversees national development imperatives in the interest of all Russian citizens. In such analysis, the American state exists as a largely abstract and holistic entity that aggressively pursues unipolar military dominance while imposing 'culturally specific' forms of neo-liberal development models and polyarchic democracy on national polities who exhibit different 'civilisational' tendencies. As I demonstrate in subsequent chapters, in the process, Russian society's transition to a market economy may occur under the aegis of the Russian state and by synthesising notions about Russia's unique culture, if not civilisation, its sovereign nature vis-à-vis the USA, and its 'alternative' development model.[14] Such representations are 'official' insofar as they come by way of state officials' efforts to accumulate, synthesise, and vet information. Moreover, prominent Russian officials have activated and embedded common-sense notions about the distinctiveness of Russian statecraft and civilisation vis-à-vis the homogenising tendencies and military, political, economic and cultural aggression found in the American hegemonic project.

The ambiguity of polysemic concepts is their strength: such a quality enables the concept to resonate with multiple subject positions in the service of a larger initiative, cementing ideological cohesion, consensus and legitimacy in the process. Rather than seeking to determine whether contemporary Russian state practices are born of invariant Russian cultural traits, a more interesting and relevant question to a political economy analysis is how Russian authority captures and deploys the language of culture in a manner consistent with its political and economic objectives. Putin deployed the language of Russian uniqueness, statism and solidarity as a means to generate legitimacy for his state building efforts and the historic task of rendering democratic ideas and market reforms palatable for a Russian populace for whom such ideas and reforms were associated with the chaos and uncertainty of the 1990s.

In addition to their obvious political roles and functions, Vladimir Putin, current President of the Russian Federation, the late Yevgeni Primakov, former Foreign Minister (1996–1998) and Prime Minister (1998–1999) of the Russian Federation, Sergei Lavrov, current Foreign Minister of the Russian Federation, and Vladislav Surkov, recently resigned Deputy Prime Minister of Russia and long-time *eminence grise* of the Kremlin, deploy polysemic concepts about international and domestic political life in a manner that stabilises regime imperatives. They selectively employ ideas about Russian culture to circumscribe the field in which debate occurs and in which political life is to be comprehended as they produce, propagate and normalise counter-(US) hegemonic world order concepts. Such figures exhibit an understanding of American hegemony that is in consistent with neo-Gramscian conceptions of the term, insofar as they emphasise the 'coercive', 'consensual', material and ideational components of American hegemonic projects (Anderson, 2002; Burron, 2012; Burron & Silvius, 2013; de Graaff & van Apeldoorn, 2011; Robinson, 1996). An examination of the capillary function of ideology and ideas in the discourse offered by political technologists and select representatives of the Russian state gives us a deeper understanding of the consensual/legitimacy-seeking components of Russian state capitalist aspirations to regional hegemony and corresponding critique of American aspirations to consolidate global hegemonic structures. In so doing, they provide greater analytical leverage than do realist accounts of hegemony, which are synonymous with unipolar military dominance (Wohlforth, 1999) or liberal accounts, in which mutual gain is presupposed for participants in American promoted multilateral fora (Ikenberry, 2004).

While much neo-Gramscian scholarship has focused on hegemonic and counter-hegemonic common sense at the 'global'/transnational level, much of post-Soviet Russia's story has been dominated by the 're-nationalisation of common sense' in the context of Russia's uneven entry into the capitalist global political economy. In this study I am concerned about what happens when Russian statist forces engage in similar discursive tactics in their critique of neo-liberal globalisation and American hegemony. For such a state project there is no direct and unproblematic correspondence between the semiotic/extra-semiotic, or ideational/material; the Russian state has managed their 'national' political economy's entrance into the capitalist global political economy in the post-Soviet period and prevented a reversal to state socialism, selectively liberalising while resisting some tenets of neo-liberal globalisation and American geopolitical and geoeconomic leadership.

Morton (2007) emphasises the extent to which Gramsci, in his reflection on the relationship between the modern Italian state, the development of capitalism, and the Italian peasantry, focused on the manner by which the Italian state 'assert[ed] itself through political consciousness in shaping the class feeling and mentality of producers, whilst peasant producers, at the same time, become transformed into propertyless individuals compelled to sell their labour' (p. 61). During this time, peasant consciousness is replete with the residue of folklore, religious beliefs, superstitions, and the like, constituting a complex moral economy within which class relations are situated and which are transformed, be it progressively or otherwise, into a 'modern outlook'. According to Morton, 'the experiential historical process of class formation is therefore recognized, situated within the lives and cognitive systems of ruler and ruled within specific contexts of antagonism and exploitation' (p. 62). Contemporary Russian citizens are not modern Italian peasants; yet the transformation from state socialism to contemporary Russian capitalism in a compressed historical period offers no less profound social and economic dislocations and relocations, social stratification, and the formation of, to a historically unprecedented magnitude in Russia, capitalist subjectivities. In such a scenario, official Russia has contributed to the historical process of collective subject formation and sought to mediate contemporary social and cognitive relations with its own particular *imprimatur*.

Hence, while we can suggest that the persistence of intersubjective ideas means that Russian responses to the advent of capitalism and democracy may be radically different from those of people in mature capitalist democracies, on the other hand we can suggest that political authority will seek to shape these ideas to ensure its continued centrality and legitimacy in contemporary political life. Borrowing from Gramsci in his urging for the use of a 'common-sense constructivism' in the case of Russia, whereby mass 'common sense' both stands in contrast to elite desire to reproduce neo-liberalism in Russia and seeps into elite discourse, Hopf (2013) suggests that 'one could conceive of a distribution of common sense, that is, the intersubjective structures of taken for granted ideas about the good life that undergird all societies and polities' as determining the stability or instability of hegemonic projects (p. 349). For Hopf, the persistence of a common sense that tolerates corruption and remains hostile to both neo-liberalism and Western forms of democracy *explains* Russia's semi-peripheral condition rather than stems from it.

Indeed, while it may be quite true that Putin/Medvedev speak frequently about how Russia is very much a part of European/Western civilisation,[15] part of the function of 'Putin era' discourse is Putin's, and, to a lesser extent Medvedev's, ability to contain in a given article, speech or news release multiple, indeed, contradictory elements that belie any form of conceptual or ideological purity. My intention in this work is to demonstrate the manner by which

Russian 'uniqueness' has been slowly, and unevenly incorporated into state-sanctioned discourse over time. Moreover, a conservative reading of Russian uniqueness has become particularly important in Putin's third term and corresponds with contemporary geoeconomic and geopolitical developments, Putin's manifest desire to mobilise his conservative and traditionalist support base, and Putin's attempt to dominate the 'discursive spectrum'. The versions of uniquely Russian 'cultural content' that come through in state discourse are less comprehensive than those which are offered by the philosopher or writer that the state official is borrowing from. Moreover, they are often instrumentalised in a manner that disrupts the historical specificity of the original work in order to speak to *contemporary* state projects. In recognising that logically and, in some ways, politically contradictory concepts are unsteadily side by side in much Putin-era discourse, my intention is to avoid essentialist positioning (Putin is/was Eurasianist, Westerniser, Statist, etc.). My preference is instead to examine how cultural content is mobilised for the purposes of various 'projects'.

By embedding common-sense understandings of multipolarity, Russian regionalism and civilisation that cohere to state strategy, official Russia invites us to efface the divide between political and scholarly practice when understanding how world order concepts are propagated and normalised. In their multifaceted critique of American post-Soviet unipolarity, key Russian figures contribute to IPE literature by unsettling the attributions made to unipolarity by defenders of Hegemonic Stability Theory (Kindleberger, 1986). They do so by questioning the assertion that American unipolarity is a net benefit to the global political economy by producing collective public goods and instead recast the American global project as military, economic *and* cultural aggression. Such a phenomenon demonstrates that Russia has not been incorporated seamlessly into global capitalism as envisioned by post-Soviet American strategists, for whom it was imperative that Russian actors forsake anti-systemic ambitions while incorporating into US-led global structures as a friendly, capitalist polyarchy (Gowan, 1999; Reddaway & Glinski, 2001). The Russian state's rhetorical and practical rejections of American unipolarity and hegemony and attempts to develop a new vernacular with which to articulate desired or existing global governance mechanisms are emblematic of this broader trend.

Analysing contemporary Russian contributions to an emerging, but contradiction ridden, multipolar global political economy in such a manner enables us to understand a shift in the global political economy. As it pertains to Russia, this shift has been the product of macro-level processes and 'ideational gestation' that have been developing since the collapse of the Soviet Union, if not before. As Russian state-guided capitalism becomes selectively integrated into the global capitalist political economy, it would appear that there is little discursive space for articulating Russia's *samobytnost'* or uniqueness, a notion derived from Russia's historical experience with modernisation and encounters with East and West. However, prominent Russian officials, in conjunction with a complex apparatus that creates Russian state-sanctioned ideas about global affairs, have rejected Western triumphalism by appealing to a longer tradition of Russian intellectual production to fashion a form of common sense about global political life. In various, and not always congruent ways, Russian officials, political technologists, and metaphysical radicals deploy concepts and ideas derived from Russian culture, history, thinking and statecraft – Eurasianism, multipolarity, civilisation – to express Russian state conduct during and before the Putin era, developing a vocabulary and conceptual apparatus to express dissatisfaction with the fundamental premises of liberal internationalism and Western-centred world order. Far from reaffirming an essentialist cultural disposition, such concepts demonstrate a polysemic and common-sensical quality, whereby they are flexibly mobilised to efface contradiction and generate legitimacy and intelligibility in the midst of a wide host of 'material' practices.

4 Critical IPE, world order and globalising capitalism

This work emerges out of debates within critical IPE concerning globalising capitalism. I add to this discussion some considerations about the need to understand wider processes concerning a particular space vis-à-vis the capitalist world economy through mediating devices: particular state–society complexes and associated representations. This reflects my suspicion that a prominent shortcoming to the world order literature is its treatment of the non-Western world with a degree of homogeneity. The prolonged Russian post-communist conjuncture comprises unique phenomena and reveals that Russian society engages with inherited and contested national legacies. The particularity of the Russian 'case' therefore might belie some of the assumptions of macro-structural IPE. My research concern is to avoid the mistake of demonstrating by theoretical fiat the place of such historically significant, non-Western cases in the contemporary global political economy. Such a concern is in itself hardly controversial, but it does have ramifications for how the international is conceived.

To start here we first must consider what is meant by internationalisation and transnationalisation. Robert Cox (1987) provides a helpful conception of the process of internationalisation, when he writes:

> The internationalising of the state is the global process whereby national policies and practices have been adjusted to the exigencies of the world economy of international production. Through this process the nation state becomes part of a larger and more complex political structure that is the counterpart to international production. The process results in different forms of state corresponding to the different positions of countries in the world economy. The reshaping of specific state structures in accordance with the overall international political structure is brought about by a combination of external pressures (external, that is, to particular countries though arising within the overall international political structure) and

> realignments of internal power relations among domestic social groups. Like the internationalising of production, the tendency toward the internationalising of the state is never complete, and the further it advances, the more it provokes countertendencies sustained by domestic social groups that have been disadvantaged or excluded in the new domestic realignments.
>
> (p. 253)

A particular state is the site of two encounters in the pressure to transform its political and economic apparatus: an *external* relation and an *internal* struggle of domestic social forces. For Cox (1987) the internationalising of the state occurs through: 'a process of interstate consensus formation regarding the needs or requirements of the world economy that takes place within a common ideological framework'; that 'participation in this consensus is hierarchically structured'; and 'the internal structures of states are adjusted so that each can best transform the global consensus into national policy and practice, taking account of the specific kinds of obstacles likely to arise in countries occupying the different hierarchically arranged positions in the world economy' (p. 254). Internationalised investors utilise or influence the state apparatus in order to facilitate accumulation. Accordingly, a state subjected to pressures of internationalisation witnesses struggles for influence in its component parts between those seeking greater and those seeking lesser internationalisation (Glassman, 1999).

The concept of transnationalisation serves to emphasise to an even greater degree the extent to which accumulation is constituted across national jurisdictions. In this reading, accumulation erases the 'inside' and 'outside' of global capitalism. Transnational social forces operate in multiple national jurisdictions simultaneously. The transnational does not constitute a 'level' as understood in IR in conventional fashion (i.e. national level; international level; European level), but rather extends across and links different territorial levels (van Apeldoorn, 2004). American political intervention and democracy promotion have been the processes by which transnationalisation has occurred in the Global South via integrative mechanisms that link local and global accumulation (Robinson, 1996). The key political question to be taken from the transnationalising problematic is to what extent the hegemony of one state–society complex is achieved through the active reformulation of another state's domestic regime, and how transformative power is operative *through* other states, rather than simply vis-à-vis other states, through the activity of such 'transnationalised kernels'. In this sense, exchange and productive relations are transformed in a host site through the actions of embedded groups, who themselves hold certain affinities and share certain objectives with wider transnational forces. A shift from internationalisation to transnationalisation signifies a *partial* eclipse of conventional ontologies of individualised nation-states within the international states system through a greater focus on the constitutive social relations between and through states and the suggestion of greater transnational functional integration of capitalist relations.

States become crucial battlegrounds between various fractions. Transnational historical materialism theorising emphasises that a division exists between national and transnational class fractions: those who rely primarily on transnational circuits of capital for accumulation and profitability – a transnational capitalist class (TCC) – and those who rely primarily on national circuits. This division cuts across and is transposed upon previously discernible national fractions of industrial, commercial and financial capital (Robinson, 2004, pp. 34–37; see also Gill & Law, 1989; Gill, 1993). In other words, the crucial class division in the contemporary age of globalisation is between those who seek greater openness in *all* national economies due to their particular accumulation needs and those who seek to close national borders and rely on the protection of the state for profitability and viability. This signifies to Robinson an eclipse of national-territorial configurations of capitalist rule. In this understanding, the American state serves as the '*point of condensation* for pressures from dominant groups to resolve problems of global capitalism and for pressures to secure the legitimacy of the system overall' (Robinson, 2005, p. 569). For Robinson (2015), the BRICS formation can be understood fully through the TCC lens, and he admonishes critical scholars who see latent, anti-imperial potential in the BRICS formation to 'expunge state centrism' and 'shift the level of analysis from nation-state capitalism in an interstate system to global capitalism in an ongoing process of capitalist class formation across countries and regions'. In such an orientation, the BRICS countries' 'interests lie in strengthening their national and regional staging platforms for ongoing global integration' (p. 3).

This formulation, though helpful, remains incomplete, particularly as it pertains to Russia. In significant ways, the social relations of capitalist production *extend* across numerous states and perform integrative functions that defy a territorial logic of power, a point emphasised by Robinson's (2004) conception of the transnational state (TNS) as an amalgam of institutions and actors that serves as a consolidated, authoritative entity separate from territorially demarcated states. The TNS is, therefore, the institutional form of TCC rule. While internationalisation/transnationalisation are helpful analytic concepts to express a state's adjustment to the global political economy and the composition of wider social relations, they are best conceived as allowing an interesting empirical question in the case of Russia concerning the extent to which such processes occur alongside Russian state capitalism and Russian political authority's reemphasis on Russia's sovereignty. Furthermore, that the Russian state leads initiatives to counteract geoeconomic and geopolitical projects of competitors in Russia's 'neighbourhood' – areas subsumed under Russian imperial ventures historically or deemed to be of deep strategic, economic and cultural significance to official Russia today – would suggest that the 'national' state's relationships with transnational loci of economic and political authority are complicated.

The Russian state has presided over the national political economy's integration into the global political economy, managing the contradictions and conflicts inherent in this broad transformation while attempting to build consensus within Russian society. The increasingly international basis for accumulation for large firms (see Chapter 3) has coexisted with the Putin regime's perceived need to reconstitute the Russian's state's domestic authority, legitimacy, capacity and security and favour Russian private and state capital. Somewhat paradoxically, the Russian political economy has become further integrated into the global political economy while Russian political authority has sought to develop a public philosophy and understanding of world order that emphasises Russia's claims to sovereignty in global politics and the right to conduct its affairs in a manner of its own choosing. The continued transition toward a market economy has intersected with the crisis of governability stemming from the 1990s and the Putin project of reconstituting central authority and managing globalisation processes to strengthen Russia's relative position amongst states and challenge American unipolarity. The Russian state,[16] resisting a strong version of the American hegemonic neo-liberal imperative, sets the parameters by which Russian and foreign, state and private actors may accumulate productive assets; challenges the geographical spread of the Western bloc – i.e. through active stances against NATO expansion to Ukraine and Georgia; and actively constructs political, economic and cultural integration initiatives in Eurasian space.

The internationalisation/transnationalisation problematic is simply one component of a configurative understanding of world order. In an application of his conception of historical structures to the study of global political and economic relations, Cox (1986) emphasises the need to understand historical structures and the configuration of world politics through analysing the interplay of material capabilities, ideas and institutions.[17] This typology is then applied to investigate three spheres of activity: 1) *social forces* (reflecting the organisation of production); 2) *forms of state* (reflecting state–society complexes); and 3) *world orders* (the configuration of forces bearing upon states) (Cox, 1986, pp. 218–221; Cox, 1987; Bieler & Morton, 2004). World orders are best understood historically and investigated according to the extent to which they are stable. For example, world orders – such as *pax Britannica* (mid-nineteenth century until World War II) and *pax Americana* (post-World War II until the contemporary period) – exhibit periods of greater, lesser, or no hegemonic leadership according to the particular constellation of material capabilities, ideas and institutions (Cox, 1996).

During periods of strong hegemonic leadership, 'concepts of control' – the world view of a particular hegemonic class, which is embedded to define the limits of the possible for society at large (van der Pijl, 1998, p. 51) – are prevalent and innocuous. This occurs at the international level, as well.[18] During the Putin era, we can see powerful fault lines develop within Russian state and society whereby the hegemonic position of the United States has been openly challenged in spite of the fact that the Russian political economy is increasingly capitalist and integrated within structures of the capitalist global political economy. In fact, official Russia has cultivated as its own vernacular to express dissatisfaction with the fundamental premises of liberal internationalism and American hegemony, thereby signifying that liberal capitalist sociability has not become fully engrained amongst the Russian elite or society as a whole and that Russian elites have not fully accepted a lesser role in international political life.

Cox (2002) has broadened the scope for investigating the ideational, cultural and intersubjective aspects of contemporary world order through an appeal for understanding how global transformations are filtered through civilisations and socio-cultural consensus. Civilisations are not territorially bounded entities and not subject to laws of development; rather, they reflect a correspondence between intersubjective ideas and material conditions, without being reduced to the latter. Cox's call for a plurality of civilisations is based on his recognition of the Western pretence to universal (business) civilisation, which is found in post-Cold War triumphalism, and the propensity for concentrated American power to enforce this civilisation throughout the world. Furthermore, the existence of multiple civilisations is obscured by the pretence of neo-liberal globalising imperatives. Civilisations are the historical dimension of culture and entities of the *longue durée*; not only are they the products of the historical dimensions of intersubjective consciousness, they are the spheres in which alternative futures can be imagined. Here I wish to contribute to an underdeveloped aspect of the Coxian tradition, as emphasised in myriad ways in his *The Political Economy of a Plural World*: the ideational and historicised component of civilisations as manifested in particular nations' contemporary encounters with global capitalism. In this work, Cox (2002) suggests that 'a sense of the uniqueness of Russian history remains latent as rejection of the West and as an alternative vision of society' in the midst of the post-Soviet emergence of Russian capitalism. Moreover, he cites the notion of the Russian Idea as that which 'appeals to an imagined past of communal values and the hope of a future good society' and serves as communal' (p. 182). Official Russia activates such historical ontologies, mobilising, crafting and guiding such sentiments in defence of material projects which may or may not demonstrate affinities with the mythical sentiments so expressed.

The internal 'state–society complex' and interstate political relationships are examples of the 'extra-semiotic' conditions that must be considered when assessing the significance of intersubjective meaning. The domestic encounter between various social forces does not occur in a vacuum but in and through manifestly political relationships within the international system. Therefore, while a framework of 'states as such' – politically and territorially sovereign units – cannot adequately capture transborder productive and economic relations, one may trace these relations as they are instantiated in a variety of state forms in any given historical epoch, under particular world orders. These state forms, though partly constituted by transnational forces, nonetheless vie with one another for supremacy in the world order. American hegemony is precarious, as the continued integration of national states into a pacified Lockean heartland of liberal-democratic states is met historically by Hobbesian contender states (van der Pijl, 1998). The history of capitalist expansion is thus marked by an economic relationship – capital's unequal exchange with labour – and a political relationship – 'an unequal exchange between the capital rich and the capital poor, including between wealthy and poor countries' (Boswell & Chase-Dunn, 2000, pp. 20–21). This becomes particularly important to any attempt to comprehend how various non-capitalist spheres have encountered political and economic forces stemming from national political 'elsewheres'. As I argue throughout this work, the incomplete incorporation of the Hobbesian contender state of Russia into the Lockean liberal democratic pact has yielded esoteric and 'pragmatic' geopolitical speculation, a mixture of compromise towards, accommodation to, and rejection of the core's dictates, and a corresponding vernacular developed to express this situation.

Hegemony in the Coxian/neo-Gramscian tradition is understood as first constituted in a particular territorial state before extending outward to establish hegemony across other state–society complexes. While such a conception allows us to consider international political, economic and social relationships stemming from a dominant state, it is incomplete. A full appreciation of hegemony requires a greater investigation of ideas, consciousness, interactive knowledge systems and the historical process (Gill, 1993). Furthermore, critical scholars must challenge the easy assumption that hegemony diffuses from North to South or from core to periphery (Pasha, 2006). Specific attention must be paid to concrete historical entities and the multifaceted relationship that ethno-national units have with global political economy. The 'state' has different connotations everywhere, and such connotations are not immediately swept aside as units become incorporated into the global political economy (van der Pijl, 2005). Historicist approaches should resist the urge to apply Western Eurocentric generalisations to the historical process of state formation and instead look at the historical specificity of states (Bilgin & Morton, 2002). The status of weak, peripheral or semi-peripheral states has been poorly understood in much contemporary critical IPE scholarship about world order (Worth, 2008). World order analyses have failed to understand the complexities of primitive accumulation and the export of capitalist sociality from the historical capitalist heartland to the global periphery (Shilliam, 2004). Further attention could be paid to the manner in which domestic social orders constitute any particular (national) state apparatus in the reformulation of policy and legal frameworks.[19] Importantly, developments out of the ashes of a previously viable *counter-hegemonic* world order warrant closer scrutiny than world order thinking has hitherto afforded.

We would do well to consider such engagements with world order thinking when examining Russia's prolonged transition from the Soviet Union to its precarious incorporation into the capitalist global political economy and contemporary geopolitical order. A deeper look at the intersubjective ideas accompanying Russia's transition is warranted: this transition has been met by the persistence and resurrection of pre-Bolshevik conceptions found in Russian cultural, historical and philosophical traditions, which have been activated within contemporary thinking and discourse. Russian thinkers and elites pay considerable attention to establishing a world order that looks radically different from that which is constituted by American unipolarity or hegemony. As the national political economy becomes (however imperfectly) integrated into the global political economy, Russian elites continue to seek a world order in which Russia has greater authority. Furthermore, long-standing traditions of the Russian/Soviet state's propensity to intervene into the domestic political economy as a means of improving its own international standing (Bunce, 1993) suggest that while the Russian political economy is subjected to the same challenges of capital accumulation and wealth creation, such processes are managed with an eye to the state's relative international standing. In other words, in the case of Russia, the general imperative of accumulation intersects with persistent challenges faced by the state to modernise and develop the economic infrastructure of a semi-peripheral power.

Such an approach to Russia enhances our understanding of world order. It involves investigating particular state–society complexes and national cultural representations to better understand global transformations in a contemporary setting. This is of crucial importance in the case of post-communist Russia amid the uncertainty of its transitional social, political and economic order. Furthermore, a focus on historical structures suggests that collective social action can and may take place at any particular level of analysis. In this sense, both the pressures exerted by the global system on a particular place and the many forms of resistance or contestation, progressive or otherwise, can be acknowledged. The relationship between the particular and the global in this sense is better understood as dialectical as opposed to determinative in any unidirectional fashion.

5 Conclusion

In this work I remain committed to understanding the material base of the prolonged Russian transition from the position of a Soviet state socialist counter hegemon to a form of state capitalism in an emerging multipolar world order. However, I seek to contribute to critical IPE literature by challenging an exclusively materialist conception of global capitalism and world order with that which is historicised through the experiences, practices and interpretations offered by the Putin regime. In other words, I seek to understand both the material processes of Russia's integration into a capitalist global political economy as a resource dependent, executive-led form of state capitalism and the intersubjective understandings and state-sanctioned representations of Russian national political life and world order that accompany these processes.

My critical reading therefore operates along two lines. First, I want to understand the ways in which representatives of an increasingly significant national political economy, which historically has existed outside of the capitalist core of the global political economy, is offering a vision of world order that questions the postulates of American liberal democratic hegemony. Second, I want to understand how such representatives have sought to legitimate their own practices within Russian society and insulate themselves from criticisms from without.

My investigation is premised neither on an economistic reading of the extension and consolidation of class forces across national boundaries, nor on an 'imperialist culturalism' that explains all social developments according to purported cultural properties. Instead, it considers both the 'semiotic' (intersubjective) and 'extra-semiotic' (social and material) elements of Russia's transition, the consolidation of state capitalism under Putin, and the Putin regime's corresponding dissatisfaction with a world order predicated on liberal democratic precepts and American hegemonic leadership. A purely materialist reading is incapable of capturing Russia's uneasy and sometimes antagonistic relationship with liberal capitalist democracies and its leaders' stubborn ambitions for power and influence in global affairs. Furthermore, explaining the practices of the Putin regime according to purportedly archetypical characteristics of Russian political culture is insufficient to understand the manner in which culture has been mobilised to suit the imperatives of political economy.

Russia's absorption into the capitalist global political economy has come as a 'Hobbesian contender state' operating vis-à-vis the 'Lockean heartland' of US-led liberal capitalist democracies. Hence, this work is a reflection on how Russia did not become a liberal, democratic, capitalist prototype and seamlessly fit into an American conception of liberal democratic world order on material or ideational levels. In historicising the notion of world order and examining it by way of the words and practices of the Putin regime, I investigate the manner in which geopolitical and geoeconomic contestation has been represented by the Russian state through a geocultural lens. The Putin regime has used the language of cultural difference to consolidate and legitimate regime state capitalist practices and challenge the liberal democratic precepts of American unipolarity and hegemony. In other words, the Putin regime is animating a series of concepts to contest American hegemony on an ideational and material basis through a thorough, albeit selective, engagement with ideas associated with Russian particularity.

Collectively, I call the products of this activity Russian alternative 'state-sanctioned' understandings of world order. They are comprised of a series of polysemic ideas and constitute a form a common sense that serves as the Putin regime's preferred representation of national and global political and economic life. Representatives of the Russian state draw on a deeper tradition of Russian cultural, political and philosophical thinking to articulate Russian particularity and sanctify a particular form of capitalism. This permits two insights that augment purely material readings of the phenomenon in question. First, the purportedly exceptional or anomalous practices of the Putin regime may be understood according to a wider and deeper array of Russian thinking and practices. Second, the Putin regime seeks to render its contemporary practices intelligible based on the argument that it legitimately represents Russian society because of its attentiveness to, and re-creation of, such traditions.

Notes

1 For a helpful overview, see Worth (2008) and Bieler & Morton (2004).

2 Note the distinction raised by Morton (2003) in defending Gramsci's purported 'absolute historicism', by which one may examine current political and social questions through historical ideas against 'austere historicism', by which the historian or thinker analyses ideas exclusively in their historical context.

3 Meiksins Wood (1995) defends a version of Marxist scholarship in the historical materialist tradition vis-à-vis accounts of unilinear capitalist evolution. She argues in favour of 'a historical materialism that allows no pre-ordained and unilinear sequence, in which the origin of capitalism – or any other mode of production – is something that needs to be explained, not presupposed, and which looks for explanations not in some transhistorical natural law but in specific social relations, contradictions and struggles' (p. 6).

4 This conception builds on a number of historicist IPE scholars, notably Cox. A very helpful summary is found in Bieler & Morton (2001).

5 According to Smith (1996), positivism entails the following: 1) logicism – that an objective confirmation of scientific theory should conform to deductive logic; 2) empirical verificationism – that only those statements which are empirically verifiable or falsifiable (synthetic) or true by definition (analytic) are considered scientific; 3) the enforcement of a theory and observation distinction – in that observation and theories are separate, with observations being theory-neutral; and 4) a Humean theory of causation – a causal relationship is established through the discovery of invariant temporal relationship between observed events (p. 15).

6 What follows is an extended version of my argument that first appears in Silvius (2015).

7 Richard Falk (1997) refers to Coxian thinking, along with the work of E.H. Carr and Hedley Bull, as comprising a 'critical realist tradition' within IR (pp. 39–45).

8 Morton (2006) emphasises the manner by which historical meaning is derived from concrete social formations, as opposed to a post-Marxist 'discursive' rendition of Gramsci's contributions.

9 I thank Randall Germain for this point.

10 Culture is conceptualised: as identity and difference (homogenising and differentiating); as webs of meaning (the semiotic dimension, as found in the interpretivism of Clifford Geertz); as material practices; as constituting the limits of rationality; and as ethical and determining values.

11 For epistemological purists, the inclusion of Jessop in a historicist reading of historical materialism may be grounds for concern given his reliance on realist epistemological premises. These are not differences that warrant charges of incompatibility. See Smith (2000) for a helpful review of the complex epistemology of Bob Jessop's state theory.

12 A similar approach (that lacks an eye to the economic 'base') may be found in Migdal (2001). By way of his 'state in society' approach, Migdal scrutinises the state's ability to impart unity and standardisation upon a complex social order.

13 Jessop (1990) adds, 'To understand the never-ending and ever-renewed process of state formation it is not enough to examine its institutional building blocks. We must also consider the "state projects" which bond these blocks together with the

result that the state gains a certain organisation unity and cohesiveness of purpose. A state without these properties is a state only in name. It does not exist' (p. 353).

14 I develop these lines of thinking in Silvius (2014).

15 I am thankful to an anonymous reviewer for emphasising this.

16 See Chapter 1 for my explanation of what I conceive of as the Russian state in this volume.

17 Cox has been accused of over-emphasising the material side of this 'trialectic' (Jessop & Sum, 2001).

18 Whether Gramsci's work can be used unproblematically to capture hegemony at the international level has been vigorously debated within critical IPE. Germain and Kenny (1998) question whether the 'new Gramscians' have adequately interpreted Gramsci's work, as they dispute that Gramsci's concepts can be legitimately 'internationalised'; that is, used to explain phenomena beyond the level of a national state–society complex. The authors are adamant in insisting that Gramscian concepts of hegemony, civil society and cultural understandings are efficacious only within national contexts. Morton (2003) defends the reflexive purposes of Gramsci's purported absolute historicism, by which the historian or thinker analyses ideas exclusively in their historical context, thereby suggesting that his thoughts and concepts can be applied fruitfully to understand the international level. Murphy (1998) suggests that the Gramsci most relevant to the study of international relations is the one who theorised and sought solutions to the problems facing Italy in its development in the early twentieth century amidst a broader capitalist economic and political order, as opposed to the one who simply focused on issues of statism. Morton (2007) presents Gramsci as a more sophisticated spatial and scalar thinker. Sassoon (2001) argues that Gramsci's concepts of hegemony and passive revolution are relevant and helpful to theorise globalisation. I prefer to view the matter in a manner similar to Cox (1983): Gramsci's works are themselves thoroughly historicised and potentially capable of offering insights into contemporary international relations.

19 One notable attempt to scrutinise thinking on internationalisation through an examination of domestic social forces can be found in Baker (1999). Through a detailed examination of Britain, Baker criticises the internationalisation literature for its imprecise handling of its core concept and ignoring the domestic base of internationalised power.

References

Amin, A., & Palan, R. (1996). The need to historicize IPE. *Review of International Political Economy*, 3(2), 209–215.

Amoore, L., Dodgson, R., Germain, R., Gills, B., Langley, P., & Watson, I. (2000). Paths to a historicized International Political Economy. *Review of International Political Economy*, 7(1), 53–71.

Anderson, P. (2002). Force and consent . *New Left Review*, 17, 5–30.

Aslund, A. (2013). Sergey Glazyev and the revival of Soviet economics. *Post-Soviet Affairs*, 29(5), 375–386.

Baker, A. (1999). Nebuleuse and the 'internationalization of the state' in the UK? The case of the HM Treasury and the Bank of England. *Review of International Political Economy*, 6(1), 79–100.

Best, J. (2012). Bureaucratic ambiguity. *Economy and Society*, 41(1), 84–106.

Best, J. & Paterson, M. (2010). Introduction: understanding cultural political economy. In J. Best & M. Paterson (Eds.), *Cultural political economy* (pp 1–25). London; New York: Routledge.

Bieler, A., & Morton, A. D. (2001). The Gordian knot of agency-structure in International Relations: a neo-Gramscian perspective. *European Journal of International Relations*, 7(1), 5–35.

Bieler, A., & Morton, A. D. (2003). Globalisation, the state and class struggle: A 'critical economy' engagement with Open Marxism. *The British Journal of Politics and International Relations*, 5(4), 467–499.

Bieler, A., & Morton, A. D. (2004). A critical theory route to hegemony, world order and historical change: Neo-Gramscian perspectives in international relations. *Capital and Class*, 28(1), 85–113.

Bilgin, P., & Morton, A. D. (2002). Historicising representations of 'Failed States': beyond the Cold-War annexation of the social sciences. *Third World Quarterly*, 23(1), 55–80.

Bonefeld, W. (1992). Social constitution and the form of the capitalist state. In W. Bonefeld, R. Gunn & K. Psychopedis (Eds.), *Open Marxism volume 1* (pp. 93–132). London: Pluto Press.

Boswell, T., & Chase-Dunn, C. (2000). *The spiral of capitalism and socialism: Toward global democracy.* Boulder: Lynne Rienner Publishers.

Bunce, V. (1993). Domestic reform and international change: The Gorbachev reforms in historical perspective. *International Organization*, 47(1), 107–138.

Burnham, P. (2002). Class struggle, states and global circuits of capital. In M. Rupert and H. Smith (Eds.), *Historical Materialism and Globalization* (pp. 113–128). London: Routledge.

Burron, N. (2012). Unpacking U.S. democracy promotion in Bolivia: From soft tactics to regime change. *Latin American Perspectives*, 39(1), 115–132.

Burron, N. A., & Silvius, R. (2013). Low-intensity democracy and political crisis in Haiti: the North American contribution. *Canadian Journal of Development Studies/ Revue canadienne d'études du développement*, 34(4), 518–532.

Carr, E. H. (1961/1983). *What is History?* New York: Penguin Books.

Casula, P. (2013). Sovereign Democracy, Populism, and Depoliticization in Russia. *Problems of Post-Communism*, 60(3), 3–15.

Chin, C., & Mittleman, J. (1997). Conceptualizing resistance to globalization. *New Political Economy*, 2(1), 25–37.

Cox, R. (1983). Gramsci, hegemony and international relations: An essay in method. *Millennium: Journal of International Relations*, 12(3), 162–175.

Cox, R. (1986). Social forces, states and world orders: Beyond International Relations theory. In R. Keohane (Ed.), *Neorealism and its critics* (pp. 204–254). New York: Columbia University Press.

Cox, R. (1987). *Production, power and world order: Social forces in the making of history.* New York: Columbia University Press.

Cox, R. (1996). Social forces, states, and world orders: Beyond international relations theory. *Approaches to world order* (pp. 85–123). Cambridge: Cambridge University Press.

Cox, R. (2002). *The political economy of a plural world: critical reflections on power, morals and civilization*. London; New York: Routledge.

de Graaff, N., & van Apeldoorn, B. (2011). Varieties of US Post-Cold War Imperialism: Anatomy of a Failed Hegemonic Project and the Future of US Geopolitics. *Critical Sociology*, 37(4), 403–427.

Eschle, C., & Maiguashca, B. (Eds.). (2005). *Critical theories, international relations and 'the anti-globalisation movement': the politics of global resistance.* London: Routledge.

Etkind, A., & Shcherbak, A. (2008). The double monopoly and its technologists: The Russian preemptive counterrevolution. *Demokratizatsiya*, 16(3), 229–239.

Falk, R. (1997). The critical realist tradition and the demystification of interstate power: E.H. Carr, Hedley Bull and Robert W. Cox. In S. Gill and H. Mittleman (Eds.), *Innovation and transformation in international studies* (pp. 39–55). Cambridge: Cambridge University Press.

Geertz, C. (1973). *The interpretation of cultures: Selected essays.* New York: Basic.

Germain, R. (1997). *The international organization of credit: States and global finance in the world economy.* Cambridge: Cambridge University Press.

Germain, R., & Kenny, M. (1998). Engaging Gramsci: International theory and the new Gramscians. *Review of International Studies*, 24(1), 3–21.

Gill, S., & Law, D (1989). Global hegemony and the structural power of capital. *International Studies Quarterly*, 33(4), 475–499.

Gill, S. (1993). *Gramsci, historical materialism and international relations.* Cambridge: Cambridge University Press.

Gill, S. (2000). Toward a postmodern prince? The battle in Seattle as a moment in the new politics of globalisation. *Journal of International Studies*, 23(3), 399–423.

Gill, S. (2012). Towards a radical concept of praxis: Imperial 'common sense' versus the post-modern prince. *Millennium-Journal of International Studies*, 40(3), 505–524.

Glassman, J. (1999). State power beyond the 'territorial trap' : The internationalization of the state. *Political Geography*, 18(6), 669–696.

Gowan, P. (1999). *The global gamble: Washington's Faustian bid for world dominance.* London: Verso.

Gramsci, A. (1971). *Selections from the prison notebooks.* London: Lawrence & Wishart.

Hollis, M., & Smith, S. (1990). *Explaining and understanding International Relations.* Oxford: Clarendon Press.

Hopf, T. (2013). Common-sense constructivism and hegemony in world politics. *International Organization*, 67(2), 317–354.

Ikenberry, G. J. (2004). Liberalism and Empire: Logics of Order in the American Unipolar Age. *Review of International Studies*, 30(4), 609–630.

Ives, P. (2006) Language, agency and hegemony: A Gramscian response to post-Marxism. In A. Bieler & A. D. Morton (Eds.), *Images of Gramsci: Connections and contestations in political theory and international relations* (pp. 60–74). London: Routledge.

Jenson, J. (2010). Diffusing ideas for after neoliberalism: The social investment perspective in Europe and Latin America. *Global Social Policy*, 10(1), 59–84.

Jessop, B. (1990). *State theory: putting the capitalist state in its place.* University Park, PA: Pennsylvania State University Press.

Jessop, B. (2004). Critical semiotic analysis and cultural political economy. *Critical Discourse Studies*, 1(2), 159–174.

Jessop, B., & Oosterlynck, S. (2008). Cultural political economy: On making the cultural turn without falling into soft economic sociology. *Geoforum*, 39(3), 1155–1169.

Jessop, B. and Sum, N.-L.,(2001). Pre-disciplinary and post-disciplinary perspectives. *New Political Economy*, 6(1), 89–101.

Jones, M. (2008). Recovering a sense of political economy. *Political Geography*, 27(4), 377–399.

Keohane, R. O. (1988). International institutions: two approaches. *International Studies Quarterly*, 32(4), 379–396.

Kindleberger, C. (1986) *The world in depression, 1929–1939*. London: University of California Press.
'Konsepsiya dolgosrochnovo sotsial'no- ekonomicheskvo razvitiya Rossiyskoy federatsii na period do 2020 goda'. (Concept of the Long-term Social and Economic Development of the Russian Federation for the Period until 2020) 2008. at www.economy.gov.ru/wps/wcm/myconnect/economylib/mert/resources/3879cd804ab8615ab426fc4234375027/kdr_171108.doc, accessed 20 November 2008.
Laffey, M. (2000). Locating identity: performativity, foreign policy and state action. *Review of International Studies*, 26(3), 429–444.
Langley, P. (2002). *World financial orders: An historical international political economy*. London and New York: Routledge.
Lawson, G. (2010). The eternal divide? History and International Relations. *European Journal of International Relations*, 18(2), 203–226.
Meiksins Wood, E. (1995). *Democracy against capitalism: renewing historical materialism*. Cambridge: Cambridge University Press.
Meiksins Wood, E. (2002). Global capital, national states. In M. Rupert and H. Smith (Eds.), *Historical materialism and globalization* (pp. 17–39). London: Routledge.
Migdal, J. (2001). *State in society*. Cambridge: Cambridge University Press.
Mitchell, T. (1999). Society, economy and the state effect. In G. Steinmetz (Ed.), *State/culture: State formation after the cultural turn* (pp. 76–97). Ithaca, NY: Cornell University Press.
Mittleman, J. (1998). Coxian Historicism as an alternative perspective in International Studies. *Alternatives*, 23(1), 63–92.
Morton, A. D. (2003). Historicizing Gramsci: situating ideas in and beyond their context. *Review of International Political Economy*, 10(1), 118–146.
Morton, A. D. (2006). The grimly comic riddle of hegemony in IPE: Where is class struggle? *Politics*, 26(1), 62–72.
Morton, A. D. (2007). *Unravelling Gramsci: hegemony and passive revolution in the global political economy*. London: Pluto Press.
Murphy, C. (1998). Understanding IR: Understanding Gramsci. *Review of International Studies*, 24(3), 417–425.
Pasha, M. K. (2006). Islam, 'soft' Orientalism and empire: A Gramscian rereading. In A. Bieler, & A. D. Morton (Eds.), *Images of Gramsci: connections and contentions in Political Theory and International Relations* (pp. 149–163). London: Routledge.
Poulantzas, N. A. (1973). *Political power and social classes*. London: New Left Books.
Poulantzas, N. A. (2000). *State, power, socialism*. London: Verso.
Reddaway, P., & Glinski, D. (2001). *The Tragedy of Russian Reforms: Market Bolshevism Against Democracy*. Washington: United States Institute of Peace Press.
"Rossiya 2020: Glavniye Zadachi Razivitiya Ctrany" ("Russia 2020: Main Objectives for the Country"). 2008. Moscow: Evropa Publishing.
Robinson, W. I. (1996). *Promoting polyarchy: globalization, US intervention, and hegemony*. Cambridge: Cambridge University Press.
Robinson, W. I. (2004). *A theory of global capitalism: Production, class and state in a transnational world*. Baltimore: The John Hopkins University Press.
Robinson, W. I. (2005). Gramsci and globalisation: From nation-state to transnational hegemony. *Critical Review of International Social and Political Philosophy*, 8(4), 559–574.
Robinson, W. I. (2015). The transnational state and the BRICS: a global capitalism perspective. *Third World Quarterly*, 36(1), 1–21.

Rupert, M. (2000). *Ideologies of globalization: contending visions of a new world order.* London: Routledge.

Rupert, M. (2003). Globalising common sense: a Marxian-Gramscian (re-) vision of the politics of governance/resistance. *Review of International Studies*, 29(S1), 181–198.

Rupert, M. (2005). Reading Gramsci in an era of globalizing capitalism. *Critical Review of International Social and Political Philosophy*, 8(4), 483–497.

Samman, A. (2014). Making financial history: the crisis of 2008 and the return of the past. *Millennium-Journal of International Studies*, 42(2), 309–330.

Samman, A. (2015). Crisis theory and the historical imagination. *Review of International Political Economy*, 22(5), 966–995.

Sassoon, A.S. (2001). Globalisation, hegemony and passive revolution. *New Political Economy*, 6(1), 5–16.

Sayer, A. (2001). For a critical cultural political economy. *Antipode, 33*(4), 687–708.

Shields, S. (2014) *The International Political Economy of Transition. Neoliberal hegemony and Eastern Central Europe's transformation*. London and New York: Routledge.

Shilliam, R. (2004). Hegemony and the unfashionable problematic of 'primitive accumulation.' *Millennium – Journal of International Studies*, 32(1), 59–88.

Silvius, R. (2014). The Russian state, Eurasianism, and civilisations in the contemporary global political economy. *Journal of Global Faultlines*, 2(1), 44–69.

Silvius, R. (2015). Understanding Eurasian integration and contestation in the post-Soviet conjuncture: lessons from geopolitical economy and critical historicism. *Research in Political Economy*, 30a, 235–258.

Sinclair, T. J. (1996). Beyond International Relations theory: Robert W. Cox and approaches to world order. In R. Cox and T. Sinclair (Eds.), *Approaches to world order* (pp. 3–18). Cambridge: Cambridge University Press.

Smith, S. (1996). Positivism and beyond. In S. Smith, K. Booth & M. Zalewski (Eds.), *International theory: Positivism and beyond* (pp. 11–44). Cambridge: Cambridge University Press.

Smith, M. (2000). *Rethinking state theory.* London and New York: Routledge.

Sum, N. L., & Jessop, B. (2013). *Towards a cultural political economy: putting culture in its place in political economy.* Cheltenham: Edward Elgar Publishing.

Sutcliffe, B. (2002). How many capitalisms? Historical materialism in the debates about imperialism and globalization. In M. Rupert and H. Smith (Eds.), *Historical materialism and globalization* (pp. 40–58). London: Routledge.

Thompson, E. P. (1978). The poverty of theory or an orrery of errors. *The poverty of theory and other essays* (pp. 1–210). New York: Monthly Review Press.

Tooze, R. (1990). Understanding the global political economy: Applying Gramcsi. *Millennium: Journal of International Studies*, 19(2), 273–280.

van Apeldoorn, B. (2004). Theorizing the transnational: A historical materialist approach. *Journal of International Relations and Development*, 7(2), 142–176.

van der Pijl, K. (1998). *Transnational classes and international relations.* London and New York: Routledge.

van der Pijl, K. (2005). Feature review of 'A theory of global capitalism: Production, class and state in a transnational world.' *New Political Economy*, 10(2), 273–277.

Wendt, A. (1999). *Social theory of international politics.* Cambridge: Cambridge University Press.

Wohlforth, W. (1999). The stability of a unipolar world. *International Security*, 24(1), 5–41.

Worth, O. (2008). The poverty and potential of Gramscian thought in International Relations. *International Politics*, 45(6), 633–649.

3 Examining Russia's post-communist transitional political economy

1 Introduction

The intention of this chapter is to give a snapshot of the 'material' or 'extra-semiotic' base upon which, and alongside which, contemporary Russian state-sanctioned understandings of world order are developed. The snapshot will emphasise that since the collapse of state socialism and the dissolution of the Soviet Union, the Russian political economy has selectively internationalised, while undergoing an uneven transition to a state capitalist economy. It is asserted here that to emphasise the extent to which Putin-era practices deviate from norms associated with liberal capitalism is to ignore the extent to which a particular form of market economy has been consolidated in Russia over the post-Soviet period, in general, and the Putin era, specifically. State measures to discipline Russia into a market economy have been an important feature of this 'transition'.

That the Russian political economy is enmeshed in the global political economy according to the tenets of market competition, albeit partly via the disciplinary functions executed by executive and bureaucratic state mechanisms, is an important observation to bring retrospectively to discussions that have unfolded across comparative political economy literature on Russia. While particularistic relations and both bureaucratic and executive decision making may have disrupted any full 'automation' of a market economy in Russia – the internalisation and self-reproduction of market norms and practices – Russian state organs and officials have been central to creating the conditions for market-based exchange and accumulation. Russian state organs and key Russian officials, therefore, have done more than obstruct the free movement of capital and the marketisation of property relations and exchange: they have participated in the historical consolidation of a market economy in Russia and created the institutional and ideational basis for capitalist accumulation while contributing to a systematic transformation out of the Soviet planned economy and corresponding social and economic provisions. Historicist analysis can contribute to the discussion by demonstrating how Russian state organs, including the office of the president, and key officials have relied on varying degrees of coercion and consent in the formation of a market economy in

Russia, even if their ability to fully discipline Russian society, including pro- and anti-market forces, into accepting such a settlement is incomplete. As I demonstrate in subsequent chapters, Russian state recourse to discourse that valorises state power, nationalism, and Russian political culture may be seen not simply as obstructing the emergence of a market economy in Russia, but rather facilitating it.

Russian capitalism both challenges and bends some of the fundamental tenets of neo-liberal globalisation while adhering to many of its precepts. In the Putin era, a degree of stability and predictability has been coupled with an emergent state-produced normative order, as the Putin regime has sought to articulate Russia's place in the contemporary global political economy. While presiding over a consolidated market economy, it has rejected many of the precepts of Western liberal world order: Western, liberal-democratic ideas and those associated with American hegemonic rule are displaced by those derived from Russian history and philosophy, primarily those which emphasise autonomy, sovereignty, and Russia's right to determine national development priorities and practices in accordance with its political culture and preferences. These ideas are central to any reflection on Russia's emergence from the Soviet system, through a period of disorder and turmoil in the 1990s into a world order deemed by the Putin regime to necessitate geopolitical power, the state's command of resources and economic competitiveness as prerequisites for the Russian state and populace's well-being. I call this position 'sovereign integrationist', one in which Russian officials articulate a perceived need to manage globalisation processes and internal political developments while selectively integrating into the global political economy according to market tenets. Such a position is partly constituted by the Russian state playing a coordinating role in domestic and external processes of capital accumulation. However, it is also partly constituted by argumentation in which Russian cultural and civilisational distinctiveness is emphasised, if not overstated, while private and state actors participate in global capitalism in a manner not entirely dissimilar to Russia's competitors.

In this chapter, I examine Russia's transitional political economy in the 1990s – its incomplete and imperfect adoption of free market principles, institutions and normative order – as well as Russia's meaningful, but uneven, 'material' resurgence in the Putin era. While at the level of national political economy, Putin-era Russia has undoubtedly witnessed an improvement in its overall material conditions, its integration into the global political economy remains dependent upon the extraction and sale of resources and uncompetitive in the production of goods. By way of its 'modernisation' paradigm, the Russian executive has sought to discipline Russian economy and society into transitioning beyond reliance on the state for social well-being while nonetheless being charged with the task of managing the displacements associated with the transition to a market economy.

In subsequent chapters I emphasise the extent to which the latter phenomenon has occurred on a semiotic and ideational level. The Russian political economy now exemplifies certain norms and understandings that condition the terms of accumulation, conditions which serve as a counterpoint to liberal-capitalist-polyarchic systems: the Russian state, led by the presidential administration, is the arbiter of who controls major productive assets. Domestic capital is to acknowledge the political supremacy of the Kremlin. International capital and political forces are to acknowledge Russia's right to construct a domestic political system that deviates from polyarchic principles.

Russia's position within the global political economy remains characterised by a semi-peripheral status that suggests resource extraction's dominant role in the state's and economy's well-being, the persistence of geoeconomic/geopolitical competition against the core, the crafting of a centralised political structure to manage economic, social and political tensions inherent in Russia's prolonged transition to a market economy, and attempts to carve out preferential zones for Russian capital through regional economic and political architecture. The Russian executive and Putin regime, meanwhile, attempt to coordinate Russian capitalism and discipline Russian society into an 'entrepreneurial' mindset and capitalist sociability so as to facilitate private capital accumulation and economic competitiveness. Meanwhile, the Russian state plays a modest role in redistribution and attenuating social conflict in the midst of a transition out of Soviet domestic and international identities and practices. These elements are investigated in this chapter and form the material basis by which Russia's alternative world order concepts are to be understood.

In Section 2, I consider Russia as one of a number of states that combine illiberal (by Western pluralist standards) political practices at the regime level amidst the consolidation of a market economy. In the case of Russia, this tendency developed in spite of the initial expectation in the post-Soviet period by the Yeltsin government, American state, and international financial institutions (IFIs) alike that Russia would follow the twin tracks of liberal-democratic and capitalist development.

In Section 3, I demonstrate the chaotic nature of the post-Soviet transition and suggest that this period was characterised by an absence of both the legitimacy and institutional basis for market practices. Putin-era efforts to consolidate authority and legitimacy are to be understood partly on this basis.

In Section 4, I consider how the Putin project consists of reconstituting state authority and providing a normative order to accompany the consolidation of capitalism through providing expectations and assumptions as to how accumulation can occur in Russia. In Section 5, I demonstrate the precarious position that Russia as 'sovereign integrationist' occupies in the contemporary global political economy. This position is characterised by an over-reliance on extracted resources, the uncompetitiveness of manufacturing, and increased autonomy vis-à-vis IFIs. The position is also characterised by a selective internationalisation of the Russian economy, the prolonged introduction of a 'modernisation' paradigm, and the prioritisation of Russia-centred regional structures. A conclusion to the chapter follows in Section 6.

2 The Russian state amidst the transition towards a market economy

History has enabled us to declare that the Russian transition from the Soviet period has violated the expectations and hopes of early liberal prognostications. Early post-Soviet thinking was dominated by the democratisation theory of the 'transitologist', 'consolidologist' or 'orthodox' schools found in comparative and Russian studies, which view the phenomenon of political transition in post-communist societies as one that may be compared to earlier democratic transitions in Southern Europe and Latin America. According to this line of thinking, post-communist transitions may be seen as a part of a wider series of regime changes that may be studied with the same conceptual tools, irrespective of the geopolitical or culture specificity of the political entity in question (Schmitter & Karl, 1994).[1] Transitologists use generalist and positivist methodologies that abstract and plot a number of variables supposedly common to all transitioning regimes.

This school of thinking cannot account for fundamental differences between post-communism and other transitions – in the nature of authoritarian rule, modes of transition, the international context of transition and the transitional agenda. Such differences render post-communist and other states beyond being comparable in any meaningful sense (Bunce, 1995 & 1999). Furthermore, post-communist states themselves varied considerably in their transition experiences according to internal and external processes, making the internal uniformity of the category of post-communist state questionable (Agh, 1999). Contrary to their assertions of using an objective, positivist methodology, orthodox approaches to democratisation remain overtly normative, as they seek the means by which authoritarian regimes achieve pluralism at the elite and party level without assessing the material conflicts accompanying such transitions (see Waylen, 1994). Orthodox approaches to democratisation neither appreciate the challenging task of constructing civil society and liberal institutions in societies that were hardly independent of the state, nor account for the role of ethno-nationalism in filling the normative void left by the collapse of a communist 'state-sustaining ideology', all of which refracted the notion of liberal democracy in the early post-Soviet period (Schöpflin, 1991, 1995 and 2000).[2]

With its focus on how best to achieve functioning institutions, domestic political stability and political pluralism, democratisation literature also cannot acknowledge that capitalism has been built in Russia historically from the state downward. Moreover, collectivist orientations and anti-market sentiments remained powerful in Russian society throughout the post-Soviet period (Nesvetailova, 2004b). Russian state organs and officials have taken on the function of managing the social dislocations and conflict endemic in comprehensive systems transformations. When viewed in terms of the *longue duree*, the imperatives of state building have trumped capital accumulation in Russia – one cannot examine Russia without understanding how geopolitics, self-preservation, and leaders' attempts to attain parity with the West have led to state incursions into the political economy (Derluguian, 2001; see also Tsygankov, 2014 and Gerschenkron, 1962).[3] Russia's historical experience has coincided with a compelling trend in the global political economy in recent years – the emergence of a series of non-polyarchic,[4] non-democratic, if not quasi-authoritarian, forms of state whose representatives selectively adopt liberalisation initiatives alongside sovereign dictates in order to manage globalisation processes for national interests with one eye towards state capacity in the context of geoeconomic and geopolitical competition with the Western core and contender states alike.

While it would be misleading to state that Russia's post-Soviet experience with democracy has been categorically poor, its engagement with polyarchic democracy and (neo)liberal economic norms has been contentious in the post-Soviet era. Russia's integration into the global political economy following the collapse of the Soviet Union would not take place according to the strong liberal reading of globalisation: unfettered market access, robust pluralism and the eradication of state ownership or management of productive industries. The reassertion of the state's presence in the Russian economy does not represent the abandonment of a broadly liberalising and marketising path, but simply re-embeds the state in the process of creating a market economy, wherein it establishes the political legitimacy and institutional basis for further liberalisation and economic restructuring (Nesvetailova, 2005). During Putin's first two presidential terms, Russia may have been on the vanguard of demonstrating the twinning of liberal economic reforms and authoritarian political inclinations: the illiberal and exceptional (i.e. the manifestation of sovereign entitlement) aspects of Putin's presidential administration were elements of Putin's liberal market reforms (Prozorov, 2008). Traits deemed exceptional to the Russian case and indicative of an inability to apply purely market and pluralist political methods are rather to be thought of as an emerging norm for a number of non-Western states now seemingly outside the reach of American hegemony.

Russia's adoption of the model of 'development state', comprised of state-directed long-term development, state mobilisation of resources to achieve development within the general framework of a market economy, and political authoritarianism, facilitates the national political economy's adaptation to global competition while distancing it from the Western model of liberal democratic capitalism (Ferdinand, 2007). In this present situation, Russia is caught between two tendencies: the fact that central leadership is buoyed by other economies' dependencies on its resources and the regime's expressed desire to liberalise the domestic economy, trade and investment climate while gradually reducing government control over productive assets (Zhuplev, 2008). Putin-era Russia exhibits what at first glance appear as contradictory tendencies: the prolonged introduction of a capitalist economy, the continued questioning of the liberal postulates of globalisation, and continued suspicion over the existence of an independent capitalist class that operates outside of the control of state mechanisms (Sakwa, 2008a).

Russia is part of a large group of emerging non-Western states who, through the use of sovereign wealth funds and state corporations, are coming to challenge Western predominance in the global political economy. While such states sometimes declare national exceptionalism and dissatisfaction with neo-liberal development, they are better understood as adhering to the strategy of acquiring assets and accepting the competitive nature of accumulation. The increased prevalence of 'statist globalisers' should not be construed as being completely hostile to foreign capital, however. In spite of highly visible acts by Putin to limit the ability of foreign energy firms to acquire productive assets in Russia, the country reveals the deepening of ties between foreign capital and Russian state capital. Nationalistic overtures on the part of the Putin regime and Russian elites are at best part of the story, as Russian firms are becoming deeply integrated into transnational networks (Harris, 2009).[5]

While the Putin era is distinct for the increasing centralisation of authority (see this chapter, below), it cannot be said that Yeltsin-era Russia was a successful case of the spontaneous development of liberal economic practices. Coercive measures by the Russian state, particularly in the position of the Russian president, have accompanied Russia's adoption of market principles since the dissolution of the Soviet Union. Contrary to assertions of the viability of Russia's liberal project of democratic elections and a burgeoning civil society (Weigle, 2000), critical scholars highlight the decidedly undemocratic measures required to push forth free market reforms in the face of strong resistance. This came through the increasingly autocratic rule of Yeltsin and intense collaboration with IFIs. The drive to free markets in the immediate post-Soviet era in Russia was a top-down process, a move that constituted the de-socialisation and de-democratisation of Russian post-Soviet transition for the purposes of the longer-term consolidation of the market economy. The process is referred to by Gowan (1999, p. 189) as 'inverted Leninism' and by Reddaway & Glinski (2001) as 'market Bolshevism'.

Neo-Gramscian scholarship focuses on the hegemonic consolidation of liberalising regimes as aspects of a broader project of transnational class power, highlighting the affinities between the Russian domestic political regime and foreign capital.[6] Neo-Gramscians locate the late Soviet era and early post-Soviet Russian transition in the context of a Western hegemonic project and the diffusion of Western cultural norms, with Yeltsin forging the stability under which a new hegemonic project of capitalist accumulation could occur. Nonetheless, acute political fragmentation, economic turmoil and lawlessness within post-Soviet Russia prevented any clear legitimacy of a hegemonic project within civil society. Yeltsin's Russia in turn served to partially legitimate the *global* project of neo-liberalism, despite the fact that efforts at instilling a mature capitalist class for whom liberal-democracy provided the accepted social, political and economic norms were only partial at best. In Gramscian terms, Yeltsin may then be viewed as a 'Caesarist' quasi-dictator, an authoritarian and executive-led response to an impasse in the struggle between social forces (Worth, 2005, pp. 93–112; see also Lester, 1995 and 2000; Simon, 2010).

This project combined the continued authority and rule of the Soviet-era *nomenklatura* system of controlled, hierarchical bureaucratic appointments with international and organic intellectuals; the latter assisted Yeltsin's regime in delegitimising potential counter-hegemonic projects found in those opposed to Yeltsin's rule, de-socialising and de-democratising the Russian post-Soviet transition for the purposes of the longer-term consolidation of the market economy. Economic liberalisation and altered domestic power relations in post-Soviet Russia and the former Soviet sphere can be understood as a part of a wider 'globally constituted process' of capitalist restructuring along neo-liberal principles with the involvement of IFIs and the United States (Bedirhanoglu, 2004). In the early 1990s Russian shock therapists, IFIs and American leaders combined with the intellectual leadership of Harvard professor Jeffrey Sachs[7] to usher in domestic institutional reform towards an open free market economy with the understanding that this would clear the vestiges of state socialist rule. Russian reformers and international colleagues sought price liberalisation and financial stabilisation prior to the privatisation of industry in order to alter power relations within the post-Soviet Russian society. They sought deep cuts in government subsidies to industry (thereby rendering them competitive), creating a market for resources. Enterprises would become dependent on private investment/credit. In the absence of subsidies, economic activity would become commercialised, with the assumption that foreign capital would enter. Foreign capital plus a nascent class of entrepreneurs would then displace rent-seeking managerial elite and state officials (Robinson, 2004a).

Putin's 'negotiation' with the oligarchs and efforts to reconstruct central authority may have changed the equation envisioned by early Russian reformers, IFIs, US leadership and liberal intellectuals. Nonetheless, in spite of some high profile cases that may suggest otherwise, such as that involving Yukos and Mikhail Khodorkovsky, it is possible to view the Yeltsin and Putin years as a settlement on the *idea* of private property in post-Soviet Russia and market economies as organising principles, insofar as the rules of the game for private ownership have been established without the possibility of a full-scale reversal to state socialised ownership or corresponding Soviet-style economic and social provisions. Practices of corporate raiding, asset stripping, short-termism, state control and particularistic forms of exchange (barter/non-monetised in-kind) witnessed over the post-Soviet period complicate, but do not obviate market relations. Moreover, Russians' livelihoods, material well-being, and struggles are increasingly shaped by the extent to which their needs and aspirations are or are not satisfied by market criteria. Such 'material' indicators constrain the extent to which cultural and civilisational difference obtain in the Putin era.

3 Disintegration and the shaky terrain of Russian capitalism

The authoritarian and international elements of Russia's initial post-communist transitions were coupled with the particular qualities of nascent Russian capitalism. The post-Soviet Russian political economy cannot be understood as a mature capitalist system, in which norms, laws and processes associated with the ownership of private property are largely internalised and uncontested, but one beset with a number of points of contestation. One must look at Russian state and society as a continuation of Soviet foundations to determine the extent to which post-Soviet conditions could produce a 'smooth' space within which capitalism can operate, for either domestic or international accumulation.

Non-monetised social relations did not simply dissolve with the Soviet Union. Rather, they constituted a phenomenon which continued well into the post-Soviet period in spite of attempts to instil market discipline in the forging of new forms of socio-economic coordination. This condition was exacerbated rather than resolved by actions undertaken to promote liberalisation. The monetarist drive along with financial liberalisation in the 1990s created severe liquidity problems in the industrial sector and the emergence of barter trade, non-payment and other forms of endogenous credit creation in Russia which were decidedly not indicative of a monetary economy (Krueger & Linz, 2002; Nesvetailova, 2004a). In light of incomplete monetarisation, the new elite in post-Soviet Russia is a complex and uneasy mix of a 'bureaucratic bourgeoisie' (which must be understood in light of the historic importance of the bureaucracy in Russia) alongside a banking/speculative sector, with close ties to international finance. Together, this suggests 'a peculiar symbiosis of the traditional corporate-bureaucratic order with the power of comprador and usurer capital' (Nesvetailova, 2004c, pp. 52–54). The contemporary Russian political economy remains thoroughly infused with bureaucratic ownership and management at all levels, as liberal commentators are quick to lament (Shevtsova, 2007, pp. 118–131).

Russia continues to violate the liberal abstractions of market transactions unfettered by political 'irrationality' or 'obstinacy'. Early Russian reformers and their international counterparts felt that if successful, the introduction of a market economy could undermine particularist relationships by universalising exchange relations and subjecting those who hold economic resources to market discipline (Robinson, 2004b, pp. 9–12). Market institutions (money and corporate ownership) have functioned at a transactional but not juridical level. Such a 'shallow marketisation' results from an imperfect grafting of a free market order on society itself. The unstable social foundations of monetary and corporate orders complicate attempts at rational, universal ordering (Woodruff, 2000). Contracts are still not consistently adhered to and property rights remain imperfectly guaranteed by law; the personal power of the executive to settle disputes between contending factions bares similarities to an historical pattern of development stretching deep into pre-Bolshevik Russia (Hedlund, 2008). The systematic, rule-based and law-backed accumulation of capital – that is, a fully institutionalised and routinised process free from particularist relations and intervening political authority – has not fully obtained in contemporary Russia.

If post-Soviet Russia was not fully capitalist in terms of the use of money for exchange and accumulation, neither was it from the standpoint of production: the majority of wealth in the 1990s was not derived from the creation and appropriation of surplus value. Rather, we can think of Russia's still emerging political economy as containing elements of a 'predatory/extractive system':

> in which the basis of the property income of the dominant class is not the present labor of the population, as is normally the case in a class system, but rather, indirectly, their past labor under the former Soviet state socialist system. This past labor, together with the gifts of nature, enables this class to derive a large income out of surplus value created in world capitalism. Perhaps the best term for this system is a predatory/extractive system, whose property-owning class is a mixture of landlords, merchants, money-lenders, speculators, revenue-skimmers, misappropriation of public funds, and extortionists, along with some capitalists.
>
> (Kotz, 2001; see also Lane, 2000)

Additional literature reinforces the view that the Russian political economy remains largely extractive in nature, with low level of investment going towards diversifying the production base (Wood, 2007). This notion is reflected in figures presented later in this chapter, which demonstrate the uncompetitive nature of Russian production and Russia's reliance on the extraction of resources.

Transitional Russia was indeed a risky place for capital, evidenced by the massive capital flight of the 1990s (Mauro & Loungani, 2001). The speculative nature of post-Soviet capitalism is reflected in patterns of foreign direct investment (FDI) that did occur. Vis-à-vis all post-communist states, FDI in Russia was comparatively lower in the late Soviet and initial post Soviet period (i.e. 1989–2001) both per capita and as a percentage of GDP. Furthermore, that which did enter Russia as 'foreign' money was often in the form of repatriated capital that once exited the country through capital flight. The above suggests that the impact of FDI in Russia has been relatively low within the post-Soviet universe (Robinson, 2004a, pp. 27–29). The influx of short-term portfolio inflows and the absence of long-term foreign investment in the productive sector reinforce Russia's peripheral status and suggest that it is not yet fully integrated into the dense webs of investment indicative of the capitalist core (Nesvetailova, 2004b). The transnationalisation of production and finance did not occur systematically in Russian space during the initial post-Soviet period and remains a protracted and uneven phenomenon while the Putin regime has negotiated the relationship between foreign investment, the security imperatives of the Russian state, and the accumulation imperatives of Russian state and private capital.

4 Putin's statism

The severe strain experienced in Russian society in the 1990s was accompanied by the collapse of state institutions and the general state of lawlessness in Russia in the transition period (Popov, 2000; 2001; 2007; Shlapentokh, 2003). One may think of Russia's early transitional, post-socialist political economy as a 'chaotic social formation', wherein institutional coordination, governing institutions and social cohesiveness were lacking (Lane, 2000). This includes the absence of both a cohesive value system for Russian capitalists and any coherently articulated dominant bourgeois class interest (Lane, 2000; Hanson, 1998). One may speak also of the 'privatisation' of government by narrow economic interests and the concomitant neo-patrimonial state as an emergent phenomenon in the 1990s with a particular logic of its own (Dutkiewicz & Popov, 2006; Yakolev, 2006; Hellman et al., 2000). Putin's efforts to restore the state's coercive, administrative and fiscal capacity were central tenets to his first two presidential terms. A reconstituted state with strong central authority and a corresponding aura of moral and practical legitimacy would come to dominate the Putin era and form the basis for political and economic competition.

Putin's centralisation of authority and autocratic tendencies have been interpreted by scholars in a number of ways. Some see the restoration of central authority under Putin as necessary given Russia's recent post-communist instabilities and diminished state capacities. According to this line of thinking, Putin's historic task was to reverse the trend of the 1990s in which the Russian state lost its capacity to govern as it was privatised and 'leased' to a group of oligarchs that had emerged from the state's privatisation scheme. Putin's group was determined to restore the integrity of the state, the 'traditional and central engine of social development in Russian history… In order to accomplish this project, they had to link the state and accumulation into one undivided whole of social power' (Dutkiewicz, 2009, n.p.). The state became the main agent of accumulation in this schema, in particular through oil and gas production, transit and sale. While it is possible to conclude that state capitalism in Russia is a marked improvement over the chaotic capitalism that prevailed during the 1990s (see Lane, 2008), less convincing is the more robust defence of the 'power vertical' – understood as a chain of command from the president to local government (Nicholson, 2001, p. 871) – that suggests that Putin's moves were necessary due to the fact that Russia has not yet achieved the level of social development necessary to use democratic institutions responsibly (Stepashin, 2008).

There is some truth to the assertion that divergent American and Russian understandings of democracy – whereby American understandings stress the de-concentration of power while Russian understandings stress efficient decision making and coherent policy outcomes – are at the root of criticisms of Putin's authoritarian backsliding. According to this logic, the most pressing issue facing Putin was to restore the legitimacy of what had been a failing state and the capacity of its institutions following the chaotic period of Russia's Yeltsin-era 'quadruple revolution' – political, economic and social change accompanied by the search for a new national identity. Having restored the state's ability for coherent policy, Putin was viewed by many

Russians as a democratic leader, and the widespread support for a strong state may be understood in this manner (see Willerton, 2007).

Putin's personality-based leadership and recourse to 'para-constitutional' and 'para-political' strategies suggest severe limitations and a shallow institutionalisation of the regime in political society (Sakwa, 2008b). Such strategies have been deployed as a means to settle questions of ownership and control over sectors of the Russian economy. Sakwa (2012) argues that the post-Soviet state may be characterised as a 'dual state', or one which demonstrates both neo-patrimonial and legal-rational elements. The neo-patrimonial element is constituted by a para-political world of informality and factions, the epicentre of which is the president's inner court. The legal-rational element is characterised by the adherence to constitutionalism. Furthermore, neo-patrimonialism is characterised by predatory behaviour, including *reiderstvo,* or raiding, whereby corporate entities attack one another, often with the backing of coercive state mechanisms. For Sakwa, such tendencies jeopardise any capability that the Russian state has to play a transparent and predictable developmental/modernising role.

A central objective of the Putin regime was to set the parameters of the oligarch–state relationship, whereby an individual's right to accumulation was predicated on political fealty to the Kremlin. One must understand the relationship between oligarchs and the Russian state in the 1990s first in order to appreciate Putin-era developments. Central to an understanding of the transitional political economy is the role of the oligarchs that rose to prominence in the 1990s. The term oligarch became central to public discourse in Russia in 1995 during the loans for shares programme and Yeltsin's 1996 presidential run, during which a number of Russian oligarchs acquired stakes in Russian firms in exchange for loans. Nonetheless, the emergence of the oligarchs predates the loans for shares programmes: individuals began amassing fortunes in Russia in the late 1980s and early 1990s (Barnes, 2006; Kryshtanovskaya & White, 1996 and 2005b; Aage, 2005; Johnson, 1997).

Conventional thinking holds that the apex of oligarchical power in the 1990s meant a conflation of economic and political power under powerful individual economic actors (see for example Kryshtanovskaya & White, 2005b), but that oligarchical power was subsequently challenged by the Russian state. In this reading, Putin's recourse to statist or authoritarian tendencies was the result of his confrontation with the oligarchs. Putin famously stated to the oligarchs in July of 2000 that he would not interfere with their business practices provided that they refrained from political adventures. The arrest of Yukos CEO Mikhail Khodorkovsky in October 2003 sent a strong signal that oligarchs were no longer able to have guaranteed access to the Kremlin nor could they challenge the Kremlin politically (Goldman, 2004). This is frequently interpreted as Putin strengthening the state apparatus against the independent power of oligarchs, thereby asserting a degree of independence in public authority over economic interests, with accompanying presidential power over 'capitalist-bureaucratic elites' (Sakwa, 2004, pp. 40–44). For some, the advent of state-centralism and state dominance of business under Putin is unprecedented – both vis-à-vis contemporary middle-income countries and otherwise comparable historical transitions under de facto one-party rule (Hanson & Teague, 2005).[8]

Studies that question the easy demarcation of state and economy are helpful to analyse the extent to which there is a fundamental contradiction between an independent, sovereign political authority and economic interests acting discretely or in tandem against state authority. However, state and economic interests do not have a clear institutional separation, even after Putin's 'renegotiation' with the oligarchs. Rather, with some notable exceptions, we can see in Putin the guarantor of property acquired by Russian elites in the 1990s and the emergence of a form of neo-patrimonial capitalism (Wood, 2007; Volkov, 1999 and 2002). Neo-Gramscian scholarship views Putin as a Caesar – one who takes authoritarian measures to cover up instabilities arising from civil society. While this is the first step towards establishing a hegemonic position, it does not constitute hegemony, as the requisite amounts of coercion and consent are lacking. Furthermore, Putin's Caesarist strategy may be viewed as strong – in which case he has successfully consolidated a coherent state mechanism in line with an underlying vision – or weak – in which reactionary attacks aimed at self-preservation become the norm. In either case, the Caesarist strategy requires an accompanying ideology. For Putin, this has consisted of drawing from sources of both a *zapadnik* (Westerniser) and *derzhavnik* (nationalist) orientation in his consolidating of a centralised state mechanism which nonetheless seeks incorporation into a more open global political economy and the attracting of foreign direct investment (Worth, 2009).[9]

Understanding the extent to which the Russian state and key Russian officials have contributed towards the consolidation of a particular form of market society enables us to question any clean demarcation between state and market and any categorical suggestion that the Russian state inhibits rather than facilitates the creation of capitalism in Russia. Such a perspective is found in some comparative political economy literature on Russia. Influenced by Tilly's model of the state as protection racket, Easter (2012) argues that the Russian state's 'revenue imperatives' – or, its imperative to strengthen itself through the coerced acquisition of wealth ('taking') – has outweighed any imperative to 'trade' according to transparent and predictable market rules.

The above perspectives understate the extent to which Putin and key Russian officials have constructed the infrastructure to undergird a market economy while being charged with the task to ameliorate poor social conditions, inequalities and displacements that accompanied Russia's transition to a market economy. Such matters warrant a chapter in their own right and cannot be fully demonstrated here,[10] however it is worth noting that they contribute to Putin's populism in two ways. First, he is responsible for socialising corporations to be more responsible in fulfilling their broader social obligations (for example, paying wages and contributing to infrastructure).

Second, he is responsible for putting populist measures into place for unpopular liberal reforms. This is witnessed, for example, in general political commitments, such as vowing to raise standards of living in the midst of increasing social inequality (Oversloot, 2006).[11] Moreover, Putin's efforts serviced the needs of domestic and international actors and foreign capital for consistent accumulation in Russia. An important element of Putin's project, therefore, was to build the institutional infrastructure and social legitimacy to enable a functioning market economy, a point that had been missed by the neo-liberal shock reforms of the early 1990s (Mommen, 2001). In other words, achieving 'stability' in the Putin era was a fundamental prerequisite to the further marketisation and liberalisation of the Russian political economy.[12]

Putin's engagement with the oligarchs constituted one measure to re-assert the Kremlin's power. His power vertical was an executive heavy strategy for the consolidation of the Russian state. The establishment of Putin's power vertical has been well documented and is considered by some a central feature of his authoritarian backsliding. Arguably, Putin initiated what was to become a discernible trend of consolidating the presidential administration's power in the spring of 2000 when presidential envoys were sent to the seven newly created federal districts to bring regional legislation in line with federal laws. In 2004, the reform of the Federation Council meant that it would now be made up of appointed representatives from regional executive and legislative branches whereas hitherto, it had been comprised of the governor and speaker of the regional legislature. This move ensured that the Council no longer served as an instrument for regional lobbying. Finally, after the school attacks in Beslan in 2004, Putin decreed that governors be Kremlin-appointed rather than elected, with only formal approval from regional legislatures. Preference would be given to those who held a majority in regional legislatures, thereby further consolidating United Russia's power in the regions (Oversloot, 2007; Sukhov, 2008). A broader, and generally pejorative, term for Putin's centralising initiatives is 'managed democracy',[13] understood to include the reestablishment of central political power, control over the media, the marginalisation of State Duma parties, and the reliance upon ideas of Great Russian nationalism (Beer, 2009).

Managed democracy also referred to the growing affiliation between Putin and the United Russia party during Putin's first two presidential terms. For some, managed democracy was brought about by the 2003 Duma victory of United Russia, which solidified its status as the party of power, followed thereafter by Putin becoming head of United Russia (Wegren & Konitzer, 2007). Putin's close association with United Russia blurred the distinction between executive and legislature and invited questions of both the competitive nature of Russia's national parties and whether the Russian president was becoming supported by a parliamentary majority. Nonetheless, it was in this period that powerful ideational elements of Putinism crystalised. In May of 2007, then head of United Russia Boris Gryzlov interpreted Putin's Plan as: 1) having Russian development correspond with Russia's status as a unique civilisation; 2) building a competitive economy, which entails moving beyond a dependence on resources towards greater innovation; 3) ensuring a new quality of life for Russian citizens, which entails the continuation of priority national projects, wage increases and pension reform; 4) establishing civil society institutions; and 5) ensuring Russia's continued development as a sovereign state in a multipolar world order (Kostenko, 2007). One may add to that an unstated adherence to broadly capitalist norms and practices in many spheres of Russian economic practice.

5 The contours of post-Soviet integration into the global political economy

In this section I outline Russia's position in the contemporary global political economy and consider some of the broad trends of the Putin era. During this time, Russia's aggregate material position has undoubtedly improved relative to the 1990s, with some important qualifications. Despite the 'great power' discourse offered by the Putin regime, Russia remains in a dependent and peripheral position in the global political economy due to its over-reliance on the extraction and sale of primary resources. Lacking a competitive manufacturing centre and only recently entering the World Trade Organisation (WTO) after a long and conspicuous absence, the Russian political economy is integrated into the global political economy but with challenges indicative of a semi-peripheral country and reflecting Soviet patterns of development.

Putin's first two presidential terms were characterised by a rebound from the poor Russian economic performance in the 1990s and Russia's bargaining power in international venues has increased accordingly. According to a number of indicators, wealth undoubtedly increased during the Putin era, as the domestic political economy was the beneficiary of high commodity prices, the devaluation of the ruble following the 1998 financial crisis and the increase in the price of oil (Hanson, 2007). Russia averaged 6.9 per cent annual growth in GDP from 1999–2008 (Table A.1 in Appendix). Russia's reliance on external finance was greatly reduced: in 2001, Russia's external public debt was 49.0 per cent of its GDP. In 2008, it was 6.5 per cent (Table A.2 in Appendix). Russia's current account surplus grew from \$35.4 billion (US) in 2003 to \$103.9 billion (US) in 2008. Its reserves (including gold) grew from \$78.4 billion (US) to \$426.3 billion (US) in the same period of time (Table A.3 in Appendix). The stabilisation fund was created on January 1, 2004 to collect export duties and extraction tax from the price of oil exceeding initially \$20, and then \$27 per barrel. The intent of the fund was to sterilise the vast sums of money entering Russia and ensure macroeconomic stability. The fund reached \$150 billion by the end of 2007, approximately 10 per cent of Russian GDP. In February 2008 this fund was divided into a Reserve Fund, with which future budget shortfalls could be cushioned and a National Welfare Fund, which would be invested in blue-chip companies (Sakwa, 2008c, pp. 303–304; Tabata, 2007).

Although an imperfect measure due to its failing to demonstrate distribution of wealth and income, GDP per capita indicates economic production per inhabitant. According to this indicator, Russia has witnessed a rebound in the Putin years after the 1990s. In 1990, per capita GDP in the Soviet Union was $3,485 (in current US$); in 1999 Russia's per capita GDP reached its post-Soviet nadir of $1,330. Per capita GDP rose steadily throughout Putin's first two presidencies to $11,635 in 2008 before receding to $8,563 in 2009 following the global financial crisis. It then rose to a post-Soviet era high of $14,487 in 2013 (see Table A.4 in Appendix). Although the corresponding data remains spotty, according to the World Bank estimate of the Gini Coefficient, Russia became a relatively less unequal place during, and immediately before, Putin's first two presidential terms compared to the earlier post-Soviet period. The figure measured 48.4 in 1993; 37.4 in 1999; and a post-Soviet low of 34.1 in 2008 (Table A.5 in Appendix).

The Russian state became increasingly involved in the oil and gas industry during Putin's first two presidential terms. Critics of Putin are quick to point out the correlation of the suppression of political freedoms in Russia (as measured by Freedom House political rights survey) and rising energy prices (Orttung, 2009). However, the Russian state's involvement in oil and gas is not so straightforward and must still be subjected to scrutiny. Majority state owned companies were responsible for 15 per cent of Russia's overall oil production in 2004. By 2007, this figure was 40 per cent. Russian oil and gas are dominated by two majority state-owned entities – Gazprom (and Gazprom Neft) and Rosneft – and three privately controlled companies – Lukoil, Surgutneftgaz and Tyumen Oil Company-British Petroleum (TNK-BP). Gazprom and Rosneft and their affiliates made major acquisitions throughout 2005–2007. Throughout this period, the Russian state used coercive pressure to challenge the ownership of those who were deemed as political adversaries (e.g. Khodorkovsky) while also acquiring assets through market means (Hanson, 2009; Pleines, 2009). Nonetheless, Russian oil and gas firms may have more private ownership than international trends suggest should be the norm. Only four out of the top 20 oil and gas companies in the world have majority private ownership (Pleines, 2009; Hanson, 2009). This may suggest the capacity of politically loyal elites to collect resource rents amidst selective direct state control of resources (Hanson, 2009), if not the existence of a sophisticated rent management system under Putin predicated on the Kremlin asserting control over administrative and information resources (Gaddy & Ickes, 2010). However, it also suggests the extent to which state finances and economic redistribution remain predicated on the energy sector.

Russia's economy is more internationalised now than it was in the earlier stages of the post-Soviet period, and by important measures Russia's economy is now more internationalised relative to other major competitors than it was in recent years. Russia's position as a capital exporter has increased significantly during the post-Soviet period. In 1992, 0.77 per cent of the world's total FDI outflows were from Russia; in 1994 this measure was at its post-Soviet low of

0.10 per cent. In the year preceding Putin's first presidential term (1999), the figure stood at 0.20 per cent. In 2009, it was 3.70 per cent, and in 2013, the figure was 6.73 per cent, slightly behind China (7.16 per cent) and over one-quarter of that of the United States (23.98 per cent) (see Table A.6 in Appendix). Russia's position as a capital importer also has been augmented since the beginning of the post-Soviet period. As a share of the world total, FDI inflows into Russia have risen: 0.69 per cent (1992); 0.27 per cent (1999); 4.11 (2008); and 5.46 (2013). Over this time frame Russia enhanced its position significantly vis-à-vis both the USA and China (see Table A.7 in Appendix). By crude measures, therefore, Russia is both a greater capital exporter and more receptive to foreign capital than it has been at any point throughout the post-Soviet period. The existence of a Russian preference for domestic capital is revealed by data on barriers to FDI.[14] Barriers preventing FDI access to national markets are considerably higher than the Organisation for Economic Co-operation and Development (OECD) average (OECD, 2009, p. 164). A May 2008 Russian law on strategic industries stipulated that the foreign purchase of controlling stake in firms in 42 strategic sectors requires special authorisation from a government commission that was headed by then Prime Minister Putin. Furthermore, foreign actors are strictly limited in their ability to acquire equity in Russian state-controlled conglomerates (OECD, 2009, p. 18; Pleines, 2009). Putin ended his first two terms as Russian president overseeing a considerably wealthier Russia, one that had vastly improved its terms of trade in the global political economy, and one that had drastically lessened its dependence on external finance.

Nonetheless, post-Soviet Russia's integration with the global political economy was, and to a great extent remains, imperiled by the uncompetitiveness of industry. This is exemplified by data on Russia's current lack of competitiveness in global markets and its over-reliance on the export of raw materials. Russia remains overwhelmingly dependent on the export of oil, gas, other natural resources, and low-value added foodstuff or primary agricultural products, and slightly more so in 2013 than in 2000 (Table A.8 in Appendix).[15] The country has a Revealed Comparative Advantage (RCA)[16] in crude materials or those subject to primary processing (Cooper, 2006a) but Russian manufacturing remains uncompetitive. Russia has no RCA in manufacturing and high technology compared with other BRIC countries, Turkey and the United States.

During Putin's first two presidential terms, Russia remained an exception to international economic integration as the largest national economy to be excluded from the WTO. While WTO Ministers finally adopted Russia's terms of entry on December 16, 2011 at the 8th Ministerial Conference in Geneva, Russia's long and conspicuous exclusion from the organisation presents a difficult case without a simple answer. As part of its accession commitments, the Russian government has agreed to a complex mix of tariff reductions, the liberalisation of financial services, banking and securities (despite the active protests of the Russian banking and insurance sectors) and the telecommunications industry (Tarr, 2007). Indeed, the Putin regime was successful in reaching a compromise between Russian sectoral lobbies, the Russian government and the WTO Working Group on Russia's entry in 2006 (Dykes, 2009). Nonetheless, subsidies to Russian agriculture, technical barriers and issues surrounding Sanitary and Phytosanitary Measures (used as non-tariff protections by Russia numerous times since 2003) were long contentious issues for critics of Russia's accession (Tarr, 2007; Aslund, 2010). Russia's short-term need to join the organisation was diminished in the 2000s by the fact that oil and gas transactions, upon which the Russian state is reliant, are largely unaffected by WTO rules and procedures (Aslund, 2010).

Russia's 'rise' during Putin's first two presidential terms must be understood within the context of such challenges. Contrary to any arguments about Putin-era Russia's rise or newly found assertiveness, post-Soviet Russia has been in danger of moving lower down the ranks of the semi-peripheral countries rather than rise to the core. The contemporary Russian economy is a bifurcated one in which a small segment of the population is integrated into global circuits of capital and consumption while the vast majority of the population experiences socio-economic stagnation, if not decline (Christensen, 2012). Historically, Russia's peripheral capitalism has been characterised by an absence of bourgeois relations in production and civil society, whereby labour has been employed more often by direct coercion than with the wage relation, and low autonomy and self-organising capacity of the Russian bourgeoisie (Kagarlitsky, 2008). The relative backwardness of the late Soviet economy has influenced post-Soviet Russian economic reforms and the social practices of barter, particularistic exchange and 'relational capital' generated in the late Soviet era have inhibited attempts to normalise and institutionalise production, exchange and finance according to market tenets. Soviet economic backwardness contributed to a disproportionately large non-tradables sector, or that which is comprised of goods and services that cannot be sold on international markets due to their naturally local or uncompetitive nature, as well as a correspondingly low internationalised sector, for an advanced industrial economy (Robinson, 2012).

Russia exemplifies many traits of a semi-peripheral country, however, one that underwent industrialisation outside of the capitalist world system. Russia's semi-peripheral status has led to the pursuit of two contradictory strategies: struggling against exclusion in the global political economy and struggling against exploitation by the core. The former involves finding a niche in the global division of labour, which entails greater exploitation by the core. The latter involves retaining or developing a division of labour autonomous from the capitalist world economy (Simon, 2009). Russia's peripheral status is reinforced by foreign investment patterns – the influx of short-term portfolio inflows and the absence of long-term foreign investment in the productive sector (Nesvetailova, 2004b). The reliance on export revenues is exacerbated by a chronic deficiency of investment capital in Russia, a structural condition that may be traced to the Soviet period (Robinson, 2009). Nonetheless, since

Primakov's time as foreign minister, Russian diplomats and policy makers have sought to craft Russia's foreign policy in a manner that prevents Russia from becoming a resource appendage to the West (Mankoff, 2009). Russian elites have resisted being relegated to a position of inferiority in the global division of labour, although the Russian state has struggled with the imperative of state-led development to prevent an over-reliance on mineral and energy wealth.

Critics have suggested that Russia continues to lag in terms of economic freedom, market attractiveness, corruption, opacity and competitiveness (see Zhuplev, 2008). Russia's position in the World Bank's 'Ease of Doing Business' rankings, a composite ranking demonstrating the ease of doing business in a national economy,[17] has fluctuated in the Putin era. It steadily deteriorated during Putin's second presidential term, from 79th in 2005 to 120th in 2008 before reaching its lowest point in 2010 (123rd). It has recently risen to a post-Soviet high of 62 in 2015. Moreover, this ranking places Russia well ahead of its BRICS counterparts China (90) and Brazil (120) (see Table A.9 in Appendix).

A recent surge in this measure of economic openness has accompanied Putin's stated priorities (see below) during his third presidential term and corresponds with long-standing efforts by the Russian executive to modernise the Russian economy epitomised by the comprehensive 'Concept 2020' ('Konsepsiya dolgosrochnovo…', 2008).[18] Written in 2008, the purpose behind the concept is to transform the Russian economy from one relying on the export of raw materials to one that is socially and economically modern, innovative and competitive in all sectors. Concept 2020 suggests that Russia can become one of the top five economies in the world by creating the conditions for competition and innovation in all sectors of the Russian economy (p. 7). It offers a development plan in which the Russian state guides the transformation of Russian society into one capable of sustaining market mechanisms, productivity and innovative development within a broadly capitalist paradigm. The sentiments of the document were encapsulated in President Dmitry Medvedev's Go Russia! article of November 2009; however, Concept 2020 reflects Russian state developmental priorities that long precede Medvedev's presidential term, thereby challenging the popular perception that as a president Medvedev was more amenable to liberalising the Russian economy than the statist Putin.

Concept 2020 foresees increased global economic competition accompanied by increased geopolitical rivalry, particularly around the control over raw materials, energy, water and food resources. In this context, Russia's low level of technological development renders it vulnerable. The plan envisions a structural reorganisation of the global economy, whereby regional economic unions coexist amidst globalisation. Regionalism is seen as a protective measure amidst strains between powerful centres and continued disparities between them (pp. 3–5). Russia's engagement with the world is to come through state support for Russian business interests to access external markets and safeguard their rights abroad. At the same time it underscores the importance of further economic integration within Eurasia and Russia's emergence as a leader in international finance, particularly within the Eurasian sphere (pp. 151–57). Concept 2020 continues the Putin era processes of Eurasian political and economic integration and precedes the intensification of such integration in Putin's third presidential term. The scope of Putin-era Eurasian integration is demonstrated fully in Chapter 5.

Concept 2020 envisions the exhaustion of the current model of energy-dependent development and stipulates the need for Russia's increased global share in the production of high technology goods, intellectual goods and services, along with its increasing its competitiveness in the traditionally important fields of energy provision, transport and agriculture (pp. 148–150). Concept 2020 cites the emergence of an 'innovative socially oriented type of economic development', a scenario whereby modernisation first occurs in the Russian economy's traditional sectors – oil and gas, raw materials, agriculture and transport – and is followed by the spread of technological innovations to further industries. This culminates in the creation of a knowledge-based economy where high technology and knowledge industries/services account for a share of the GDP comparable to that of oil and gas (p. 11). More specifically, this scenario is comprised of six components:

1 The development of human potential in Russia and human capital. This includes improving the quality of life of Russian citizens, while stabilising and eventually increasing the population, and overtures towards the social rights and material prosperity of Russians.
2 Creating a competitive institutional environment to attract capital into the Russian economy and stimulate entrepreneurial activity, including a reduction of state role in the economy and the self-organisation of the business community, transparency in business, etc.
3 Economic diversification based on innovative scientific and technological development, including the development of a national innovative system, which is based on the advancement of Russian scientific research and development and its translation into high-tech sectors and a knowledge economy.
4 The strengthening and expansion of Russian industry's traditional competitive advantages in energy, agricultural sector, transport and the processing of natural resources.
5 The expansion and strengthening of Russia's external economic position through increased share in foreign markets and a stronger position in the international division of labour (through the attraction of capital, technology and personnel). This includes integration of Eurasian space and Russia becoming an international financial centre. This also entails diversifying Russia's external relations so as to mitigate against future global risks.
6 A new concept for the spatial development of Russia, whereby regional disparities are reduced through the increasing of each territory's competitive potential (pp. 12–16).[19]

2020 therefore signals the intention to create a Russian economy that is competitive in traditional and new sectors, through the incorporation of advanced technology and the development of human capital.[20] Concept 2020 correspondingly emphasises the need for Russia to adopt the institutional framework befitting a state overseeing and fostering a competitive national political economy that attracts investments by securing private property rights, reducing the seizure of property, reforming the Russian court system, fighting corruption, increasing transparency, reducing the state's ownership of productive enterprises and enabling market entry for private actors (pp. 82–86).

The executive-led modernisation impulse carried into Putin's third presidential term. Putin's so-called May Decrees are a large number of decrees announced and signed by Putin shortly upon his taking the office of president on May 7, 2012. In addition to their populist hue, the 2012 May decrees are notable as part of a series of decrees and executive mechanisms that have been enacted in order to facilitate a propitious climate for accumulation in Russia. The decrees may be considered a prolongation of the Russian government's ongoing modernisation strategy, an effort to foster the conditions for human capital development and institutional change deemed necessary to facilitate the transition to a post-resource dependent economy.

Amongst the so-called May decrees is the *Executive Order on Long-Term Economic Policy* (EOLTEP) (President of Russia, 2012), which aimed 'to step up the rate of stable and consistent economic growth, increase people's real incomes, and make Russia's economy a technological leader'. Amongst the efforts are those that aim to increase the general ease with which to conduct business, including increasing Russia's ranking from 120th place (2011) to 50th (2015) to 20th (2018) in the World Bank's ease of doing business index, as well as propitious conditions for accumulation, including increasing labour productivity 1.5 fold from 2011 to 2018. Also included was the goal of reducing business tax evasion through the use of offshore and shell companies and rendering business financial activities more transparent. Moreover, the EOLTEP contains numerous instructions to improve the ease of doing business, including the establishing of an ombudsman for entrepreneurs. EOLTEP also contains a series of measures to hasten the modernisation of the Russian economy, including developing a national innovation system and approving the state programme for Industrial Development and Competitiveness.

The Putin era has been characterised partly, if unevenly, by the state's role in disciplining society into accepting capitalist norms. Similarly, there are grounds for qualifying the place of the state sector in the Russian economy over this period, as the Putin years reflected the long-term post-Soviet trend of the diminishing of the state sector as employer for the Russian populace. In 1992, 49,660,000 people were employed in the Russian state sector (constituting 69 per cent of the Russian population's employment), whereas 13,887,000 were employed in the private sector (19.3 per cent of the Russian population's employment). In 2000, the numbers were 24,371,000 (37.8 per cent) for the state sector and 29,773,000 (46.1 per cent) for the private sector. The percentage of Russians employed in the private sector grew relative to that of those employed in the state sector through Putin's first two presidential terms until reaching numbers of 19,221,000 (28.4 per cent) in the state sector and 40,684,000 (60 per cent) in the private sector in 2013 (see Table A.10 and A.11 in Appendix). In short, a significantly greater proportion of working Russians' livelihoods are now derived from the private vs. the state sector in the first instance.

6 Conclusion

In this chapter, I sketched Russia's material position in the contemporary global political economy as well as the challenges inherent in this position. I did so by positioning Russia as a sovereign integrationist, a state which articulates the need to manage globalisation processes and internal political developments while selectively integrating into the global political economy. The Russian state is one of numerous states that combine illiberal (by Western pluralist standards) political practices with broad market developments. This tendency developed in Russia in spite of the initial expectation in the post-Soviet period by the Yeltsin government, American state, and IFIs alike that Russia would follow the twin tracks of liberal-democratic and capitalist development.

Furthermore, Putin's efforts to consolidate authority and legitimacy are to be understood against the particularities of Russian capitalism that developed in the 1990s, a period that lacked both the legitimacy and institutional/routinised basis for market practices. However maligned by Western liberal-democratic standards, Putin created a normative and institutional order and a relatively stable set of expectations and assumptions by which accumulation can occur in Russia.

Russia occupies an improved (over the 1990s) position in the contemporary global political economy, albeit one marked by the over-reliance on mineral and energy resources, uncompetitiveness of manufacturing, increased autonomy vis-à-vis IFIs and selective internationalisation. Finally, such internationalisation occurs with the Putin-era state occupying a central role in consolidating free market norms and practices despite remaining an active economic agent in its own right. This material position corresponds to the world order concepts elaborated upon throughout this work.

Notes

1 See also O'Donnell, Schmitter & Whitehead (1986) and Huntington (1991).

2 According to Schöpflin, Soviet communism's position as a 'state-sustaining ideology' was precarious: perceived economic and technological failures in the Soviet Union undermined the state's legitimacy, particularly when ethno-national affective bonds between state and society were absent. The emergence of a previously suppressed ethno-nationalism challenged the emergence of a democratic political system in post-Soviet Russia.

3 Derluguian suggests that Russia was capable of achieving strategic parity with the West three times: under Ivan IV ('the Terrible') in the sixteenth century; under Peter I and Catherine I (both 'the Great') in the eighteenth century and under Stalin and Khrushchev in the twentieth century. In each case, the state orchestrated massive incursions into Russian society at the expense of an enormous number of lives.

4 I use polyarchic in the same manner as Robinson (1996), a form of low-intensity democracy that comprises American foreign policy with the intention of containing statist or redistributive alternatives. See also Burron (2013).

5 According to Harris, most conspicuous in this regard is numerous Western banks financing *Rosneft* for the latter to acquire components of Yukos after its breakup by the Russian state.

6 Attempts at viewing transitional political economies in Central and Eastern Europe through the 'internationalisation' lens include Shields (2014) on Poland and Petrovic and Solingen (2005) on the Czech Republic.

7 On Sachs' proposed institutional reform as accompaniment to shock therapy, see Gowan (1999, pp. 192–199).

8 For a contrasting view, however, see Shleifer and Treisman (2004), for whom Russia represents a 'normal' middle-income country in key political and economic indicators.

9 See also Neumann (1996) for a prolonged discussion of the *zapadnik/dherzhavnik* tradition in Russia.

10 But see Lane (2013, Chapter 17) for a comprehensive account of the mostly negative changes in a variety of economic and social indicators between socialist countries, including Russia, in the early 1990s and their post-Socialist equivalents at the end of the first decade of the 2000s.

11 It is also evident in the specific example of the highly unpopular Benefits Bill of 2006, which monetised social benefits previously enjoyed as in kind or subsidies. Putin ensured the delivery of billions of dollars to provinces and cities to ease the adjustment while continuing with the bill (Oversloot, 2006).

12 That Putin's actions were conducive to growth is not uniformly accepted. McFaul and Stoner-Weiss (2008) challenge the notion that authoritarian government or 'market authoritarianism' is conducive to stability and economic growth. They attribute Russia's economic turnaround to fiscal austerity and the reduced role of the state introduced by Minister Primakov's government following the 1998 collapse. According to Hanson (2007), the functioning of Putin's 'weak state authoritarianism' should be called into question due to an absence of any of Weber's tripartite definition of political legitimacy: traditional (Hanson sees as 'traditional authoritarianism'), procedural ('modern democratic proceduralism'), and charismatic ('charismatic utopianism').

13 Mandel (2005) offers a different interpretation of managed democracy, with Gramscian overtones about the weakness of state and oligarchical bourgeoisie in civil society, thereby leading to authoritarian drift: '"Managed democracies" retain the trappings of democracy and tolerate, to varying degrees, political rights and organized political opposition. However, those in control of the apparatuses of state violence do not hesitate to violate the law and accepted democratic norms to ensure the continuity of their tenure' (pp. 117–118).

14 'The indicator for barriers to foreign direct investment measures the extent to which legal restrictions apply on foreign acquisition of equity in public and private firms in general, and in the telecommunications and airlines sectors in particular' (OECD, 2009, p. 164).

15 In 2000, the four categories of 1) Mineral products; 2) Metals, precious stones, articles thereof; 3) Food stuffs and agricultural raw materials; and 4) wood, pulp

and paper products comprised 88.6 per cent of Russian exports. In 2013, they comprised 89.9 per cent.

16 RCA is a particular country's share of world export in a particular good divided by its share of total world exports.

17 In the 2011 survey, the ease of doing business overall ranking was comprised of the following factors, with Russia's ranking in parentheses: starting a business (108), dealing with construction permits (182), registering property (51), getting credit (89), protecting investors (93), paying taxes (105), trading across borders (162), enforcing contracts (18), and closing a business (103).

18 The author would like to thank Marina Sabanadze and Viktoriya Neadow for their guidance with translating the Concept 2020 document. Mistakes and omissions remain the lone fault of the author.

19 The end result is a new paradigm for development, evident in the following: 'Russia will be able to realize its potential abilities and occupy a deserved place among the leading world countries only by having fully embodied the formula "democracy – the person – technology" into the practice of everyday life' (p. 28).

20 This thinking is encapsulated in the following: 'The increase of national competitiveness is a complex task, the success of which is determined by the development of human capital, economic institutions, the realization and strengthening of Russia's already existing competitive advantages in energy, raw materials and transport infrastructure, as well as the creation of new competitive advantages connected with the diversification of the economy and the formation of a powerful scientific-technological complex and knowledge economy' (p. 108).

References

Aage, H. (2005). The triumph of capitalism in Russia and Eastern Europe and its Western apologetics. *Socialism and Democracy*, 19(2), 3–36.

Agh, A. (1999). Processes of democratisation in the East Central European and Balkan states: Sovereignty-related conflicts in the context of Europeanization. *Communist and Post-Communist Studies*, 32(3), 263–279.

Aslund, A. (2010). Why doesn't Russia join the WTO? *The Washington Quarterly*, 33(2), 49–63.

Barnes, A. (2006). *Owning Russia: the struggle over factories, farms and power*. Ithaca, NY: Cornell University Press.

Bedirhanoglu, P. (2004). The nomenklatura's passive revolution in Russia in the neoliberal era. In L. McCann (Ed.), *Russian transformations: Challenging the global narrative* (pp. 19–41). London and New York: Routledge.

Beer, D. (2009). Russia's managed democracy. *History Today*, 59(5), 37–39.

Bunce, V. (1995). Should Transitologists be grounded? *Slavic Review*, 54(1), 111–127.

Bunce, V. (1999). The political economy of postsocialism. *Slavic Review*, 58(44), 756–793.

Burron, N. A. (2013). *The new democracy wars: the politics of North American democracy promotion in the Americas*. Burlington, VT: Ashgate Publishing, Ltd.

Christensen, P. (2012). Russia as semiperiphery: Political economy, the state and society in the contemporary world system. In Neil Robinson (Ed.), *The Political Economy of Russia* (pp. 169–189). Plymouth: Rowman and Littlefield Publishers, Inc.

Cooper, J. (2006a). Can Russia compete in the global economy? *Eurasian Geography and Economics*, 47(4), 407–425.

Cooper, J. (2006b). Of BRICs and brains: Comparing Russia with China, India and other populous emerging economies. *Eurasian Geography and Economics*, 47(3), 255–284.

Derluguian, G. (2001). Recasting Russia. *New Left Review*, 12(5), 5–31.
Dutkiewicz, P., & Popov, V. (2006). Ahead or behind? Lessons from Russia's post-communist transformation. In A. Kuklinski, & B. Skuza (Eds.), *Turning points in the transformations of the global scene* (pp. 233–251). Warsaw: The Polish Association of the Club of Rome.
Dutkiewicz, P. (2009). Missing in translation: Re-conceptualization of Russia's development state. *Russia in Global Affairs*, 7(4).
Dykes, D. (2009). Will Russia ever join the WTO? *The Hague Journal of Diplomacy*, 4 (1), 83–101.
Easter, G. (2012). Revenue imperatives: State over market in postcommunist Russia. In Neil Robinson (Ed.), *The Political Economy of Russia* (pp. 51–68). Plymouth: Rowman and Littlefield Publishers, Inc.
Ferdinand, P. (2007). Russia and China: Converging responses to globalisation. *International Affairs*, 83(4), 655–680.
Gaddy, C., & Ickes, B. (2010). Russia after the global financial crisis. *Eurasian Geography and Economics*, 51(3), 281–311.
Gerschenkron, A. (1962). *Economic Backwardness in Historical Perceptive: A Book of Essays*. Cambridge, MA: Harvard University Press.
Goldman, M. (2004). The Yukos affair. *Current History*, 103(675), 319–323.
Gowan, P. (1999). *The global gamble: Washington's Faustian bid for world dominance*. London and New York: Verso.
Hanson, S. E. (1998). Development, dependency, and devolution: the anomalous political economy of communist and postcommunist societies. *Environment and Planning C: Government and Policy*, 16(3), 225–246.
Hanson, P. (2007). The Russian economic puzzle: Going forwards, backwards or sideways? *International Affairs*, 83(5), 869–889.
Hanson, P. (2009). The resistible rise of state control in the Russian oil industry. *Eurasian Geography and Economics*, 50(1), 14–27.
Hanson, P. & Teague, E. (2005). Big business and the state in Russia. *Europe-Asia Studies*. 57(5), 657–680.
Harris, J. (2009). Statist globalisation in China, Russia and the gulf states. *Science and Society*, 73(1), 6–33.
Hedlund, S. (2008). Such a beautiful dream: How Russia did not become a market economy. *The Russian Review*, 67(2), 187–208.
Hellman, J., Jones, G. & Kaufmann, D. (2000). Seize the state, seize the day: State capture, corruption and influence in transition. World Bank Policy Research Working Paper No. 2444.
Huntington, S. (1991). *The Third Wave: democratisation in the late twentieth century*. Norman: University of Oklahoma Press.
Johnson, J. (1997). Russia's emerging financial-industrial groups. *Post-Soviet Affairs*, 13(4), 333–365.
Kagarlitsky, B. (2008). *Empire of the periphery Russia and the world system*. London; Ann Arbor, MI: Pluto Press.
'Konsepsiya dolgosrochnovo sotsial'no- ekonomicheskvo razvitiya Rossiyskoy federatsii na period do 2020 goda' (2008). Retrieved 20 November 2008. http://www.economy.gov.ru/wps/wcm/myconnect/economylib/mert/resources/3879cd804ab8615ab426fc4234375027/kdr_171108.doc.
Kostenko, N. (2007). Atmospherics of United Russia 22 May session adopting 'Putin plan' viewed. *World News Connection*, 25 May 2007.

Kotz, D. (2001). Is Russia becoming capitalist? *Science and Society*, 65(2), 157–181.

Krueger, G., & Linz, S. J. (2002). Virtual reality: Barter and restructuring in Russian industry. *Problems of Post-Communism*, 49(5), 31–44.

Kryshtanovskaya, O., & White, S. (1996). From Soviet nomenklatura to Russian elite. *Europe-Asia Studies*, 48(5), 711–733.

Kryshtanovskaya, O., & White, S. (2004). Putin's militocracy. *Post-Soviet Affairs*, 19 (4), 289–306.

Kryshtanovskaya, O., & White, S. (2005a). Inside the Putin court: A research note. *Europe-Asia Studies*, *57*(7), 1065–1075.

Kryshtanovskaya, O., & White, S. (2005b). The rise of the Russian business elite. *Communist and Post-Communist Studies*, 38(3), 293–307.

Lane, D. (2000). What kind of capitalism for Russia? A comparative analysis. *Communist and Post-Communist Studies*, 33(4), 485–504.

Lane, D. (2008). From chaotic to state-led capitalism. *New Political Economy*, 13(2), 177–184.

Lane, D. (2013). *The capitalist transformation of state socialism: The making and breaking of state socialist society, and what followed*. London: Routledge.

Lester, J. (1995). *Modern tsars and princes: the struggle for hegemony in Russia*. London & New York: Verso.

Lester, J. (2000). *The dialogue of negation: Debates on hegemony in Russia and the West*. London: Pluto Press.

Mandel, D. (2005). 'Managed democracy': Capital and state in Russia. *Debatte*, 13(2), 117–136.

Mankoff, J. (2009). *Russian foreign policy: The return of great power politics*. New York: Rowman and Littlefield Publishers.

Mauro, P., & Loungani, P. (2001). Capital flight from Russia. *The World Economy*, 24(5), 689–706.

McFaul, M & Stoner-Weiss, K. (2008). The myth of the authoritarian model. *Foreign Affairs*, 87(1), 68–84.

Mommen, A. (2001). Russia's responses to globalisation. *International Journal of Political Economy*, 31(4), 53–78.

Nesvetailova, A. (2004a). Coping in the global financial system: The political economy of nonpayment in Russia. *Review of International Political Economy*, 11(5), 995–1021.

Nesvetailova, A. (2004b). From 'transition' to dependent development: The new periphery in global financial capitalism. In N. Robinson (Ed.), *Reforging the weakest link: Global political economy and post-soviet change in Russia, Ukraine and Belarus* (pp. 127–161). Aldershot and Burlington, VT: Ashgate.

Nesvetailova, A. (2004c). Globalisation po-Russki, or What really happened in August 1998? In L. McCann (Ed.), *Russian transformations: Challenging the global narrative* (pp. 42–62). London: Routledge.

Nesvetailova, A. (2005). Globalisation and post-Soviet capitalism: Internalising neoliberalism in Russia. In S. Soederberg, G. Menz & P. G. Cerny (Eds.), *Internalising globalisation: The rise of neoliberalism and the decline of national varieties of capitalism* (pp. 238–260). New York: Palgrave MacMillan.

Neumann, I. (1996). *Russia and the idea of Europe: A study in identity and International Relations*. London: Routledge.

Nicholson, M. (2001). Putin's Russia: Slowing the pendulum without stopping the clock. *International Affairs*, 77(3), 867–884.

O'Donnell, G., Schmitter, P. & Whitehead, L. (eds) (1986). *Transitions from Authoritarian Rule*. Baltimore: John Hopkins University Press.

OECD (2009). Russian Federation. *OECD Economic Surveys*, 29(6).

Orttung, R. (2009). Energy and state-society relations: Socio-political aspects of Russia's energy wealth. In J. Perovic, R. Orttung & A. Wagner (Eds.), *Russian energy power and foreign relations: Implications for conflict and cooperation* (pp. 51–70). London: Routledge.

Oversloot, H. (2006). Neo-liberalism in the Russian Federation. In R. Robison (Ed.), *The neoliberal revolution: Forging the market state* (pp. 58–79). Houndsmills: Palgrave MacMillan.

Oversloot, H. (2007). Reordering the state (without changing the constitution): Russia under Putin's rule, 2000–2008. *Review of Central and East European Law*, 32(1), 41–64.

Petrovic, B., & Solingen, E. (2005). Europeanisation and internationalisation: The case of the Czech Republic. *New Political Economy*, 10(3), 281–303.

Pleines, H. (2009). Developing Russia's oil and gas industries: What role for the State? In J. Perovic, R. Orttung & A. Wagner (Eds.), *Russian energy power and foreign relations: Implications for conflict and cooperation* (pp. 71–86). London: Routledge.

Popov, V. (2000). Shock therapy versus gradualism: The end of the debate (explaining the magnitude of the transformational recession). *Comparative Economic Studies*, 42(1), 1–51.

Popov, V. (2001). Russia: Inconsistent shock therapy with weakening institutions. In G. A. Cornia, & V. Popov (Eds.), *Transition and institutions: The experience of gradual and late reformers* (pp. 29–54). Oxford and New York: Oxford University Press.

Popov, V. (2007). Russia redux. *New Left Review*, 44, 36–52.

President of Russia (2012). Executive order on long-term state economic policy. Available at: http://eng.kremlin.ru/acts/3758. Accessed 2 February 2015.

Prozorov, S. (2008). The paradox of infra-liberalism: Towards a genealogy of 'managed democracy' in Putin's Russia. In A. Woll, & H. Wydra (Eds.), *Democracy and myth in Russia and Eastern Europe* (pp. 186–202). New York: Routledge.

Reddaway, P. & Glinski, D. (2001). *The tragedy of Russian reforms: Market Bolshevism against democracy*. Washington: United States Institute of Peace Press.

Renz, B. (2006). Putin's militocracy? An alternative interpretation of siloviki in contemporary Russian politics. *Europe-Asia Studies*, 58(6), 903–924.

Robinson, N. (2004a). A fickle benefactor: Russia and the global political economy as a resource for change. In N. Robinson (Ed.), *Reforging the weakest link: Global political economy and post-soviet change in Russia, Ukraine and Belarus* (pp. 22–45). Aldershot and Burlington, VT: Ashgate.

Robinson, N. (2004b). Global economy, the USSR and post-soviet change. In N. Robinson (Ed.), *Reforging the weakest link: Global political economy and post-soviet change in Russia, Ukraine and Belarus* (pp. 1–21). Aldershot and Burlington, VT: Ashgate.

Robinson, N. (2009). August 1998 and the development of Russia's post-communist political economy. *Review of International Political Economy*, 16(3), 433–455.

Robinson, N. (2012). The contexts of Russia's political economy. In Neil Robinson (Ed.), *The Political Economy of Russia* (pp. 15–50). Plymouth: Rowman and Littlefield Publishers, Inc.

Robinson, W. I. (1996). *Promoting polyarchy: globalisation, US intervention, and hegemony*. Cambridge: Cambridge University Press.

Sakwa, R. (2004). *Putin: Russia's choice.* London: Routledge.
Sakwa, R. (2008a). Myth and democratic identity in Russia. In A. Woll, & H. Wydra (Eds.), *Democracy and myth in Russia and Eastern Europe* (pp. 203–218). New York: Routledge.
Sakwa, R. (2008b). Putin's leadership: Character and consequences. *Europe-Asia Studies.* 60(6), 879–897.
Sakwa, R. (2008c). *Russian politics and society.* 4th. London: Routledge.
Sakwa, R. (2012). Systemic stalemate: Reiderstvo and the dual state. In Neil Robinson (Ed.), *The Political Economy of Russia* (pp. 69–96). Plymouth: Rowman and Littlefield Publishers, Inc.
Schmitter, P. & Karl, T. (1994). The conceptual travels of Transitologists and Consolidologists: how far to the East should they go? *Slavic Review*, 54(1), 173–185.
Schöpflin, G. (1991). Obstacles to liberalism in post-communist polities. *East European Politics and Societies*, 5(1), 189–194.
Schöpflin, G. (1995). Nationhood, communism and state legitimation. *Nations and Nationalism*, 1(1), 81–91.
Schöpflin, G. (2000). *Nations, Identity, Power.* New York: New York University Press.
Shevtsova, L. (2007). *Russia: Lost in transition. The Yeltsin and Putin legacies.* Washington: Carnegie Endowment for International Peace.
Shields, S. (2014). *The International Political Economy of Transition*. London and New York: Routledge.
Shlapentokh, V. (2003). Hobbes and Locke at odds in Putin's Russia. *Europe-Asia Studies*, 55(7), 981–1007.
Shleifer, A. & Treisman, D. (2004). A normal country. *Foreign Affairs*, 83(2), 20–38.
Simon, R. (2009). Upper Volta with gas? Russia as a semi-peripheral state. In O. Worth and P. Moore (Eds), *Globalisation and the 'new' semi-peripheries* (pp. 120–137). New York: Palgrave Macmillan.
Simon, R. (2010). Passive revolution, perestroika, and the emergence of the new Russia. *Capital and Class*, 34(3), 429–448.
Stepashin, S. (2008) Do we have to seal the retort? *Russian Politics and Law*, 46(5), 41–46.
Sukhov, I. (2008). The power vertical and the nation's self-consciousness. *Russia in Global Affairs, 2*.
Tabata, S. (2007). The Russian stabilisation fund and its successor: Implications for inflation. *Eurasian Geography and Economics*, 48(6), 699–712.
Tarr, D. (2007). Russian accession to the WTO: An assessment. *Eurasian Geography and Economics*, 48(3), 306–319.
Taylor, B. (2011). *State building in Putin's Russia: Policing and coercion after communism*. Cambridge: Cambridge University Press.
Tsygankov, A. P. (2014). *The strong state in Russia: Development and crisis.* New York: Oxford University Press.
Volkov, V. (1999). Violent entrepreneurship in post-communist Russia. *Europe-Asia Studies*, 51(5), 741–754.
Volkov, V. (2002). The selective use of state capacity in Russia's economy: Property disputes and enterprise takeovers after 2000. *PONARS Policy Memo*, 273, 1–4.
Waylen, G. (1994). Women and democratisation: Conceptualizing gender relations in transition politics. *World Politics*, 46(3), 327–354.
Weigle, M. (2000). *Russia's liberal project: State society relations in the transition from communism*. University Park, PA: Pennsylvania State University Press.

Wegren, S. & Konitzer, A. (2007). Discussion Article: Prospects for managed democracy in Russia. *Europe-Asia Studies*, 59(6), 1025–1047.

Willerton, J. (2007). The Putin legacy: Russian-style democratisation confronts a 'failing state'. *The Soviet and Post Soviet Review*, 34(1), 33–54.

Wood, T. (2007). Contours of the Putin era: A response to Vladimir Popov. *New Left Review,* 44, 53–68.

Woodruff, D. M. (2000). Rules for followers: Institutional theory and the new politics of economic backwardness in Russia. *Politics and Society*, 28(4), 437–482.

World Bank (2008). *Russian Economic Report #16*. June 2008. http://siteresources.worldbank.org/INTRUSSIANFEDERATION/Resources/rer16_Eng.pdf.

Worth, O. (2005). *Hegemony, international political economy and post-communist Russia*. Ashgate: Aldershot.

Worth, O. (2009). Unraveling the Putin myth: Strong or weak Caesar? *Politics*, 29(1), 53–61.

Yakolev, A. (2006). The evolution of business-state interaction in Russia: From state capture to business capture? *Europe-Asia Studies*, 58(7), 1033–1056.

Zhuplev, A. (2008). Economic internationalisation of Russia: Roots, trends and scenarios. *International Political Science Review*, 29(1), 99–119.

4 The embedding of Russian state-sanctioned multipolarity in the post-Soviet conjuncture

1 Introduction

Are we living in a multipolar world? Russian President Vladimir Putin thinks so. In his 2012 Address to the Federal Assembly, Putin stated, 'It is absolutely obvious to everyone that the modern world is becoming increasingly multipolar' (Putin, 2012). But what does that signify? What signifies *that*? Putin's statement is part of a broader trend in which key Russian officials cast multipolarity as a state of affairs that warrants little elaboration. Ambiguously but consistently, multipolarity has figured prominently in various iterations of official Russia's desired world order throughout the post-Soviet period.

In excavating the post-Soviet conjuncture for Russian state-sanctioned uses of multipolarity, this chapter contributes to a nascent 'multipolar turn' in International Relations (IR) and International Political Economy (IPE) literature. The intention behind this chapter is twofold. First, it is meant as a theoretical contribution to broader discussions about globalisation, neo-liberalism, unipolarity and multipolarity. The historicist approach offered here invites us to problematise, if not efface, the divide between scholarly and political practices that produce concepts, theories and ideas pertaining to how the global political economy functions.

Second, it is meant as an empirical 'corrective' to the aforementioned discussions through its demonstration of the longer-run tendencies of Russian state organs and prominent Russian officials to embed multipolar discourse in their respective visions of world order (Silvius, 2014; 2015). Russian state movements towards multipolarity gestate in the midst of, if not previous to, scholarship pertaining to 'globalisation debates', multipolarity, the emergence of the BRICS framework of global governance, and the 2007–2008 financial crisis. Such a corrective demonstrates that at a 'political' level, the Russian state has been embedding multipolarity in a 'polysemic' fashion before important scholarship deemed it warranted or possible. For the Russian state, the multipolar world order becomes over laden with signifiers that are as much normative and axiomatic as they are measurable. In the process multipolarity is portrayed as an objective material condition predicated on the dispersal of economic and political power beyond the Western core, a defense of cultural integrity, and a solution to problems of global governability instigated by unipolarity.

This chapter proceeds as follows. Section 2 considers the extent to which Russian state practices of multipolarity challenge or contribute to globalisation paradigms in IPE. In Section 3, I consider how official Russia's post-Soviet discourse and practices contribute to a nascent multipolar turn in IR/IPE. In Section 4, I demonstrate how major developments during the post-Soviet conjuncture shaped key elements of a discursive strategy of multipolarity: cultural and civilisational integrity, geopolitics, geoeconomics, and the promise of a just and better functioning world order. Section 5 contains the deeper empirics: analysis of statements and documents by Russian officials and Russian state organs which demonstrate how multipolarity has stabilised at the discursive level as a multifaceted critique of American unipolarity. Section 5 also demonstrates the 'overdetermined' nature of multipolarity: the range of qualitative, technical and normative qualities ascribed to multipolarity by Russian officials. Section 6 concludes the piece.

2 Multipolarity, the Russian state and IPE's globalisation debates

Post-Soviet Russia serves as an interesting case to the 'globalisation debates' that proliferated during the 1990s and initially coalesced around those who envisioned technical, economic and cultural integration beyond the 'level' of the state (cf. Held & McGrew, 2000; Friedman, 2000; Ohmae, 1995), and those who disputed the extensity and intensity of such processes (Hirst & Thompson, 1995; Weiss, 1998). Interlocutors in the initial debates and those that elaborated upon it have expanded our understanding of 'multiple globalisations' paradigms (cf. Gills, 2000; Mittleman, 2004; van Apeldoorn, 2004; Appelbaum & Robinson, 2005; Held & McGrew, 2007; James & Steger, 2014), and worked to disassociate globalisation from neo-liberalism (Gills, 2014). Indeed, to firmly historicise globalisation processes is to resist the idea that such processes presuppose straightforward global flattening, the creation of global monocultures, or unproblematic relationships with global institutions (see Eley, 2007). When examining the engagement of official Russia with globalisation concepts and practices, it is entirely possible to see the embedding of a multipolar paradigm even as the Russian leaders have pursued and achieved entrance in global clubs such as the World Trade Organisation (WTO), or those historically intrinsic to Western power (G-8).

Scholars have challenged aspects of globalisation paradigms by foregrounding multipolarity as a prism through which the contemporary global political economy is understood (Ambrosio, 2005; Amin & Camiller, 2006; Cooper & Flemes, 2013; Desai, 2013; Keohane et al., 2009; Stephen, 2014; Wade, 2011; Zakaria, 2011). Multipolarity is a particularly significant concept for understanding emerging debates on Russian foreign policy. Multipolarity has been considered as a threat to the West's 'collective unilateralism' by prominent Russian thinkers and policy makers (Makarychev & Morozov, 2011).

It has emerged as a central plank in the Russian–Chinese relationship following the collapse of the Soviet Union (Turner, 2009). It has been juxtaposed to, if not deemed corrosive of, liberal internationalist, multilateral structures of global governance (Laïdi, 2014). Russia's current foreign policy options are often expressed as a choice *between* multipolarity and multilateralism (Tsygankov, 2009) in spite of official Russia's having attempted to demonstrate the two as mutually constitutive. Multipolarity has emerged as a prism through which to critique the ideational components of Western and American hegemony (Kurowska, 2014). The multipolar challenge is at once considered 'epistemological' (Makarychev & Morozov, 2013) and predicated on more 'mundane' discussions of contemporary global economic governance based on the *objective* phenomenon of emerging economies becoming disproportionately responsible for driving global growth (Mundial, 2011).

We may relate to the explicit 'multipolarity' literature that which focuses upon the further disarticulation of American unipolarity, globalisation and global governance on two fronts in the latter half of the first decade of the 2000s. The first emphasises the evolution of the 'BRICS' (Brazil, Russia, India, China and South Africa; originally 'BRIC') framework (Ban & Blyth, 2013; Mielniczuk, 2013; Nadkarni & Noonan, 2012; Roberts, 2010; Vezirigiannidou, 2013). Arguably, Russia has been the most active in converting the 'BRIC' hypothesis offered by Goldman Sachs analyst Jim O'Neill (2001) – that Brazil, Russia, India and China were poised to become increasingly responsible for global economic growth and seek greater say in global governance mechanisms – from an *analytical* structure to a *political* one (Luckhurst, 2013).

The second is the profound effect that the 2007–2008 financial crisis had on globalised neo-liberal finance and corresponding governance structures (cf. Germain, 2012; Nesvetailova & Palan, 2013; Brenner et al., 2010; Peck et al., 2010). Analysing the post-Soviet conjuncture reveals that key Russian officials have considered multipolarity prior to the evolving 'multipolar turn' in IR/IPE scholarship. That Russian officials engaged with and propagated the notion of multipolarity first in the 1990s and intensively during Putin's first two presidential terms demonstrates an earlier practical, strategic and rhetorical disarticulation of globalisation, neo-liberalism, unipolarity and hegemony[1] than that forecasted in the above literature.

Key Russian officials have selectively mined Russian culture to circumscribe the field in which debate occurs and in which political life is to be comprehended, foregrounding a state-sanctioned conception of Russia in a multipolar world, guiding Russian public political consciousness in a particular fashion, and activating notions about national and international political and social life in a manner that serves regime imperatives. That they have done so in various ways since the mid-1990s signals the extent to which the 'formal' extension of American empire over the post-Soviet landscape constituted a 'failed crusade' (Cohen, 2001) shortly after Russia's post-communist nadir, if by crusade we understand an attempt to incorporate Russia seamlessly into

Western institutions and relegate it to a lower rung on the international division of labour. Multiple post-Soviet Russian understandings of multipolarity – both academic (Shakleyina & Bogaturov, 2004; Lukyanov, 2010; Subacchi, 2008) and state-sanctioned – contribute to the multipolar turn by demonstrating the uneven ideational and material gestation of a multipolar world. With a political strategy of multipolarity, key Russian officials proclaimed a 'post-mortem' to the more strident forms of globalisation theory well before IR/IPE scholars did (Rosenberg, 2005). Earlier post-Soviet Russian officials may have been the first to declare such theory's stillbirth in a manner then unrecognised.

Multipolarity is amongst numerous concepts embedded in Russian state-sanctioned discourse that frame Russia's prolonged and multifaceted transition from state socialism to a particular form of capitalism in a manner that legitimates Russian state conduct while critiquing American unipolarity.[2] Russian officials offer a 'home-grown' ideology to combat the USA's global project, which is predicated on polyarchic, Anglo-American capitalist postulates, including a bending, if not negation, of some of the main tenets of globalisation in favour of reconstituting the global political economy on a multipolar and 'multicivilisational' basis. Russian state officials have borrowed selectively from Russian political, cultural and philosophical debates to assert the historical and ethical basis for the Russian state's domestic and international involvement, including the restoration of a highly centralised state apparatus and state involvement in the Russian economy (see Chapter 3). According to key Russian officials, Russia could be capitalist provided that it was also a great power, 'sovereign' in its conduct vis-à-vis the USA, and able to demonstrate to its public the compatibility of a market economy with Russian cultural and political traditions. Russian state officials' self-representations in the post-Soviet period can assist us in understanding what Gills and Philip (1996) refer to as the 'historicity of divergent development trajectories'. To understand Russia's prolonged transition from state-socialist counter-hegemon, through a period of state collapse and social anomie, to one of a number of powerful non-Western centres with an ambiguous relationship with liberal democratic precepts of world order, one might examine how prominent Russian officials activate common-sense notions about the ethical and technical superiority of multipolarity vis-à-vis American unipolarity.

A deeper examination of the Russian state's fashioning of capitalism, its facilitating of Russia's uneven entry into global capitalism and its efforts to attenuate profound social conflict beginning in the 1990s exceeds this chapter's scope (but see Chapter 3). Nonetheless, insofar as such a political project coincided with a geopolitical or geoeconomic architecture, that architecture is multipolar in nature. Vocal proponents of multipolarity can be found in various iterations of the post-Soviet Russian state. Vladimir Putin, current President of the Russian Federation, the late Yevgeni Primakov, former Foreign Minister and Prime Minister (1998–1999) of the Russian Federation, and Sergei Lavrov, current Foreign Minister of the Russian Federation are all active public proponents of multipolarity. We may add the former Deputy Prime Minister of Russia, Vladislav Surkov, a self-styled public intellectual who sought to cement Russian society's transition to a market economy by synthesising notions about Russian culture, if not civilisation, its 'sovereign' nature vis-à-vis the USA, and its 'alternative' development model (see Chapter 7). Throughout Putin's first two presidential terms, Surkov valorised the cultural parameters of Russia's development trajectory while bending the 'speculative' aspects of the Russian philosophical tradition to suit the utilitarian ends of modernisation. The above are joined by numerous Kremlin-affiliated 'political technologists' who constitute the social and material basis for intellectual production and leadership on politically and economically sensitive questions associated with Russian political and economic transitions. Such figures distanced post-Soviet-era ideology from Soviet internationalism by representing multipolarity in the global political economy as taking place on material (state-state) and cultural (civilisation–civilisation) terrain and largely devoid of class inequality.

Such individuals cultivate multipolarity as both ideology and strategy. Multipolarity may be considered polysemic in nature (Jenson, 2010). To revisit: a polysemic concept is a 'quasi-concept', the fluidity of which enables disparate groups to ascertain and support it irrespective of its internal inconsistencies and lack of 'measurability'. In spite of their being anchored in 'material reality', polysemic concepts are largely volitional and performative in nature: they correspond with the contours of a desired political reality as uttered by their defenders and proponents. The 'political' strength of a polysemic idea may be found in its ambiguity and capacity to resonate with multiple subject positions in the service of a larger political project. Containing such attributes, polysemic ideas may be deployed to construct ideological cohesion, consensus and legitimacy. That a concept may be polysemic is not dissimilar to Gramsci's notion of common sense, 'an ambiguous, contradictory and multiform concept' which comprises 'a chaotic aggregate of disparate conceptions, and one can find there anything one likes' (Gramsci, 1971, pp. 422–423). Hence, multipolarity becomes a durable component of official Russia's lexicon precisely because it is ambiguous, imprecise, and seemingly inoculated against counterfactuals.

Embedding common-sense understandings of multipolarity that cohere to state strategy, Russian officials invite us to efface the divide between political and scholarly practice when understanding how world order concepts are propagated and normalised. Russian state officials contribute to IR and IPE literature by inverting the attributions made to unipolarity by contributors to Hegemonic Stability Theory (Kindleberger, 1981; 1986). Such a phenomenon demonstrates that Russia has not been incorporated seamlessly into the global political economy as envisioned by post-Soviet American strategists (Gowan, 1999; Reddaway & Glinski, 2001) and that Russian elites have rejected the notion that American unipolarity is a net benefit to global political economy for producing collective public goods. The Russian state's rhetorical and practical rejections of American unipolarity and hegemony and attempts to develop a new vernacular with which to articulate global governance are emblematic of this broader trend. Multipolarity is central to this wider initiative.

3 Dimensions of Russia's state-sanctioned multipolarity

Multipolarity is but one term employed in the production of Russian state-sanctioned visions of contemporary world order. Official Russia has ascribed a series of 'objective', subjective, ethical and technical attributes to both unipolarity and multipolarity: polarity is both 'objectively' based on the calculus of relative economic or military power and something beyond this. A multifaceted treatment of multipolarity does not render it analytically dubious; rather, it cements its importance as a common-sense and polysemic understanding of global political affairs serving an explicit political function. Four interrelated elements of multipolarity as Russian state-sanctioned discursive strategy will be examined here.

The first is the appeal to civilisational diversity vis-à-vis American unipolarity, hegemony, democracy promotion and regime change. Such efforts are directed against the sovereign integrity of political states and the moral integrity of particular cultures constituted as civilisations. Russia is one of the aggrieved parties disdainful of liberal capitalist aggression and pledges to construct an order in which states, cultures and civilisations have sovereign authority over their own affairs, including culturally constituted development trajectories.

Two 'civilisational' elements inform Russia's post-Soviet multipolar turn. The first is the emphatic articulation of cultural and civilisational difference. This is done in part as a 'negative' project – a defensive principle against perceived US economic, political and cultural aggression – and a 'positive' project – re-asserting the common cultural and civilisational heritage of Russia's historical area of influence in order to facilitate contemporary regional integration (Silvius, 2015). The second is the *effacing* of such substantive difference when enlisting a variety of agents in the multipolar project, whereby cultural or civilisational difference does not preclude any collective entity from joining in the multipolar project. Russia's multipolar project therefore simultaneously involves the assertion of irreconcilable cultural difference and its negation.

The 'civilisational question' pertains most directly to Russia's myriad Eurasian integration initiatives. Having recently (May 2014) signed the Eurasian Economic Union Treaty alongside the President of Kazakhstan, Nursultan Nazarbayev and the President of Belarus, Aleksandr Lukashenko (Nazarbayev et al., 2014) and pursuing a comprehensive Eurasian Union, Putin legitimately may be viewed as representing 'the triumph of Eurasianism' during his third term (Pryce, 2013). However, the Eurasian groundwork was laid much earlier (as demonstrated in Chapter 5). Russia's 'turn to the east' in foreign policy under Primakov has been considered emblematic of a 'pragmatic Eurasianism' in action (RFERL, 1997, Jan. 9; Rangsimaporn, 2006, p. 378). Russia's deepening of ties with Central Asia – through the Shanghai

Cooperation Organisation (SCO), the Collective Security Treaty Organisation (CSTO) and the Eurasian Economic Community (EurAsEC) – has also been construed as multipolar and Eurasian in nature (Torbakov, 2004). However, the *embedding* of Eurasianism civilisational discourse – whereby Putin and Russian officials positively invoke the Eurasianist philosophical tradition to demonstrate the cultural basis of contemporary Eurasian integration initiatives in the fashioning of a multipolar world order – has intensified in Putin's third term (Silvius, 2015).

The second is distinctly geopolitical in nature: official Russia's strategic response to perceptions of American unipolar aggression since at least Primakov's tenure as foreign minister in the mid-1990s. For many Primakov represented a shift in Russia's international orientation from the liberal internationalist position of Andrei Kozyrev, Yeltsin's foreign minister until 1996, although some argue that Kozyrev drifted towards multipolarity before Primakov (Mikhailenko, 2003; Ambrosio, 2005). Nonetheless, Primakov's symbolic importance to the question of multipolarity is widely accepted, as he is associated with having orchestrated a shift from Russia's eager embrace of Western civilisation, institutions and norms (having briefly returned to the fold after a 70-year hiatus during the 'Bolshevik interregnum') to a more independent statist position through which Russia sought greater autonomy in global affairs vis-à-vis institutions and practices associated with American hegemony (O'Loughlin, 2001). Primakov's statism and multipolar orientation were enshrined in the 1997 National Security Concept of the Russian Federation (Wallander, 1998), well before Putin's arrival as president, the emergence of the BRIC(S) formation, or the global financial crisis.

In the late 1990s fear of US unilateral domination became a consensus position within Russian elite circles (Mikhailenko, 2003). Primakov was representative of this position and credited with having developed a distinct multipolarity position in the Primakov Doctrine (Ambrosio, 2005; Katz, 2006). Primakov and Yeltsin both argued that multipolarity would enable Russia to check the hard-military security threats emanating from the American-dominated NATO bloc and the creation of a 'NATO-centric' world order (RFERL, 1998, May 12; RFERL, 2001, 2 February), seeking a Russia–Germany–France axis, enhancing relations with China, India and the Islamic world, and opposing NATO's campaign against Slobodan Milosevic (Kolossov & Turovsky, 2001, pp. 160–161).

The language of multipolarity appeared in joint Chinese–Russian declarations prior to the emergence of the BRICS framework. This includes the 1997 'Joint Russian-Chinese Declaration about a Multipolar World and the Formation of a New World Order' and the 2001 'Sino-Russian Treaty on Good Neighbourliness, Friendship and Cooperation'. The Bishkek Declaration, signed in 1999 by the Shanghai Five emphasised a commitment to political and military cooperation in the 'general trend' towards multipolarity. Pursuing multipolarity has been a main objective for both Russia and China within the Shanghai Cooperation Organisation (SCO), the successor to the Shanghai

Five. Putin and then Chinese President Hu Jintao signed a joint declaration supporting a multipolar world in May 2003 (Turner, 2009; RFERL, 2003, 29 May).

The third is the notion that multipolarity *objectively* reflects the dispersal of economic and political power beyond the core of Western states, seemingly independent of political volition. Putin and Russian officials suggest that the emerging objective material conditions in the global political economy, whereby Western political economies are losing their position of dominance vis-à-vis those of emerging states. Russia was a component of this: during its 'resurgence', Russia's domestic political economy improved in the aggregate, suggesting that the Russian state improved its terms of engagement with Western-led international financial institutions (see Chapter 6).

Russian–Chinese cooperation is deepening following the intensification of Russia's conflict with the West over Ukraine. Such a deepening may lead to a qualitatively and quantitatively different form of integration between the two non-Western political economies and a different dimension to economic mutlipolarity. Nonetheless, the language used to express such cooperation remains similar to that of previous years ('China to Push Strategic Partnership with Russia', 2014). In February 2015, China's Foreign Minister pledged support to Russia following sanctions against Russia and a collapse in oil prices ('China's Xinjiang-Russia Trade', 2014). In May 2014, Putin visited China and signed over 50 agreements, including a 30-year, $400 billion gas contract signed between state-controlled Gazprom and the China National Petroleum Corporation ('China and Russia Sign Gazprom', 2014). Amidst the flurry of developments, Russia is overcoming a previous aversion to a Chinese presence in the Russian automobile industry, allowing China's automaker Great Wall to invest in a project in the Tula region (Kashin, 2014).

Finally, Russian officials portray multipolarity as enabling a more efficient and just international system that can solve a series of technical and ethical dilemmas pertaining to global security and governability, whereby the multipolar world is equated with stability, cooperation and global security and entails neither anarchy nor 'zero-sum' security policy (Bordachev, 2009). In such a fashion have they inverted Hegemonic Stability Theory, which holds that preponderant power must provide international public goods in order to prevent the proliferation of rival, if not autarkic, blocs. For official Russia, not only does American hegemony fail by silencing great powers and smaller states and forcibly transforming the cultural, religious and moral basis of discrete development models, it also works less efficiently.

4 Embedding a multipolar world order

In addition to reflecting the objective dispersal of economic and political power beyond the Western core, multipolarity contains a volitional element for official Russia. In August 1999 Yeltsin suggested that the main task of Russia's foreign policy lay in 'the creation of a multipolar world order that must be based on the principles and norms of international law and the mutual interest of all states'. In the late 1990s both Yeltsin and then Russian Foreign Minister Igor Ivanov deemed Russia's main foreign policy task to be the *construction* of the multipolar world (de Weydenthal, 1998; RFERL, 1999, 1 September).

While multipolarity therefore clearly constitutes a way of thinking that predates Putin's first presidential term, which began in 2000, it becomes further embedded in Russian state discourse during the 'Putin era'. Putin is reported to have issued a decree to amend the 2000 National Security Concept in order to emphasise multipolarity (RFERL, 2000, 13 January). This precedes the neoconservative unilateralism of George W. Bush being enshrined in the 2002 US National Security Strategy. Russia's 2000 National Security Concept analyses the system of international relations according to two major tendencies. The first

> manifests itself in the strengthened economic and political positions of a significant number of states and of their integrative associations and in improved mechanisms for multilateral governance of international processes. Economic, political, science and technological, environmental and information factors are playing an ever-increasing role. Russia will help shape the *ideology* behind the rise of a multipolar world on this basis.
>
> (The Russian Federation, 2000b; emphasis added)

In this formulation, the objective and the subjective elements of multipolarity coincide. The multipolar condition results from particular states enhancing their respective positions in the global economic and political order. Based on such comments, it is difficult to determine which is leading and which following: impersonal processes and factors that contribute to the rise of states or an enabling ideology that contributes to the legitimacy and desirability of such an order.

The document continues and lists the second tendency, which

> manifests itself in attempts to create an international relations structure based on domination by developed Western countries in the international community, under US leadership and designed for unilateral solutions (primarily by the use of military force) to key issues in world politics in circumvention of the fundamental rules of international law.
>
> (The Russian Federation, 2000b)

According to official Russia, in the midst of various processes which led to the rise of non-Western political economies, American attempts to reassert hegemony are anachronistic, resulting not from preponderant American power but from the desire to suppress rising states. Moreover, they are predicated on a narrowly conceived base of Western-dominated institutions and therefore not representative of the general global will:

> The strategy of unilateral actions can destabilise the international situation, provoke tensions and the arms race, aggravate interstate contradictions, national and religious strife. The use of power methods bypassing existing international legal mechanisms cannot remove the deep socio-economic, inter-ethnic and other contradictions that underlie conflicts, and can only undermine the foundations of law and order.
>
> Russia shall seek to achieve a multi-polar system of international relations that really reflects the diversity of the modern world with its great variety of interests.
>
> (The Russian Federation, 2000a; see also The Russian Federation, 2008)

A host of negative qualities are attributed to American unipolarity in contrast to a multipolar world order. A multipolar system is known predominantly as the opposite of unipolar aggression and more accurately reflects a plurality of interests in the modern world. States including Russia must contribute to the multipolar world order to more effectively address contemporary problems of global systems management, addressing both the technical requirements of global governance and a normative imperative to improve a conflict-ridden state of affairs. Normatively, multipolarity represents a more just, inclusive and representative world order than unipolarity. Instrumentally, it simply works better. Putin offered more strident criticism of unipolarity in his second term, during which time Russia acquired greater material resources with which to project economic and political influence in the world (Monaghan, 2006; Yefremenko, 2010) and responded vociferously to a series of 'colour revolutions' on its periphery.[3] Sergey Yastrzhembskiy, Special Representative of the Russian President for the Development of Relations with the EU, stated as much in 2007:

> The basic trend is to turn the world – which objectively, by virtue of globalisation, is becoming increasingly multipolar – into a unipolar world in which all the rules of the game, the rules of life, the rules of behavior are defined by just one player, who, moreover, does not care about the code of laws enshrined in international law. That is what we categorically disagree with. Many others also disagree with it, only they say so quietly, as we used to do previously, in the days of the Soviet Union, in our own kitchen.
>
> ('Sergey Yastrzhembskiy', 2007)

We are perhaps left to assume that the 'many others' are those dissatisfied with, but not yet openly confronting, American rule who are enlisted by Putin-era Russian officials in the multipolar project. Larger states able to translate economic power into political authority are considered by Russia as significant assets, the poles which constitute multipolarity. Such centers are frequently invoked as the emerging alternative to the present state of unipolar dominance (RFERL, 2004, 27 October; RFERL, 2005, 4 January; RFERL, 2000, 4 December; 'Russian, Brazilian Foreign Ministers', 2003).

Putin utilises the polysemic quality of multipolarity to appeal to audiences that are either overtly hostile or at best lukewarm towards America's global stewardship, representing a wide array of developments in multiple states, not simply those in larger ones, as indicative of these states' commitment to multipolarity. Putin routinely appeals to a variety of institutional forms, political entities and political relationships for the multipolar enterprise. Putin has courted partners and participants for the multipolar vision in a variety of forms: within a trilateral project (China, Russia and India or Russia, France and Germany); a bilateral project (China and Russia; India and Russia); within the BRICS formulation; as an institutional pooling of sovereignties in which Russia participates (for example the CSTO); and as a regional agency or civilisational entity that Russia seeks to engage (The President of the Russian Federation, 2000; 2001; 2008). All multilateral venues of which Russia is a part, regardless of the degree of formalised activity and decision-making authority they represent, become forums in which Russia may construct multipolarity. So too are various international venues of which Russia is not a formal member – the Association of Southeast Asian Nations (ASEAN), whom Sergei Lavrov considered an 'important partner in creating a multipolar world and a common regional security system' (RFERL, 2005, 12 December); MERCOSUR (The President of the Russian Federation, 2007); 'Latin America' (RFERL, 2008, 26 September); and the League of Arab States ('Putin Objects', 2007).

That multipolarity had become a reality is a position stated with some frequency in 2007, during which time numerous Russian officials portrayed multipolarity as in line with the redistribution of wealth and power to non-Western countries. The 2008 Review of Foreign Policy of the Russian Federation clearly expresses this notion:

> The increasing processes of globalisation, in spite of their contradictory consequences, led to the more even distribution of resources, influence and economic growth, *laying an objective foundation for the multipolar construction of international relations.*
>
> (italics added; see also Lavrov, 2007a, 2007b, 2007c)

Centres of economic growth may see their economic might translated into political clout and thereby create a multipolar system. Putin emphasises that India's and China's combined GDP (in terms of purchasing power parity – PPP) exceeds that of the United States and that that of the BRIC countries surpasses that of EU countries. Putin declares, 'There is no reason to doubt that the economic potential of the new centres of global economic growth will inevitably be converted into political influence and will strengthen multipolarity' (The President of the Russia Federation, 2007). According to Sergei Lavrov, the United States should drop its pretensions to unilateral leadership and instead accept the reality of multipolarity and its place in it (Lavrov, 2007a, 2007b, 2007c).

Beyond appealing to a complex institutional and material basis for multipolarity, Putin has laden multipolarity and unipolarity with other attributes. In his 2007 'Munich Speech', Putin criticised unipolarity for exhibiting numerous subjective, moral and technical failings. According to Putin, the unipolar model 'is flawed because at its basis there is and can be no moral foundations for modern civilisation' and because it imposes foreign political systems and development models while ignoring historical, cultural and religious elements (The Russian Federation, 2007). For Putin, to recreate a unipolar world is to contribute to global crises by inhibiting cultural and socio-economic development (World News Connection, 24 January 2007). The decisive turn to multipolarity has coincided with the call for an 'intercivilisational consensus' in state-sanctioned discourse (Lavrov 2007a). The 2008 Foreign Policy Concept of the Russian Federation (The Russian Federation, 2008) echoes this sentiment, stating, 'It is for the first time in the contemporary history that global competition is acquiring a civilisational dimension which suggests competition between different value systems and development models within the framework of universal democratic and market economy principles'. Moreover, 'As the constraints of the bipolar confrontation are being overcome, the cultural and civilisational diversity of the modern world is increasingly in evidence'. Hence, multipolarity acquires a civilisational dimension as the appropriate form by which to secure culturally specific developmental trajectories.

Lavrov refutes the notion that multipolarity necessitates great power confrontation and competitive bloc formation and inscribes multipolarity with attributes ascribed to unipolar structures by defenders of unipolarity. In a 2007 article he suggests that the alternative to unipolarity was a chaotic system of international relations and instead offered a model for governance and security provision predicated on informal leadership and international institutions:

> I cannot agree with the opinion that a real alternative to a 'unipolar world' is 'chaotisation' of international relations due to a 'vacuum' of governability and security… It is understandable that many people across the Atlantic still cannot make themselves say the word 'multipolar'. But it is absolutely groundless to suggest that multipolarity increases the likelihood of confrontation.
>
> (Lavrov, 2007c)

Similarly, for Primakov, multipolarity denoted neither anarchy nor rival blocs but a condition of *economic interdependence* (RFERL, 2008, February 1). Instead, it represented a more democratic distribution of economic resources beyond the West via globalisation processes, depriving the West of its 'monopoly' on globalisation processes (World News Connection, 30 April 2007).

For Putin, unipolarity is a destabilising force that provokes defensive moves by threatened states. In contrast, a multipolar world order would bring with it promises of a unified security regime. There is no indication of the precise nature of a unified security arrangement in a globalised world; rather, the positive qualities are attributed to the multipolar world order by virtue of it being the opposite of unipolarity. The notion that multipolarity can counter international anarchy is somewhat of a conceptual innovation of Russian officials in the Putin era. Multipolarity reflects democratic plurality (if not outright consensus) and anarchy mitigating interdependence amongst states and a plethora of economic and political institutions (President of the Russian Federation, 2003; RFERL, 2003, 12 February; RFERL, 2003, 7 April; Yakovenko, 2005, p. 9.)

Urging 'broad multilateral cooperation', Lavrov suggested, 'it is difficult to avoid the conclusion that the ultimate foreign policy objective of the US administration is to perpetuate America's sole leadership in world affairs *despite the fact that countering terrorism and other new challenges and threats can be objective [sic] achieved solely on the basis of broad multilateral* cooperation' (Lavrov, 2007a). A more negative scenario is one in which the United States, or the West, dominates as global monopolist. This situation is untenable as it entails the ideological and material suppression of other states. In 2007, Lavrov stated:

> The paradigm of contemporary international relations is rather determined by competition in the broadest interpretation of the word, particularly when the object of competition is value systems and development models. However, this is not at all equivalent to confrontation. The novelty of the situation is that the West is losing its monopoly on the globalisation process. This explains, perhaps, attempts to present the current developments as a threat to the West, its values, and very way of life.
>
> (Lavrov, 2007c)

For key Russian officials, a multipolar world order represents a consensus position amongst a number of states prior to the 2007–2008 financial crisis and its aftermath. When asked whether there was anything sensational in the contents of a communiqué from a meeting between Russian, Indian and Chinese foreign ministers in 2007, Foreign Minister Lavrov said, 'Naturally. Don't the phrases – a multipolar world, the democratisation of international relations, multilateral diplomacy as a key to everything, the need to seek a collective solution to all problems without dual standards, resisting terrorism – sound familiar? President Putin spoke of the same things in Munich.' He continued, 'This goes to prove that what he said is on everyone's mind, many countries have been speaking of that for long and consistently' (World News Connection, 16 February 2007). The Russian position on multipolarity and the associated instruments of international relations are envisioned as representing a consensus amongst important powers, with Russia having helped to bring about this consensus position.

5 Conclusion

Multipolarity is now firmly entrenched in official Russia's discourse. The 2013 Foreign Policy Concept of the Russian Federation (The Russian Federation, 2013) is emblematic for the manner in which multiple elements of the multipolar world order coincide while echoing themes found in the 2008 variant. In addition to emphasising the need to create a polycentric (multipolar) world order and denouncing unilateralism, the concept reinforces the 'civilisational turn', stating, 'For the first time in modern history, global competition takes place on a civilisational level, whereby various values and models of development based on the universal principles of democracy and market economy start to clash and compete against each other. Cultural and civilisational diversity of the world becomes more and more manifest'.[4] Moreover, 'the reverse side of the globalisation processes is the increased emphasis on civilisational identity'. The manageability of global development 'requires collective leadership by the major states of the world, which, in turn, should be representative in geographical and civilisational terms' and utilise UN, BRICS, G20 and SCO frameworks.

The result of post-Soviet Russia's gradual and uneven rejection of American hegemonic leadership has been an unleashing of concepts, rhetoric and practices by Russian officials testifying to some combination of the veracity, immanence and desirability of a multipolar world order in which 'alternative' (non-neo-liberal and non-polyarchic) development models may be legitimated and 'civilisational' autonomy respected. On an ideational and material level, the Russian political state has launched a challenge to US hegemonic leadership. On a theoretical level, Russian officials invite us to consider the extent to which globalisation paradigms were disarticulated and rearticulated before the disciplines took notice.

Notes

1 I utilise these terms in the following manner: unipolarity denotes a condition of preponderant material power; hegemony denotes both the coercive and consensual tactics employed to incorporate states and social forces into the USA's global project; and neo-liberal globalisation denotes a condition whereby state-based impediments to the capital mobility and capital accumulation are removed.

2 Considerable literature explores the composition of contemporary Russian capitalism and the extent to which it breaks with Soviet-era practices and norms. See: Dawisha (2014); Dzarasov (2013); Lane (2013).

3 Most significant in this regard were: the 2003 Rose Revolution in Georgia, which ousted Eduard Shevardnadze in favour of the pro-American Mikhail Saakashvili; the 2004 Orange Revolution in Ukraine, during which Russia openly supported Viktor Yanukovych for president yet witnessed the victory of Viktor Yushchenko, and the 2005 Tulip Revolution in Kyrgyzstan, which ousted pro-Kremlin Askar Akayev.

4 The 2008 Foreign Policy Concept of the Russian Federation contains a near verbatim statement.

References

Ambrosio, T. (2005). *Challenging America's global pre-eminence: Russia's quest for multipolarity.* Burlington: Ashgate.

Amin, S., & Camiller, P. (2006). *Beyond US hegemony? Assessing the prospects for a multipolar world.* London: Zed Books.

Appelbaum, R. P., & Robinson, W. I. (2005). *Critical globalization studies.* New York: Routledge.

Ban, C., & Blyth, M. (2013). The BRICs and the Washington Consensus: An introduction. *Review of International Political Economy*, 20(2), 241–255.

Bordachev, T. (2009). Multipolarity, anarchy and security. In I. Krastov, M. Leonard & A. Wilson (Eds.), *What does Russia think?* (pp. 60–66). London: European Council on Foreign Relations.

Brenner, N., Peck, J. & Theodore, N. (2010). After neoliberalization? *Globalizations*, 7(3), 327–345.

Channel TF-1 & The President of the Russian Federation. (2003, 11 February). Interview with French Television Channel TF-1 (Interview transcript). Retrieved from http://eng.kremlin.ru/transcripts/7289.Accessed January 2012.

'China and Russia sign Gazprom supply agreement'. (2014, 21 May). *The Moscow Times: Reuters.* Retrieved from http://www.themoscowtimes.com/business/article/china-and-russia-sign-gazprom-supply-agreement/500571.html.

'China to push strategic partnership with Russia: Foreign ministry'. (2014, 5 December). *The BRICS Post.* Retrieved from http://thebricspost.com/china-to-push-strategic-partnership-with-russia-foreign-ministry/ #.VQ8x7dLF9IE.

'China's Xinjiang-Russia trade rose 374% in 2014.(2014, 14 February). *The BRICS Post.* Retrieved from http://thebricspost.com/chinas-xinjiang-russia-trade-rose-374-in-2014/#.VQ8tD9LF9IE.

Cohen, S. (2001). *Failed crusade: America and the tragedy of post-communist Russia.* New York: W.W. Norton.

Cooper, A. F., & Flemes, D. (2013). Foreign policy strategies of emerging powers in a multipolar world: an introductory review. *Third World Quarterly*, 34(6), 943–962.

de Weydenthal, J. (1998, 9 October). Russia: Foreign Minister rules out membership in NATO and EU. *RFERL.* Retrieved from http://www.rferl.org/content/article/1089823.html.

Dawisha, K. (2014). *Putin's kleptocracy: Who owns Russia?* New York: Simon and Schuster.

Desai, R. (2013). *Geopolitical economy: After US hegemony, globalization and empire.* London: Pluto.

Dzarasov, R. (2013). *The conundrum of Russian capitalism: The Post-Soviet economy in the world system.* London: Pluto.

Eley, G. (2007). Historicizing the global, politicizing capital: Giving the present a name. *History Workshop Journal*, 63(1), 154–188.

Friedman, T. (2000). *The Lexus and the olive tree.* New York, NY: Random House.

Germain, R. (2012). *Global politics and financial governance.* New York: Palgrave Macmillan.

Gills, B. K. (2000). *Globalization and the politics of resistance.* London; New York: Macmillan; St. Martin's Press.

Gills, B. K. (2014). Barry K. Gills. *Globalizations*, 11(4), 561–572.

Gills, B., & Philip, G. (1996). Editorial: Towards convergence in development policy? Challenging the Washington Consensus and restoring the historicity of divergent development trajectories. *Third World Quarterly*, 17(4), 585–592.
Gowan, P. (1999). *The global gamble: Washington's Faustian bid for world dominance.* London: Verso.
Gramsci, A. (1971). *Selections from the prison notebooks.* London: Lawrence & Wishart.
Held, D., & McGrew, A. (2000). *The global transformations reader: An introduction to the globalisation debate.* Malden, Mass: Polity Press.
Held, D., & McGrew, A. (2007). *Globalization/anti-globalization: Beyond the great divide.* Cambridge: Polity.
Hirst, P., & Thompson, G. (1995). Globalization and the future of the nation state. *Economy and Society*, 24(3), 408–442.
James, P., & Steger, M. B. (2014). A genealogy of 'globalization': The career of a concept. *Globalizations*, 11(4), 417–434.
Jenson, J. (2010). Diffusing ideas for after neoliberalism: The social investment perspective in Europe and Latin America. *Global Social Policy*, 10(1), 59–84.
Kashin, V. (2014, 27 May). Russia's rapprochement with China runs deep. *The Moscow Times.* Retrieved from http://www.themoscowtimes.com/opinion/article/russias-rapprochement-with-china-runs-deep/500998.html.
Katz, M. (2006). Primakov redux? Putin's pursuit of 'multipolarism' in Asia. *Demokratizatsiya*, 14(1), 144–152.
Keohane, R. O., Macedo, S. & Moravcsik, A. (2009). Democracy-enhancing multilateralism. *International Organization*, 63(1), 1–31.
Kindleberger, C. (1981). Dominance and leadership in the international economy: Exploitation, public goods, and free rides. *International Studies Quarterly*, 25(2), 242–254.
Kindleberger, C. (1986). *The world in depression, 1929–1939.* London: University of California Press.
Kolossov, V., & Turovsky, R. (2001). Russian geopolitics at the fin-de-siecle. *Geopolitics*, 6(1), 141–164.
Kurowska, X. (2014). Multipolarity as resistance to liberal norms: Russia's position on responsibility to protect. *Conflict, Security & Development*, 14(4), 489–508.
Laïdi, Z. (2014). Towards a post-hegemonic world: The multipolar threat to the multilateral order. *International Politics*, 51(3), 350–365.
Lane, D. (2013). *The capitalist transformation of state socialism: The making and breaking of state socialist society, and what followed.* New York: Routledge.
Lavrov, S. (2007a). Global politics needs openness and democracy. World News Connection. Retrieved from http://wnc.dialog.com.proxy.library.carleton.ca/April 30.
Lavrov, S. (2007b, July 19). The article by Russian Minister of Foreign Affairs Sergey Lavrov 'Containing Russia: Back to the future?' Retrieved from http://www.mid.ru/brp_4.nsf/0/8F8005F0C5CA3710C325731D0022E227.Accessed January 2012.
Lavrov, S. (2007c, May 13). The present and the future of global politics. *Russia in Global Affairs.* Retrieved from http://eng.globalaffairs.ru/number/n_8554.Accessed January 2012.
Luckhurst, J. (2013). Building cooperation between the BRICS and leading industrialized states. *Latin American Policy*, 4(2), 251–268.
Lukyanov, F. (2010). Russian dilemmas in a multipolar world. *Journal of International Affairs*, 63(2), 19–32.

Makarychev, A., & Morozov, V. (2011). Multilateralism, multipolarity, and beyond: A menu of Russia's policy strategies. *Global Governance*, *17*(3), 353–373.
Makarychev, A., & Morozov, V. (2013). Is "Non-Western theory" possible? The idea of multipolarity and the trap of epistemological relativism in Russian IR. *International Studies Review*, 15(3), 328–350.
Mielniczuk, F. (2013). BRICS in the contemporary world: Changing identities, converging interests. *Third World Quarterly*, 34(6), 1075–1090.
Mikhailenko, V. I. (2003). Russia in the new world order: Power and tolerance in contemporary international relations. *Demokrtizatsiya*, 11(2), 198–211.
Mittelman, J. H. (2004). Globalization debates: Bringing in microencounters. *Globalizations*, 1(1), 24–37.
Monaghan, A. (2006). Calmly critical: Evolving Russian views of US hegemony. *Journal of Strategic Studies*, 29(6), 987–1013.
Mundial, B. (2011). *Global development horizons 2011. Multipolarity: the new global economy*. Washington DC: World Bank.
Nadkarni, V., & Noonan, N. C. (2012). *Emerging powers in a comparative perspective: The political and economic rise of the BRIC countries*. New York: Bloomsbury Academic.
Nazarbayev, N., Putin, V., & Lukashenko, A. (2014, May 29). Press statements following the Supreme Eurasian Economic Council meeting. Speech presented in Astana. Retrieved from http://eng.kremlin.ru/transcripts/22404.
Nesvetailova, A., & Palan, R. (2013). The end of liberal finance? The changing paradigm of global financial governance. *Millennium – Journal of International Studies*, 38(3), 797–825.
Ohmae, K. (1995) *The end of the nation state: The rise of regional economies*. New York, NY: Free Press.
O'Loughlin, J. (2001). Geopolitical fantasies, national strategies and ordinary Russians in the Post-Communist era. *Geopolitics*, 6(3), 17–48.
O'Neill, J. (2001). *Building better global economic BRICs*. London: Goldman Sachs.
OECD. (2009). Russian Federation. *OECD Economic Surveys*, 29(6), 21–24.
Peck, J., Theodore, N., & Brenner, N. (2010). Postneoliberalism and its malcontents. *Antipode*, 41(S1), 94–116.
The President of the Russian Federation. (2000, October 27). Vladimir Putin congratulated Austrian President Thomas Klestil and Federal Chancellor Wolfgang Schuessel on the republics national holiday: Adoption of law on the permanent neutrality of Austria. Kremlin, Moscow: The President of the Russian Federation. Retrieved from http://eng.kremlin.ru/news/15062.Accessed January 2012.
The President of the Russian Federation. (2001, 14 May). Statement for the Press and Answers to Questions at the Joint Press Conference with President Hugo Chavez of Venezuela. Kremlin, Moscow: The President of the Russian Federation. Retrieved from http://eng.kremlin.ru/transcripts/8944.Accessed January 2012.
The President of the Russian Federation. (2007, 18 December). President Vladimir Putin sent a message of congratulations to the delegates at the MERCOSUR Latin American common market summit. N.p. The President of the Russian Federation. Retrieved from http://eng.kremlin.ru/news/17194.Accessed January 2012.
The President of the Russian Federation. (2008, 4 December). Interview for Indian Broadcasting Corporation Doordarshan. N.p. The President of the Russian Federation. Retrieved from http://eng.kremlin.ru/transcripts/9919.Accessed January 2012.

Pryce, P. (2013). Putin's third term: The triumph of Eurasianism? *Romanian Journal of European Affairs*, 13(1), 25–43.
Putin, V. (2012, 12 December). Address to the Federal Assembly. Speech presented in Moscow. Retrieved from http://eng.kremlin.ru/news/4739.
'Putin objects to use of force'. (2007, 29 March). Interfax. Retrieved from World News Connection. Accessed January 2012.
Rangsimaporn, P. (2006). Interpretations of Eurasianism: Justifying Russia's role in East Asia. *Europe-Asia Studies*, 58(3), 371–389.
Reddaway, P., & Glinski, D. (2001). *The tragedy of Russian reforms: Market Bolshevism against democracy*. Washington: United States Institute of Peace Press.
RFERL. (1997, 9 January). Newsline. RFERL. Retrieved from http://www.rferl.org/content/article/1141324.html.Accessed January 2012.
RFERL. (1997, 24 September) Newsline. RFERL. Retrieved from http://www.rferl.org/content/article/1141501.html.Accessed January 2012.
RFERL. (1998, 12 May). Newsline. RFERL. Retrieved from http://www.rferl.mobi/a/1141653.html.Accessed January 2012.
RFERL. (1999, 1 September). Newsline. RFERL. Retrieved from http://www.rferl.org/content/article/1141982.html.Accessed January 2012.
RFERL. (2000, 13 January). Newsline. RFERL. Retrieved from http://www.rferl.org/content/article/1142071.html.Accessed January 2012.
RFERL. (2000, 4 December). Security Watch. RFERL. Retrieved from http://www.rferl.org/content/article/1344757.html.Accessed January 2012.
RFERL. (2001, 12 February). Security Watch. RFERL. Retrieved from http://www.rferl.org/content/article/1344696.html.Accessed January 2012.
RFERL. (2003, 7 April). Newsline. RFERL. Retrieved from http://www.rferl.org/content/article/1142892.html.Accessed January 2012.
RFERL. (2003, 29 May). Newsline. RFERL. Retrieved from http://www.rferl.org/content/article/1142925.html.Accessed January 2012.
RFERL. (2004, 27 October). Newsline. RFERL. Retrieved from http://www.rferl.org/content/article/1143271.html.Accessed January 2012.
RFERL. (2005, 4 January). Newsline. RFERL. Retrieved from http://www.rferl.org/content/article/1143310.html.Accessed January 2012.
RFERL (2005, 12 December). Newsline. RFERL. Retrieved from http://www.rferl.org/content/article/1143536.html.Accessed January 2012.
RFERL. (2008, 1 February). Newsline. RFERL. Retrieved from http://www.rferl.org/content/article/1144043.html.Accessed January 2012.
RFERL. (2008, 26 September). Putin Offers Nuclear Help to Chavez. RFERL. Retrieved from http://www.rferl.org/content/Putin_Offers_Nuclear_Energy_Help_To_Chavez/1291733.html.Accessed January 2012.
Roberts, C. (2010). Russia's BRICs diplomacy: Rising outsider with dreams of an insider. *Polity*, 42(1), 38–73.
Rosenberg, J. (2005). Globalization Theory: A post mortem. *International Politics*, 42(1), 2–74.
The Russian Federation. (2000a, 28 June). The Foreign Policy Concept of the Russian Federation: Approved by the President of the Russian Federation V. Putin. Fas.org. Retrieved from http://fas.org/nuke/guide/russia/doctrine/econcept.htm.Accessed January 2012.
The Russian Federation. (2000b, 10 January). National Security Concept of the Russian Federation: Approved by Presidential decree No. 24 of 10 January 2000. N.p. The

Ministry of Foreign Affairs of the Russian Federation official site. Retrieved from http://www.mid.ru/ns-osndoc.nsf/osnddeng.Accessed January 2012.

The Russian Federation. (2007). 2007 review of the foreign policy of the Russian Federation (ОБЗОР ВНЕШНЕЙ ПОЛИТИКИ РОССИЙСКОЙ ФЕДЕРАЦИИ). (Author's translation). Retrieved from http://www.ln.mid.ru/brp_4.nsf/sps/3647DA9748A106BC32572AB002AC4DD.Accessed January 2012.

The Russian Federation. (2008, 12 July). The Foreign Policy Concept of the Russian Federation. Kremlin.ru. Retrieved from http://archive.kremlin.ru/eng/text/docs/2008/07/204750.shtml.Accessed January 2012.

The Russian Federation. (2013, 18 February). Concept of the Foreign Policy of the Russian Federation: Approved by President of the Russian Federation V. Putin on 12 February 2013. The Ministry of Foreign Affairs of the Russian Federation official site. Retrieved from http://www.mid.ru/brp_4.nsf/0/76389FEC168189ED44257B2E0039B16D.Accessed January 2012.

Russian, Brazilian foreign ministers confirm adherence to multipolar order. (2003, 17 February). *Moscow Interfax in English*. Retrieved from World News Connection.

Sergey Yastrzhembskiy: Gentlemen, Russia is back! (2007, 26 February). *Rossiyskaya Gazeta*. Retrieved from World News Connection.

Shakleyina, T. A., & Bogaturov, A. D. (2004). The Russian Realist school of international relations. *Communist and Post Communist Studies*, 37(1), 37–51.

Silvius, R. (2014). The Russian state, Eurasianism, and civilizations in the contemporary global political economy. *Journal of Global Faultlines*, 2(1), 44–69.

Silvius, R. (2015). Eurasianism and Putin's 'embedded civilisationalism'. In D. Lane & V. Samokhvalov (Eds.), *The Eurasian project and Europe: Regional discontinuities and geopolitics* (pp. 75–88). London: Palgrave MacMillan.

Stephen, M. D. (2014). Rising powers, global capitalism and liberal global governance: A historical materialist account of the BRICs challenge. *European Journal of International Relations*, 20(4), 912–938.

Subacchi, P. (2008). New power centres and new power brokers: Are they shaping a new economic order? *International Affairs*, 84(3), 485–498.

Torbakov, I. (2004). Russia's Eastern Offensive: Eurasianism versus Atlanticism. *Eurasia Daily Monitor,* 1(38). Retrieved from http://www.jamestown.org/single/?no_cache=1&tx_ttnews%5Btt_news%5D=30001#.U5NM_nKwKXs. Accessed January 2012.

Tsygankov, A. P. (2009). Russia in global governance: multipolarity or multilateralism? In D. Lesage & P. Vercauteren (Eds.), *Contemporary global governance: Multipolarity vs. new discourses on global governance* (pp. 51–62). Brussels: P.I.E. Peter Lang, S.A.

Turner, S. (2009). China and Russia and the multipolar world order: The danger in the undefined. *Asian Perspective*, 33(1), 159–184.

van Apeldoorn, B. (2004). Theorizing the transnational: A historical materialist approach. *Journal of International Relations and Development*, 7(2), 142–176.

Vezirgiannidou, S. (2013). The United States and rising powers in a post-hegemonic global order. *International Affairs*, 89(3), 635–651.

Wade, R. H. (2011). Emerging world order? From multipolarity to multilateralism in the G20, the World Bank, and the IMF. *Politics & Society*, 39(3), 347–378.

Wallander, C. (1998). The Russian national security concept: A liberal-statist synthesis. PONARS Policy Memo 30, Ponars: Harvard University.

Weiss, L. (1998). *The myth of the powerless state.* Ithaca, NY: Cornell University Press.

World Bank. (2009, November). *The World Bank in Russia: Russian Economic Report No 20*. Retrieved from http://siteresources.worldbank.org/INTRUSSIANFEDERATION/Resources/305499-1245838520910/rer20fulltext_eng.pdf. Accessed January 2012.

World News Connection. (2007, 24 January).

World News Connection. (2007, 30 April).

World News Connection. (2007, 16 October).

Yakovenko, A. (2005) Russia-India-China meeting. *Current Digest of the Post-Soviet Press*, 57(22), 9.

Yefremenko, D. (2010). Forced or desired modernity? *Russia in Global Affairs*, 8(4). Retrieved from http://eng.globalaffairs.ru/number/Forced-or-Desired-Modernity-14996. Accessed January 2012.

Zakaria, F. (2011). *The Post-American world: Release 2.0*. New York: WW Norton & Company.

5 The Russian state, Eurasianism and civilisations in the contemporary global political economy

1 Introduction

During a post-Cold War era in which numerous academics and commentators have debated the veracity and extensity of American hegemony, liberal democratic norm diffusion, and neo-liberal globalisation, the Russian state has been seeking to negate or challenge all three tendencies. Open geopolitical conflicts, witnessed in Georgia in 2008 and Ukraine at present are particularly 'material' examples of this challenge. But Russia has offered a considerable 'ideational' challenge to the West, as well, a challenge predicated on the insistence of the intrinsic virtues of Russian, if not Eurasian, culture and civilisation. In being, to borrow a term from Morozov (2009), 'obsessed with identity', the Russian state has echoed scholarly tendencies in the broad fields of international relations and international political economy.

Such an 'obsession' and the scholarship, concepts and practices it has unleashed have been accompanied by attempts by select Russian officials to augment Russian influence in the former Soviet sphere via a series of geopolitical and geoeconomic initiatives. Russian forays into Eurasian space have been accompanied by the language of cultural particularity and Russian/Eurasian civilisational distinctiveness. In utilising such language, Russian officials borrow selectively from the heterogeneous corpus of scholarship of Eurasianism. Eurasianism and associated debates about the place of civilisations in the contemporary global political economy offer official Russia the lexicon to demonstrate that its practices adhere to a longer Russian tradition of statecraft. Moreover, they provide the rationale that geopolitical and geoeconomic pursuits are at their heart *cultural* affairs and predicated on the cultural predispositions that obtain in geographical space.

Far from being merely the fashion of a post-global age, such a 'cultural turn' is in myriad ways apparent in Eurasianists' suggestions that liberalism, ethical relativism and their Western cultural substratum have in one way or another confronted Russia and Eurasia as civilisational difference in different historical epochs. Alleged civilisational incommensurability is a curious counterpoint to official Russia's efforts to consolidate Eurasian space under

Russian leadership as a modern, 'pragmatic' form of regionalism that allows for the further development of Russian state capitalism. And yet the 'material' and 'ideational', the 'semiotic' and 'extra-semiotic' components of Eurasian integration need not perfectly align: the result is what might appear to be an irreconcilable tension between Eurasianism as both a civilisational and technocratic/institutional project. This project is what I refer to as 'embedded civilisationalism', and it forms the basis of this chapter.

Russian Eurasianism is a multifaceted intellectual and political project, but, ultimately, its various strands share a common orientation: articulating a cultural plurality in Eurasian space that has obtained over the longue duree by way of Russia's historical role as the integrator of disparate peoples. Whether this serves as cover for Russian ethno-nationalism or a 'positive' project of Russian multiculturalism depends upon the author in question. What is clear is that it offers a more palatable option with which to articulate regional integration efforts than narrowly conceived Russo-centrism. The key to Eurasianism's hegemonic function is found in this realisation. Eurasianism as embedded civilisationalism is the manner by which official Russia absorbs and diffuses what are otherwise the more potentially radical and unsanctioned strains of Eurasianism for the purposes of establishing ideological hegemony and legitimacy. It does so in two ways: negatively, and defensively, as an aggrieved party to US liberal-capitalist and unilateral global hegemonism and positively, as the architect of a Russia-centred regional order on Eurasian space. While the Eurasianist/civilisational line of thinking has found particular traction in the Putin era, during which the Russian president and former prime minister has sought to recapture influence in the former Soviet sphere via numerous Eurasian integration initiatives, its gestation has been occurring much longer.

This chapter proceeds in the following manner. In Section 2, I set up the problem of civilisations within the context of critical historicism and IPE. In Section 3, I demonstrate the political philosophy of Classical Eurasianism, the Bolshevik-era precursor to contemporary Eurasianism and neo-Eurasianism, all of which serve as an historical repository of ideas that has been selectively mined by Russian officials and political technologists for practical and ideological purposes. In Section 4, I turn to an analysis and demonstration of the prevalence and function of Eurasianist ideas in Putin-era, state-sanctioned discourse. A conclusion follows.

2 Russia, civilisations and international political economy

The Russian case of Eurasianist thinking demonstrates the renewed politicisation and significance of historical, non-Western subjectivities following the apex of globalisation thinking and assertions of the arrival of a 'borderless' age in the 1990s (Friedman, 2000). Thinking about civilisations is not only the domain of macrohistorians like Arnold Toynbee (1957) and Fernand Braudel (1994), who sought to understand the dynamics of previous empires and civilisations. Culture and civilisation talk filters into officially sanctioned state discourse, whereby states claim the responsibility of defending the morals, cultural particularity and geographical integrity of a civilisation alongside proclamations of more utilitarian political and economic matters. Moreover, talk of the significance of civilisations is not confined to a United States seeking to extend the unipolar moment amid an uncertain post-Cold War geopolitical settlement (see Huntington, 1996). Rather, concepts pertaining to culture and civilisation are being employed by non-Western states and actors, including those of Russia, to critique American hegemony, consolidate the domestic political apparatus, and achieve legitimacy at home and abroad.

Select Russian state officials' and political technologists' engagement with civilisational discourse alongside projects of political, security and economic integration on Eurasian space demonstrates that emerging fault lines in Eurasia have complex material and ideational dimensions. By analysing contending visions of world order on the terrain of intersubjective ideas as well as material factors (Cox, 1986), it is possible to gauge the stability or instability of hegemonic world orders. Important in this regard is the perception of, and response to, cultural imperialism – which is often overlooked by overtly materialist accounts of world order (Germain, 2011). An historicist analysis of contemporary Russian state-sanctioned political and economic projects and accompanying discourses, propagated in this case by Russian officials and political technologists, enables us to demonstrate how historical national knowledge production has been reactivated for the purposes of imagining and constraining contemporary political possibilities across Eurasian space.

A profound polarisation of Russian society between those seeking Russia's integration into Western liberal institutions and those advocating for the reconstitution of Russia from a variety of nationalist, communist and conservative positions occurred in the 1990s. Furthermore, this period saw the collapse of Russian public authority and the 'privatisation' of Russian government, as well as the absence of norms governing the accumulation process in Russia (see Chapter 3). It is in such a context that the revalorising, if not 'mythologising' (Urban, 1998) of the Russian state was carried out, a trend that has continued to the present. During this time, Russian state officials have borrowed selectively from broader Russian political, cultural and philosophical debates in order to assert the historical and ethical basis for Russian state conduct in national and international affairs, which includes a departure from liberal norms. Eurasianism has emerged as a central component of Russian officials' attempts to articulate an alternative world order that departs from the tenets of polyarchic liberal internationalism. Indeed, Eurasianist discourse and thinking offers much for Russian state projects for which both internal (within Russia) and external (to a non-Russian audience) validity is sought.

Post-Soviet Russia demonstrates that the semiotic and extra-semiotic dimensions of 'transition' need not align. Polysemic ideas pertaining to culture, civilisation and intersubjectivity may be cultivated from a distant past to inoculate against the effects of profound social and economic dislocation. The extent to which such ideas are in sync with aspirations to hegemonic leadership demonstrate the contours of coercion and consent at international, national and regional levels. During periods of strong hegemonic leadership, 'concepts of control' – the world view of a particular hegemonic class, which is embedded to define the limits of the possible for society at large (van der Pijl, 1998, p. 51) – are prevalent and innocuous. Arguably, in Russia, the high water mark of liberal internationalism's domestic appeal occurred in the immediate aftermath of the collapse of the Soviet Union, during which time it was not uncommon for Anglo-American scholarship to proclaim that neo-liberal globalisation had no durable intellectual or practical rivals.

During the Putin era, we can see the proliferation of state-sanctioned discourses pertaining to Russia's place in 'world order', whereby the hegemonic position of the United States has been challenged in spite of the fact that the Russian political economy is increasingly capitalist and integrated within structures of the capitalist global political economy. Since the 1990s, Russian officials have cultivated a home-grown vernacular to express dissatisfaction with the fundamental premises of neo-liberal accumulation strategies, polyarchic democracy and American hegemony, thereby signifying that liberal capitalist sociability has not become fully engrained amongst the Russian elite or society as a whole and that Russian elites have not fully accepted a lesser role in international political life. Furthermore, alongside a variety of efforts towards politically and economically integrating Eurasia under Russian leadership, Putin-era Russian officials emphasise Russia's cultural affinities and civilisational compatibilities with its Eurasian neighbours. By way of Eurasian terrain, therefore, Putin, Russian officials and regime supporting political technologists contest American hegemony on both material and ideational levels, while nonetheless being subject to the constraints and opportunities of participating in regional and global economic structures along increasingly capitalistic lines.

Official Russia's aspirations for domestic and Eurasian hegemony occur by displacing the Soviet-era propensity of geopoliticising class conflict and recasting international amity and enmity as occurring on grounds of cultural/civilisational compatibility or incompatibility. Russia's contemporary international conduct, including a cultivation of, and response to, a Eurasianist revival, offers a radical departure from Soviet state-socialism. An historicist analysis of this revival warrants an investigation of the conservative pre-Bolshevik and Bolshevik-era conceptions found in Russian thinking and political practice that contemporary ideas are grafted on.

3 Original and contemporary Eurasianism

This section demonstrates the gestation of Eurasianism/civilisational thinking in Russia. A note on terminology is warranted. A Eurasianist tradition is first discernible through a broad body of ideas originally elaborated by émigré Russian writers in the 1920s and 1930s, which focused on Russia's combined European and Asian geographical identity, as well as its relationship vis-à-vis

Europe. In this chapter, 'original Eurasianism' denotes the initial elaboration of Eurasianist ideas. 'Contemporary Eurasianism' denotes subsequent attempts to elaborate upon or utilise Eurasianist concepts and is comprised of two categories. 'Neo-Eurasianism' denotes subsequent and primarily post-Soviet attempts to develop these ideas in a comprehensive manner. It is primarily, but not entirely, post-Soviet because of the need to trace the intellectual heritage to the Soviet-era ethnologist Lev Gumilyov. Neo-Eurasianism primarily refers to the various post-Soviet attempts at elaborating Eurasianism ideas into a more comprehensive philosophical or political doctrine. Eurasianist/Eurasianism here more generally refers to a continental orientation towards geographical identity and related notions of Russian/Eurasian particularity in any number of spheres – political, cultural, ethnic, geoeconomic, etc. – without a corresponding commitment to a more elaborate political philosophy. For example, Vladimir Putin would hardly be called a neo-Eurasianist, insofar as he exhibits no continual orientation towards a comprehensive Eurasianist doctrine. However, he may exhibit Eurasianist inclinations in suggesting that questions of multipolarity and unipolarity have a cultural, civilisational and moral dimension. Hence, there can be many Eurasianist sentiments and positions exhibited in post-Soviet Russia; neo-Eurasianism, however, is a greater intellectual and/or political commitment, to the extent that its adherents demonstrate a desire to fundamentally challenge modern liberal political thought and practice.

Original Eurasianism emerged in 1921 with the publishing of *Ishkod k Vostoku* (Exodus to the East), a collective volume published by four men who can be considered as the first Eurasianists: Prince Nikolay Sergeevich Trubetskoy, a linguist; Pyotr Nikolaevich Savitsky, an economist and geographer; Pyotr Petrovich Suvchinsky, a music critic; and Georgy Vasileyvich Florovsky, a theologian. Several subsequent Eurasianist joint volumes would follow, and Eurasianism attained a degree of popularity amongst Russian exiles living throughout Europe in the 1920s and 1930s. Original Eurasianism's contribution to the Russian history of ideas is in its theorising on the contribution of Mongol political rule to the history of the Russian state and providing an extended critique of Western colonialism. Early Eurasianists built upon previous critiques of Europe, including those of the Slavophiles, defenders of Official Nationality, and conservatives Constantine Leontyev and Constantine Pobedonostsev, who still had Russia identifying with Europe in a 'fraternal' conflict (Riasanovsky, 1967).

Original Eurasianism reflects, but exceeds, the nineteenth-century division between Westernisers and Slavophiles found in Russian political philosophy. Savitsky maintained the distinction in an article titled 'Two Worlds', published in the second Eurasian symposium in 1922. The two worlds consisted of, first, that of Russian spirituality represented by authors such as Nikolai Gogol and Fyodor Dostoyevsky, the Slavophiles, the philosophers Vladimir Solovyev and Constantine Leontyev, and second, that of the Westernisers, such as writers/critics Nikolai Dobrolyubov and Dmitri Pisarev, the theorist

N.K. Mikhaylovksy, and the world of positivism, scientism and nihilism. The key distinguishing characteristic between the two is the former's anti-state religiosity and the latter's belief in the power and significance of the state, which inspired, *inter alia*, the Bolshevik revolution (Riasanovsky, 1967, pp. 58–60; see also Paradowski, 1999, p. 21).

Insofar as they posit irreconcilable civilisational conflict between Russia (now as Eurasia) and the West, the Eurasianists resemble Nikolai Danilevsky, the nineteenth-century writer whose *magnum opus, Russia and Europe*, divided humanity into distinct cultural and civilisational types analogous to different species of a genus and varying according to naturalistic principles (Danilevskii, 2013). For Danilevsky, civilisations were closed areas between which values were non-transmittable. Danilevsky first conceived of Russia as a cohesive 'natural-geographic region' upon which a historical-ethnographic unity – the Russian-Slav people – was based. This vision was opposed to the idea that Russia constituted two geographic halves – the European and the Asiatic – a notion held by many Russians since Peter the Great's time (Bassin, 1991, p. 11). For Danilevsky, the driving force of history was to be found in the divide between the Romano-Germanic people, who used coercive tactics and suffered from pretensions to universality in seeking to reproduce all other cultures in their image, and the Slavic type. Only the Slavic culture/civilisation, of which Russia was the largest member and therefore the guarantor of its integrity, demonstrated a fully balanced civilisation which included religious, cultural, political and social and economic endeavors (see also Utechin, 1964, pp. 86–87; Laruelle, 2007, pp. 21–23).

Ideas about civilisational conflict between Russia and Europe predate Eurasianism. The original Eurasianists expand on this theme by speaking of the dying of the West and the imminent rise of the East. Their body of work may thus be considered a prolonged critique of Europe in which Russia is conceived as a distinct geocultural entity outside of the sphere of European civilisation. Russia as Eurasia is viewed as comprising an original and independent zone in which Russians/Slavs, Finno-Ugric, and Turkic people combine to establish a culture that is neither reducible to that of Russian-Slav, nor compatible with that of Europe. The original Eurasianists were centrally concerned with understanding the Russian Revolution and distinguished two main aspects of it. First, it represented the culmination of the Westernising trend in Russian history initiated by Peter the Great's reforms. For the Eurasianists, this constituted not only a rebellion against God for the sake of secular aims, but the beginnings of a deep division between an educated elite and government and the mass of Russians. Second, the Revolution destroyed the old order and brought popular forces into Russian political life. However, being foreign to the Russian people, Bolshevism served only a temporary function and would be replaced by Eurasianism, an organic and religious ideology closer to the outlook of the Russian people. By supplanting the Bolsheviks, Eurasianists would ensure the stability of an 'organic' Russian statehood (see also Mazurek, 2002). Eurasianism constituted a version of Russian ideocracy – the reign of a comprehensive idea, employed by a ruling class (in this case the Eurasianists) and safeguarded by an autocratic state.[1]

Following World War I, Eurasianists suggested that a Russian revolt against European dominance would be strengthened by enlisting the support of colonial peoples. In his 1920 book *Europe and Mankind*, Trubetskoy argues that European colonisation did not bring universal civilisation and progress, but rather constituted a form of domination of coloniser over colonised. Eurasianists regarded it not as the triumph of Enlightenment ideals and progress, but as the imposition of the coloniser's culture on the colonised. Trubetskoy defended cultural relativity and particularity, with a now defeated and weakened Russia leading a colonial revolt against the 'Romanogermanic colonisers' (Riasanovsky, 1967, p. 56). Strategically, Eurasianism can be understood as a defense of the territorial integrity of the Russian state and empire amidst great geopolitical upheaval, uncertainty and Russian weakness (Bassin, n.d.). Its similarities to contemporary Eurasianism in both content and context should be noticeable.

Contemporary neo-Eurasianists sought to articulate Russia's place in an emerging world order during a time in which diminished international prestige and domestic upheaval elicited speculation on what constituted authentic Russian statecraft. In such a way did contemporary neo-Eurasianist thinking filter into post-Soviet debates about Russia's position in the world, and, in the process, contribute ideas that subsequently would be developed by Russian politicians to achieve ideological hegemony over Russian, if not *Eurasian*, civil society. Contemporary neo-Eurasianism is represented here by three authors: Lev Gumilyov, Aleksandr Panarin and Aleksandr Dugin. The affinities among and difference between what we may refer to as a Eurasianist conception of world order and certain orientations of the Putin regime, in its most statist and strident moments and during its attempts to consolidate Eurasian space under Russian leadership, necessitate reflection.

Gumilyov's work has swung from being received as heretical during Soviet times to unassailable and strongly supported institutionally in the latter half of post-Soviet era. Gumilyov's (1990) main contribution to the Eurasianist canon is to be found in his 'objectivist' theorising on ethnicity. Social, economic and linguistic forms do not alone determine an ethnic grouping, as they are prone to variation in history and not of objective causes. Nor are ethnic groupings reducible to race. For Gumilyov, ethnic groupings (ethnoi; singular = ethnos) are products of nature and undergo a process of ethnogenesis, which takes place over 1200–1500 years, the lifespan of an ethnos. Ethnoi display the quality of *passionarnost'*, or drive, to act upon their environment, consolidate the group, and propel it through the ethnogenetic cycle. During this process, as natural phenomena, ethnoi are subject to laws of entropy, and their drive and energy diminish (Bassin, 2009, p. 135; Paradowski, 1999; Gumilyov, 1990, Chapter 5). For Gumilyov ethnicity is organised hierarchically. The ethnos is the central unit, roughly analogous to a national grouping that fuses through historical, geographical and biological processes and differentiation (Gumilyov, 1990, p. 44). Underneath them are subethnoi (subsidiary groupings, which are incapable of surviving without the unity imparted by an ethnos). Above them are superethnoi. A superethnos is: 'a group of ethnoi that has arisen at the same time in a region and which manifests itself in history as a mosaic unity of ethnoi' (Gumilyov, 1990, p. 106). Superethnoi are major groupings of ethnoi, fused through shared cultural experiences and affinities and capable of achieving world historical significance (Bassin, 2009, p. 136). For Gumilyov, as only two of the seven superethnoi[2] – the Russian and Steppic – *only* inhabit the area of Eurasia/Soviet Union, the history of the Russian Empire is the history of these two superethnoi converging on the Russian steppe (Laruelle, 2008, p. 71).

Gumilyov upholds the original Eurasianists' contention that the very existence of the Russian state is owed to the Mongol empire, which, rather than having a negative effect on Russia's Orthodox Christian culture, acted as its protector against European encroachment via a positive symbiosis of Mongols and Russians that led to the creation of a Russian/Mongol 'superethnos' (Shlapentokh, 2012). While Gumilyov's scientific-naturalistic conceptions and hierarchical ordering of human ethnicities have elicited considerable controversy,[3] his thinking has also provided the basis for a Russian imagining of the ethnic basis for contemporary geopolitics and the compatibility between Russian culture and that of areas the Russian state seeks to incorporate into Eurasian integration initiatives.

The work of the late Aleksandr Panarin, former Chair of Political Science at Moscow State University's Philosophy Department, is integral to the development of post-Soviet Eurasianism.[4] Panarin developed his contributions to neo-Eurasianism as a philosophical component for Russian post-Soviet rehabilitation, with a particular emphasis on Russia's role in maintaining a global system of checks and balances and thus resisting American-led unipolar globalisation efforts (Solovyev, 2004). In Panarin's works, Russia is to be understood as a civilisation unto itself, whose moral basis is found in Russian Orthodoxy. Civilisations are irreducible entities, to be understood spatially with no temporal standard for analysis. This means that civilisations are not to be slotted on a continuum from archaic to modern and that the technological and economic superiority of the West does not constitute advanced civilisation. Nor are we to assume that civilisations which are not yet modern are destined to become so.

Eurasian pluralism entails the safeguarding of regional and national-cultural rights under an autocratic state. In *Revansh istorii: Rossiiskaya strategicheskaya initsiativa v XXI veke* (The revenge of history: The Russian strategic initiative in the 21st century), Panarin calls for the moral and religious-based rejection of Westernism through, among other things, a 'spontaneous people's conservatism' (an ascetic disavowal of materialism and commercialism) and 'ecological abstinence' (see Bazhanov, 1999). A strong reading of his work might imply that communication and moral judgement across discrete, if not incommensurable, civilisations is impossible. Russia, therefore, reserves the right to reject Western development models and indeed has a moral duty to construct a multipolar world order as the material shell by which Russian/ Eurasian civilisation is safeguarded. Particularly by way of the concept of Sovereign Democracy (Okara, 2007; see also Chapter 7), the Putin regime has echoed this sentiment when calling for an international political architecture and normative order to accommodate and legitimate different development models under multipolarity.

Writing in 1994, Panarin suggested that the heart of his Christian Eurasianism was predicated on 'the idea of a supreme power as the defender of the weak before the strong, who are inclined to be remiss' (p. 73). Panarin's Eurasianism is to be contrasted to that of the original Eurasianists, who 'succumbed to the Bolshevik temptation'. Historically, it was best exemplified by pre-Bolshevik Russia, which was a 'supra-ethnic collectivity, governed not by a national monarchy but by a special kind of 'civilisational' monarchy, which was liberal in a very specific sense of the word: in the sense that it tolerated pluralism in regard to ways of life, beliefs, and ethnic traditions' (p. 71). For Panarin, Eurasianism signifies a civilisation not simply reducible to Russia, Slavic culture, or Orthodoxy, but nonetheless safeguarded by Russian *political* authority.

The work of Aleksandr Dugin, a publicist, strategist and thinker of myriad interests, has attracted considerable attention in the West.[5] The full trajectory of Dugin's thought, his personality, and his relationship to the Kremlin will be explored in Chapter 6. At present it is worth emphasising that Eurasianism, and *Dugin's* Eurasianism in particular has received a disproportionate amount of attention as *political ideology*. The 'pragmatic Eurasianism' of actual emerging economic interdependencies has received comparatively little attention. It is difficult to square the ideological aspects of Eurasianism with ongoing processes of regional integration. Anti-Western, 'mythical', and esoteric Eurasianism has little to say about the region as both inheritor to the Soviet legacy and that which has become the new arena for competition amongst, and collaboration with, non-Russian political economies and the manner by which they fit into international or regional market structures. Vinokurov and Libman (2012), self-declared 'pragmatic Eurasianists', go so far as to claim, 'In Eurasia one is more likely, in fact, to encounter purely market-based international cooperation than in the EU' (p. 27; see also Libman & Vinokurov, 2012; Libman, 2015).[6]

For Dugin, as for many Eurasianists, globalisation is an extension of American unilateralism and hegemony born of the desire of cultural homogenisation. Russia must resist this, both for the sake of preserving its own ethnicity and for defending a form of federalism in the Eurasian space within which individual ethnicities may be preserved in commonwealth form (Shlapentokh, 2007, pp. 232–233). It is therefore reasonable to consider the extent to which talk of 'culture' in the Eurasianist paradigm is placed into the service of those undertaking geostrategic and geoeconomic projects on Eurasian space, whereby culture serves as a unifying element to court other countries against Western hegemony.

4 The Russian state, Eurasianism and the idea of civilisations

The more philosophically and politically adventurous Eurasianists have an ambiguous relationship with Russia's state structures. Nonetheless, 'Eurasianism' came to signify a general statist direction in Russian Foreign Policy exhibited by Foreign Minister Yevgeni Primakov in the mid-1990s, which directed Russia towards greater cooperation with Central and East Asia and away from the enthusiastic embrace of the West exhibited by his predecessor, Andrei Kozyrev. In this sense, a 'pragmatic' Eurasianism came to dominate Russian foreign policy discourse. While some claim that Eurasianism has been eclipsed in recent Russian foreign policy discourse (Morozova, 2009), and in the minds of Russian elites by 'Byzantism', which emphasises Russian Orthodoxy and Russian language and culture as the quintessential elements of Russian civilisation (Shlapentokh, 2013), this chapter makes a contrary claim. While one should question the extent to which the many facets of Eurasianist thinking have influenced and continue to influence Putin's administrations in terms of concrete political orientation and decisions, one need not look solely to such an orientation and decisions to gauge the significance of these various strands of Eurasianist discourse for Russian state conduct, particularly in the context of its efforts to integrate Eurasia under Russian leadership.

'Embedded civilisationalism' refers to the increased significance of both the myriad projects for Eurasian integration that are central to Putin's geoeconomic and geopolitical initiatives and a corresponding valorisation of the distinctiveness of Russian/Eurasian civilisation in official pronouncements and documents. It is argued here that select Putin-era Russian officials, Russian state organs and political technologists have incorporated Eurasianist discourse through the practice of embedded civilisationalism in three manners: 'positively', to serve as the ideological cement in Russian state-led projects of Eurasian political and economic integration; 'negatively', to critique and resist American influence into the Eurasian areas of the former Soviet Union; and 'nationally', to sanctify contemporary state practices by weighing in on broader post-Soviet debates on Eurasianism, Russian identity and civilisations.

Embedded civilisationalism has crept into Russia's official Foreign Policy Concepts. Indeed, the 2008 Concept (The Russian Federation, 2008) attempts to recast the entire post-Soviet period in civilisational terms. It states that 'As the constraints of the bipolar confrontation are being overcome, the cultural and civilizational diversity of the modern world is increasingly in evidence'. The 2013 Concept (The Russian Federation, 2013b) goes further by recasting the notion of globalisation in the context of civilisations, stating:

> The reverse side of the globalization processes is the increased emphasis on civilizational identity. Desire to go back to one's civilizational roots can be clearly seen in recent events in the Middle East and North Africa where political and socioeconomic renewal of society has been frequently carried out under the banner of asserting Islamic values. Similar processes

> can be observed in other regions as well, which makes it a priority for world politics to prevent civilizational fault line clashes and to intensify efforts to forge partnership of cultures, religions and civilizations in order to ensure a harmonious development of mankind. In these circumstances imposing one's own hierarchy of values can only provoke a rise in xenophobia, intolerance and tensions in international relations leading eventually to chaos in world affairs.

Moreover, the 2013 Concept states, echoing a similar depiction in the 2008 concept:

> For the first time in modern history, global competition takes place on a civilizational level, whereby various values and models of development based on the universal principles of democracy and market economy start to clash and compete against each other. Cultural and civilizational diversity of the world becomes more and more manifest.

While its contributors tend to de-radicalise and sanitise their brand of embedded civilisationalism from the more philosophically adventurous and anti-systemic qualities of Eurasianist discourse, we can find direct praise for, and invocations of, the Eurasianist legacy in the highest echelons of the Russian state. Therefore, it is possible to see Eurasianism as having been successfully incorporated into the ideological mainstream of the Putin regime, giving it the ambiguous status of 'being both marginalised and fashionable, dissident and official' (Laruelle, 2012). In August 2005 during a speech at the millennial celebration of Kazan, the capital of the Republic of Tatarstan, Putin paid tribute to Gumilyov's Eurasianism, affirming that the Russian state's 'imperial conscience' was adopted from the Mongol Golden Horde (see RFERL, *Newsline* 2005, August 25). Such praise for Gumilyov indicates Putin's willingness to make more forthright invocations of Eurasianism when framing contemporary global political and economic trends. In his 2012 Address to the Federal Assembly, he states:

> Global development is becoming increasingly unequal. This creates a fertile ground for new economic, geopolitical and ethnic conflicts. Competition for resources is becoming more intense. And I can assure you and want to emphasise that this competition will not be limited only to metals, oils and gas, but above all will focus on human resources and intelligence. Who will take the lead and who will remain outsiders and inevitably lose their independence will depend not only on the economic potential, but primarily on the will of each nation, on its inner energy which Lev Gumilev termed 'passionarity': the ability to move forward and to embrace change.
>
> (The President of the Russian Federation, 2012a)

In spite of appealing to the legacy of Gumilyov in the speech, Putin's 2012 Address to the Federal Assembly is perhaps better characterised as being preoccupied with Russia's demographic crisis and its need to move to a post-resource dependent economy. In utilising Gumilyov's thinking for the purposes of Russia's economic modernisation Putin continues in the broader practice of bending Russian cultural and philosophical legacies – including but not limited to Eurasianism – to more utilitarian dimensions of political economy, a move frequently employed by regime-friendly political technologists and select Russian officials, such as Vladislav Surkov (see Chapter 7).

Such a propensity demonstrates the dual reality of embedded civilisationalism. On the one hand, it is a political necessity for Vladimir Putin to appeal to a constituency that is favourable to talk of Russian 'civilisational projects' and exceptionalism as he proceeds with the more complex, technical and negotiated aspects of Eurasian integration. On the other hand, observers of Russia who wish to find in the Russian president's conduct and words evidence of the same exceptional Russia that does not play by Western standards amplify the significance of conduct deemed to be distinctly Russian to the level of cultural essentialism. It therefore represents the propensity of Putin to co-opt the language of Russian nationalists and 'civilisationalists', while satisfying those who are keen to suggest that Putin is either reconstituting the Soviet Union or a counter-hegemonic system, the qualities of which differ immensely from others operating in the same capitalist global political economy.

Putin's programmatic statements on Eurasian integration are replete with the language of the economic benefits of integration, reading more like the stuff of economic policy wonks than one concerned with asserting irreconcilable civilisational differences. Take for example Putin's October 2013 speech in Minsk at a meeting of the Supreme Eurasian Economic Council. Putin states: 'The Eurasian Economic Union is designed to ensure maximum freedom for the movements of goods, services, capital and labour.' Partners need to create 'a level playing field'. Creating Eurasian energy, transport and telecommunications networks 'will create the most favourable conditions for our economies; developmental potential'. This is important, because 'Regional integration is the most effective way to maximise the use of internal growth resources and increase competitiveness in global markets' ('Supreme Eurasian Economic Council Meeting', 2013).

Adopting the mundane language of technocracy, institution building and regional integration, on the one hand, and that of collaboration, non-Russian consent, and cultural compatibilities in the project, Putin's aim is to demonstrate not only that the Eurasian project meets the criteria of other contemporary regional integration projects. It is to demonstrate that it does not constitute a form of Russian imperial restoration. Supporting Eurasian integration is tantamount to 'playing by the rules' of the contemporary capitalist global political economy, and therefore of limited *counter hegemonic potential.* Nonetheless, the 'alternative' potential in Eurasian integration is found precisely in the forms of collective subjectivities that Russian officials mobilise or appeal to in their attempts to fashion a regional integration project predicated on the economic potential of Russian state capitalism.

Strident interpretations of the Eurasian Union as analogous to the Russian empire can be found. For example, Igor Panarin, a Moscow State University professor who is perhaps best known for once predicting the dissolution of the United States into six discrete parts, suggested in April 2012 that 'Russia is building a Eurasian Union from Scotland to New Zealand' as part of its new 'imperial breakthrough'. Russia, Belarus and Kazakhstan would form the core of the union in December 2012, with the following countries acceding: Ukraine, Armenia, Tajikistan (by December 30, 2013); Serbia, Slovakia and Montenegro (by December 30, 2016); Kyrgyzstan, Mongolia and Uzbekistan (by December 30, 2016); and Turkey, Ireland, Scotland, New Zealand, Vietnam and 'a number of other states' joining eventually ('Eurasian Union – Rising empire or Delusion?' 2012).

Prominent Russian academic figures have likewise taken up the cause of 'values and civilisations'. Alexander Lukin, for example, is Vice President of the Diplomatic Academy of the Russian Ministry of Foreign Affairs, and Director of the Center for East Asian and Shanghai Cooperation Organisation Studies at the Moscow State Institute of International Relations (MGIMO-University). In an article titled 'Eurasian Integration and the Clash of Values', Lukin (2014) suggests that Eurasian integration is emblematic of a larger clash of values between Western moral relativism and individualism, on the one hand, and collectivist cultural and religious systems indigenous to the non-West and often obtaining at the level of the nation within rising national political economies. Moreover, Lukin asserts that substantial portions of populations in Eurasia have chosen leaders as a way to demonstrate their preference for such value systems: Putin, former Ukrainian President Viktor Yanukovich, Belarusian President Alexander Lukashenko and Moldovan communist leader Vladimir Voronin 'have come to power on a wave of popular sentiment favouring a separate identity and a special relationship with Russia, and fears that Europe might absorb them too completely' (Lukin, 2014, p. 49).

Given the centrality of Eurasian integration initiatives to Putin's third tenure as Russian president, it is not misleading to question whether, at the geopolitical and geoeconomic level, Putin's third term is evidence of the 'triumph of Eurasianism' (Pryce, 2013). Putin's Eurasian integration project is actually comprised of a number of discrete initiatives – some completed, others underway – to unify Eurasian space in political, economic and security terms, as detailed below. However, Eurasianism as a form of economic integration is hardly the purview of Putin and Putin alone. As President of the Russian Federation, Dmitry Medvedev extolled the virtues of Eurasian integration. In 2011, while signing the Declaration on Eurasian Economic Integration and the Treaty on the Eurasian Economic Commission with Nazarbayev and Lukashenko, Medvedev proclaimed that as stated by the Declaration, the main aims of further integration were 'ensuring the effective functioning of the common market for goods, services, capital and labour; the formation of a coherent industrial, transport, energy and agricultural policy; further harmonisation of national legislations; strengthening cooperation in the monetary sphere and in [the] area of economic security'. Moreover, he extolled the virtues of the then already created Customs Union, stating that 'it has already boosted our economies' investment attractiveness and is encouraging economic modernisation, which is a paramount goal in today's world', while reminding listeners of the goal of creating the Eurasian Economic Union by 2015 ('Meeting of the presidents of Russia, Belarus and Kazakhstan', 2011).

In both language and practice, then, Russian state efforts towards Eurasian integration precede Putin's third presidential term and the person of Putin. These include, but are not limited to, the following, the intricacies of which exceed the scope of this work. The Eurasian Economic Community (EurAsEC) was founded in 2000 with the intention of achieving the harmonisation of foreign economic, tariff and price policies. It has included Belarus, Kazakhstan, Kyrgyzstan, Russia and Tajikistan. Uzbekistan joined EurAsEC in 2006 prior to having its membership suspended in 2008 (The Russian Federation, 2013a). The Customs Union (CU), founded in 2009, and the Eurasian Economic Union (EEU), which was brought into force on January 1, 2015 are both comprised of Russia, Belarus and Kazakhstan as founding members, with Kyrgyzstan and Armenia joining subsequently (The President of the Russian Federation, 2012b). The Commonwealth of Independent States Free Trade Agreement (CISFTA) was founded in 2011 and is comprised of Armenia, Belarus, Kazakhstan, Kyrgyzstan, Moldova, Russia, Tajikistan and Ukraine (The President of the Russian Federation, 2012a; 2012b). The Eurasian Union (EaU) is frequently conflated with the EEU but signifies a more comprehensive economic and political union project with a common normative and ideational underpinning (The President of the Russian Federation, 2013b).

It is in the context of Russian-led Eurasian integration that one sees the potential efficacy of Eurasianism as a body of ideas deployed to articulate both discrete and comprehensive regionalisation initiatives. Distancing themselves from charges that Eurasian integration is tantamount to neo-Soviet revisionism, Russian officials require ideational, if not 'spiritual' (Salin, 2013) content to unify Russian and non-Russian populations and elites. Narrowly conceived (ethnic) Russian nationalism and 'Byzantine' philosophies (Karaganov, 2013; Shlapentokh, 2013), which extol the virtues of Russian Orthodoxy and ethnic Russian civilisation and enjoy a certain amount of traction in elite circles, are ill-suited to serving as the ideational basis of an initiative which, while spearheaded by Russia, nonetheless requires some degree of consent on the part of non-Russian states and populations. Putin and his supporters have been at pains to demonstrate that the Eurasian Union does not constitute a form of imperial restoration. The Russian president has positioned the initiative as a 'powerful supranational union capable of becoming an anchor in the modern world that serves as an effective bridge between Europe and the dynamic Asia-Pacific region… Our goal is not to revive the Soviet Union in some form or other'. Similarly, Andrei Ilnitsky, deputy head of United Russia's central executive committee suggested that the initiative required rebranding from 'Back to the USSR' to 'Forward to the 21st century Eurasian Union' to diminish any calls for imperial restoration amongst pro-Russian forces in Eurasia ('Eurasian Union – Rising empire or Delusion?' 2012).

Official publicity and commentary concerning the gestation of the Eurasian Union highlights the extent to which the project has non-Russian politicians and populations at its centre.[7] For example, the President of Kazakhstan, Nursultan Nazarbayev (2011), claims that he first conceived that a 'Eurasian Union of States' would evolve from the platform of the CIS as early as 1994. Moreover, while Eurasian integration is to proceed primarily on the grounds of economic pragmatism, Nazarbayev suggests that 'our peoples increasingly perceive themselves as part of an emerging Eurasian identity that is culturally, religiously and linguistically diverse, but united by the common pursuit of fruitful economic cooperation and neighborly relations' (p. 6).

Select Russian officials have mined Russian philosophical and cultural knowledge, both contemporary and historical, for the purposes of legitimating regime imperatives. This group is comprised of such individuals as Putin, Lavrov, the late Primakov and Surkov, who in addition to their past or present regime functions, have been charged with the task of framing public thinking about contemporary domestic, regional and global political affairs through their representation of Russian state actions in light of Russian cultural traditions. It is also comprised of 'moderate' and reputable public intellectuals such as Sergei Karaganov, who is emblematic of the interpenetration of contemporary Russian state and knowledge structures. Reportedly once a close associate of Primakov, Karaganov is credited with creating the neo-Eurasianist 'Karaganov Doctrine', which 'holds that the Russian Federation should position itself as the defender of ethnic Russian minority rights throughout the former Soviet republics, asserting its influence wherever ethnic Russians are subjected to perceived discrimination by the authorities of the state in question' (Pryce, 2013, p. 33).

As reported by his personal website,[8] Karaganov has occupied key roles both inside and outside Russia that leaves him both deeply tied to present and past state structures and capable of providing intellectual direction in academic and broader civil society. In 1993–1999, he served as Member of the Presidential Council of the Russian Federation. Since 1993, Karaganov has served as Member of the Advisory Committee of the Security Council of the Russian Federation. He was a foreign policy advisor to the presidential administrations of both Putin and Dmitry Medvedev from 2001–2013. Since 2009 he has been Member of the Advisory Board of majority state owned *Vnesheconombank*. From 1995–2005, Karaganov served as Member of the International Advisory Board of the Council on Foreign Relations in New York. Karaganov performs a role in the Russian state's broader post-Soviet posturing as that entity which ensures Russian social and cultural harmony against dangerous anti-systemic, if not anti-social, elements born of Russia's post-Soviet transition to a consolidated state capitalism.

Karaganov also served as the Chairman of the Valdai International Discussion Club from 2004 to 2013. Supported by the Kremlin, 'Valdai' highlights topical matters in a manner that both invites discussion and limited debate while expounding state-sanctioned discourse. It is therefore a useful gauge of the manner by which 'official Russia' aims to create thinking around a particular matter. Moreover, in addition to its high profile annual meetings, 'Valdai' solicits and publishes a wide range of material on its website from Russian and non-Russian authors in English. It can be distinguished from the more recently established Izborski Club. Involving the likes of Aleksandr Dugin, who is the subject of a subsequent chapter, Izborski is an attempt to reconcile Eurasianist ideas with 'those of Tsarist Russia', or 'Slavophile Orthodox Empire' (Tsygankov, 2014).

'Valdai' is at once a frank discussion forum involving Russian state officials and foreign dignitaries, journalists and academics and an opportunity for Russian state officials to put their 'ideational brand' on contemporary global political and economic issues. In his 2013 Valdai speech, titled, 'Why do we need national identity?' Karaganov unapologetically drafts from Gumilyov-style Eurasianist discussions of civilisations as naturalistic phenomena. He states:

> we still don't know what history we should associate ourselves with, whether we are an independent but peripheral part of Europe, and whether we want to become this. Nor have we defined our connection to our own culture. Russia's great literature of the 19th and early 20th century – its biggest contribution to world civilization – is losing popularity in Russian society. Even the majority of thinking Russians do not feel our culture's connection to antiquity. But it is antiquity that bears the *genetic code of our civilization and culture*, (emphasis added) including modes of behavior that were reproduced and further developed in Christianity.
>
> (Karaganov, 2013)

Karaganov's 2013 Valdai foray into Eurasianism and civilisationalism is in line with similar displays by Russian state officials. In his own 2013 Valdai speech, Putin is concrete with his Eurasianist/proto-Eurasianist cultural markers. Midway through the speech he suggests that 'Russia – as philosopher Konstantin Leontyev vividly put it – has always evolved in "blossoming complexity" as a *state-civilisation* (emphasis added), reinforced by the Russian people, Russian language, Russian culture, Russian Orthodox Church and the country's other traditional religions. It is precisely the state-civilisation model that has shaped our state polity.' Putin's invocation of the proto-Eurasianist Leontyev is not accidental. In the latter half of the nineteenth century, the Conservative and ascetic Leontyev criticised European liberal-bourgeois development, valorised hierarchical culture, and saw promise in a Russia that retained the possibility of coercive power (see Utechin, 1964, pp. 164–66). In the same Valdai speech, Putin's foray into political philosophy precedes an emphasis on Eurasian integration projects. The following selection is worth quoting at length:

> I would like to touch on another topic. The 21st century promises to become the century of major changes, the era of the formation of major geopolitical zones, as well as financial and economic, cultural, *civilisational* (*emphasis added*), and military and political areas. That is why integrating with our neighbours is our absolute priority. The future Eurasian Economic Union, which we have declared and which we have discussed extensively as of late, is not just a collection of mutually beneficial agreements. The Eurasian Union is a project for maintaining the identity of nations in the historical Eurasian space in a new century and in a new world. Eurasian integration is a chance for the entire post-Soviet space to become an independent centre for global development, rather than remaining on the outskirts of Europe and Asia.
>
> I want to stress that Eurasian integration will also be built on the principle of diversity. This is a union where everyone maintains their identity, their distinctive character and their political independence. Together with our partners, we will gradually implement this project, step by step. We expect that it will become our common input into maintaining diversity and stable global development.
>
> (The President of the Russian Federation, 2013a)

Combining references to conservative philosophical figures and concrete political projects in embedded civilisationalism constitutes an effort on the part of Russian officials to assert the multipolar and multicivilisational content of the contemporary global political economy, to defend the ethical basis of 'alternative' (i.e. non-polyarchic, non-neo-liberal) development models, and to suggest that American hegemony constitutes a failed moral, intellectual, political and economic project, whose origins, like that of nineteenth- and twentieth-century Western imperialism, has its origins in cultural aggression. Lavrov stated as much in 2012 with the following:

> We have come a long way from the idea, widespread in the early 1990s, that the world is moving towards some unified model, replicated from the Western model and coupled with local folklore. Now it is clear that, apart from the recognition of the market economy and democratic principles of the state as the main course of the historical process, the multiplicity of centers of power and influence presupposes a multiplicity of development models. Moreover, the trend towards higher significance of the civilizational identity factor, sagaciously predicted by Samuel Huntington, has become much more distinct. It was hard to imagine in the era of the decline of colonial empires and the domination of nationalist or revolutionary (in any case, Western in origin) ideologies that such a powerful renaissance of the Islamic identity would take place half a century later. The growing desire to rely on one's civilizational roots is seen in Asia and other parts of the world. In international politics, it may result in more

> conflicts or in realization of the need for partnership on a new basis, meeting the modern realities.
>
> (Lavrov, 2012)

In other words the embedded civilisationalism of Russian officials is the latest in a longer-running Putin-era trend of casting American hegemony as cultural aggression. Such a discourse has resonated with Russian state officials and is included in invectives against American unipolarity that have become more forceful since Russia's 'resurgence' during the first decade of the 2000s. Moreover, it has featured prominently since the Russian state's concerns about the proliferation of pro-Western governments on its periphery were at their highest (see below). Both elements are captured emblematically in Putin's 2007 'Munich Speech',[9] which has been received broadly as indicating that Russia had achieved sufficient enough strength and stability to resist Western incursions into its 'neighbourhood' after having been largely incapable of doing so since the end of the Cold War (see Yefremenko, 2010). Furthermore, it signals the Putin regime's disillusionment with an explicitly 'integrationist' (into historically Western-centred regional and global institutions) foreign policy and its renewed focus on constructing Russian national power (Lukyanov, 2010) and multipolarity. As it pertains to Eurasian space, Eurasianism is yet another ideational correlate to the ideas and practices pertaining to multipolarity.

5 Conclusion

According to select Russian officials and political technologists, contemporary Russia, like that of the original Eurasianists, finds itself amongst a group of powers that are distrustful of military, economic and cultural dominance from the West. In language that is reminiscent of Eurasianist works, Russian officials speak of cultural and civilisational exclusivity, in that civilisations are irreducible to a common substratum from which universal norms can be derived, and plurality, in that such units are therefore destined to coexist, to their mutual exclusion. They do so when appealing to the need to protect the civilisational diversity inherent in the contemporary world order, a condition that is similarly threatened by the presence of a unipolar hegemon. The moral imperative extends to safeguarding the rights of a multitude of discrete civilisations against American or Western hegemonism, democracy promotion and the use of force. Liberal capitalism, therefore, is viewed as a failed geopolitical and geocultural project that operates both through coercion and as an ideological weapon. In either case, according to Russian officials, these are directed against the sovereign integrity of political states and the ethical-moral integrity of particular cultures constituted as civilisations. That Russian officials have incorporated talk of the plurality of civilisations into their contemporary discourse suggests that speculation on the compatibility or incompatibility of civilisations is not the exclusive domain of Eurasianists.

As such, an historicist analysis of Eurasianism and its relationship to contemporary Russian state practices demonstrates emerging global political, economic, military and cultural fault lines in a post-hegemonic world in a number of ways. First, it demonstrates that contemporary 'global fault lines' are constituted by complex material and ideational factors. Second, it enables us to see the extent to which intellectual traditions – in this case, those which emphasise Russian civilisational particularity and dissatisfaction with Western hegemony and dominance – become activated and appropriated in a contemporary context within state-driven political and economic projects. Third, it demonstrates a broader turn to cultural relativism as an ethical basis for modern state conduct on the part of powers outside of the consolidated Western bloc, whereby abstract notions of liberal capitalism and polyarchy become recast as forms of geopolitical and geocultural hegemonic aggression. To the extent that the Russian state and executive have established a dividing line in global politics, it is now between those in favour of an aggressive liberal hegemon in the United States. The language is subtler – it is not Danilevsky- or Gumilyov-like talk of a genetic difference between civilisations, nor that of Panarin's insistence on religious pluralism – but the impact on our understanding of contemporary global fault lines is not less significant as a result. In fact, such language warrants our attention precisely because it has been displaced from the realm of philosophical speculation to become intertwined with concrete political and economic projects deemed central to Putin's legacy, projects which will attract considerable material and ideational resources from the Russian state in the coming years.

Notes

1 The original Eurasianists' relation to Bolshevism is a source of debate. Shlapentokh (1997) argues that the original Eurasianists eventually accepted the Soviet regime after perceiving, and approving of, the latter's increased nationalism and corporate-authoritarianism. Senderov (2009) suggests that classical and contemporary Eurasianism are both variants of Bolshevism, presumably for their anti-liberal, statist and ideocratic qualities.

2 The others are Circumpolar, Muslim, European, Buddhist, Byzantine (Caucasian Christian) and Jewish.

3 His work has been criticised for using a scientific basis to justify the degradation of particular ethnicities (Paradowski, 1999), as well as for its methodological shortcomings (Shnirelman and Panarin, 2001).

4 The synopsis on Panarin is derived from Laruelle (2008), unless otherwise stated.

5 Laruelle (2008, pp. 107–144), Dunlop (2001) and Sedgwick (2004) offer succinct political biographies of Dugin.

6 See also the legal-institutionalist scholarship of Dragneva and Wolczuk, who emphasise that two decades worth of post-Soviet regional projects may be characterised as 'declarative and ultimately insubstantial initiatives" with "weak and ineffective institutional frameworks' which 'delivered limited economic results' (2013, p. 2).

7 One should not overstate the extent to which Eurasianism is merely a form of Russian dominance. Voting schemes in the various bodies of Eurasian integration

are heterogeneous, with some weighted disproportionately towards smaller members. See Yesdauletova & Yesdauletov, 2014.

8 http://karaganov.ru/en/pages/biography; accessed 18 January 2014.

9 This was Putin's address to the Munich Security Conference on 10 February 2007.

References

Bassin, M. (1991). Russia between Europe and Asia: The ideological construction of geographical space. *Slavic Review*, 50(1), 1–17.

Bassin, M. (2009). The emergence of Ethno-Geopolitics in Post-Soviet Russia. *Eurasian Geography and Economics*, 50(2), 131–149.

Bassin, M. (n.d.). *Classical Eurasianism and the geopolitics of Russian identity.* Unpublished manuscript.

Bazhanov, V. A. (1999). A note on A. S. Panarin's Revansh Istorii. *Europe-Asia Studies*, 51(4), 705–708.

Braudel, F. (1994). *A history of civilisations.* New York: Allen Lane.

Cox, R. (1986). Social forces, states and world orders: Beyond International Relations theory. In R. Keohane (Ed.), *Neorealism and its Critics* (pp. 204–254). New York: Columbia University Press.

Danilevskii, N. I. (2013). *Russia and Europe: The Slavic world's political and cultural relations with the Germanic-Roman West*. Bloomington, IN: Slavica Publishers.

Dragneva, R., & Wolczuk, K. (Eds.). (2013). *Eurasian economic integration: Law, policy and politics.* Cheltenham, UK: Edward Elgar Publishing.

Dunlop, J. (2001). Aleksandr Dugin's 'Neo-Eurasian' textbook and Dmitrii Trenin's ambivalent response. *Harvard Ukrainian Studies*, 25(1/2), 91–127.

Eurasian Union: Rising empire or delusion? (2012). The Current Digest of the Post-Soviet Press, 14(64), 3–5.

Friedman, T. (2000). *The Lexus and the olive tree.* New York, NY: Random House.

Germain, R. (2011). New Marxism and the problem of subjectivity: Towards a Critical and Historical International Political Economy. In S. Shields, I. Bruff & H. Macartney (Eds.), *Critical International Political Economy: Dialogue and dissensus* (pp. 61–79). New York, NY: Palgrave Macmillan.

Gumilyov, L. (1990). *Ethnogenesis and the biosphere.* Moscow: Progress Publishers.

Huntington, S. L. (1996). *The clash of civilizations and the remaking of world order.* New York, NY: Simon and Schuster.

Karaganov, S. (2013, 2 October). Why do we need national identity? N.p. *Russia in Global Affairs.* Retrieved from http://eng.globalaffairs.ru/pubcol/Why-do-we-need-national-identity-16140.

Laruelle, M. (2007). The Orient in Russian thought at the turn of the century. In D. Shlapentokh, (Ed.), *Russia between East and West: Scholarly debates on Eurasianism* (pp. 9–37). Boston, MA: Brill.

Laruelle, M. (2008). *Russian Eurasianism: An ideology of empire.* Washington, DC: Woodrow Wilson Center Press.

Laruelle, M. (2009). (Neo-)Eurasianists and politics. *Russian Politics and Law*, 47(1), 90–101.

Laruelle, M. (2012). Larger, higher, farther north … Geographical metanarratives of the nation in Russia. *Eurasian Geography and Economics*, 53(5), 557–574.

Lavrov, S. (2012, 27 December). Russia in the 21st-century world of power. N.p. *Russia in Global Affairs.* Retrieved from http://eng.globalaffairs.ru/number/Russia-in-the-21st-Century-World-of-Power-15809.

Libman, A. (2015). Supranational organizations: Russia and the Eurasian Economic Union. In A. Obydenkova & A. Libman (Eds.), *Autocratic and democratic external influences in Post-Soviet Eurasia* (pp. 133–158). Farnham, Surrey; Burlington, VT: Ashgate.

Libman, A., & Vinokurov, E. (2012). *Holding-together regionalism: Twenty years of post-Soviet integration.* Basingstoke, UK: Palgrave Macmillan.

Lukin, A. (2014). Eurasian integration and the clash of values. *Survival,* 56(3), 43–60.

Lukyanov, F. (2010). Russian dilemmas in a multipolar world. *Journal of International Affairs, 63*(2), 19–32.

Mazurek, S. (2002). Russian Eurasianism: Historiosophy and ideology. *Studies in East European Thought,* 54(1–2), 105–123.

Morozov, V. (2009). Obsessed with identity: The IR in Post-Soviet Russia. *Journal of International Relations and Development,* 12(2), 200–205.

Morozova, N. (2009). Geopolitics, Eurasianism and Russian foreign policy under Putin. *Geopolitics,* 14(4), 667–686.

Nazarbayev, N. (2011). Eurasian Union: from idea to future history. *The Current Digest of the Russian Press,* 43(63), 5–9.

Okara, A. (2007). Sovereign democracy: A new Russian idea or a PR project? Russia in Global Affairs. Retrieved from http://eng.globalaffairs.ru/number/n_9123.

Panarin, A. (1994). A design for Russia: Fundamental liberalism or liberal fundamentalism? *Russian Politics & Law,* 32(5), 56–79.

Paradowski, R. (1999). The Eurasian idea and Lev Gumilev's scientific ideology. *Canadian Slavonic Papers,* 41(1), 19–32.

The President of the Russian Federation. (2011, 18 November). Meeting of the Presidents of Russia, Belarus, and Kazakhstan. Kremlin, Moscow: The President of the Russian Federation. Retrieved from http://en.kremlin.ru/events/president/news/13581.

The President of the Russian Federation. (2012a, 12 December). Address to the Federal Assembly. Kremlin, Moscow: The President of the Russian Federation. Retrieved from http://eng.kremlin.ru/transcripts/4739.

The President of the Russian Federation. (2012b, 7 May). Executive order on measures to implement foreign policy. N.p. The President of the Russian Federation. Retrieved from http://en.kremlin.ru/events/president/news/15256.

The President of the Russian Federation. (2013a, 19 September). Meeting of the Valdai International Discussion Club. Novgorod Region: The President of the Russian Federation. Retrieved from http://eng.kremlin.ru/news/6007.

The President of the Russian Federation. (2013b, 12 December). Presidential address to the federal assembly. Kremlin, Moscow: The President of the Russian Federation. Retrieved from http://eng.kremlin.ru/news/6402.

Pryce, P. (2013). Putin's third term: The triumph of Eurasianism? *Romanian Journal of European Affairs,* 13(1), 25–43.

RFERL. (2005, 25 August). Newsline. RFERL. Retrieved from http://www.rferl.org/content/article/1143467.html.

Riasanovsky, N. V. (1967). The emergence of Eurasianism. *California Slavic Studies,* 4, 39–72.

The Russian Federation. (2008, 12 July). The foreign policy concept of the Russian Federation. N.p. Kremlin.ru. Retrieved from http://archive.kremlin.ru/eng/text/docs/2008/07/204750.shtml.

The Russian Federation. (2013a). Eurasian Economic Community (EurAsEC). Retrieved from http://eng.kremlin.ru/terms/E#term_12.

The Russian Federation. (2013b, 18 February). Concept of the foreign policy of the Russian Federation: Approved by President of the Russian Federation V. Putin on 12 February 2013. The Ministry of Foreign Affairs of the Russian Federation official site. Retrieved from http://www.mid.ru/brp_4.nsf/0/76389FEC168189ED44257B2E0 039B16D

Salin, P. (2013, 26 October). Spiritual values to cement Eurasian Union. Russia in Global Affairs. Retrieved from http://eng.globalaffairs.ru/number/Spiritual-Values-to-Cement-the-Eurasian-Union-16163.

Sedgwick, M. (2004). *Against the modern world: Traditionalism and the secret intellectual history of the twentieth century.* New York, NY: Oxford University Press.

Senderov, V. (2009). Neo-Eurasianism: Realities, dangers, prospects. *Russian Politics and Law*, 47(1), 24–46.

Shlapentokh, D. (1997). Eurasianism past and present. *Communist and Post-Communist Studies*, 30(2), 129–151.

Shlapentokh, D. (2001). Russian nationalism today: The views of Alexander Dugin. *Contemporary Review*, 279(1626), 29–37.

Shlapentokh, D. (2007). Dugin Eurasianism: A window on the minds of the Russian elite or an intellectual ploy? *Studies in Eastern European Thought*, 59(3), 215–236.

Shlapentokh, D. (2012). Lev Gumilev: The ideologist of the Soviet Empire. *History of European Ideas*, 38(3), 483–492.

Shlapentokh, D. (2013). The death of the Byzantine empire and construction of historical/political identities in late Putin Russia. *Journal of Balkan and Near Eastern Studies*, 15(1), 69–96.

Shnirelman, V., & Panarin, S. (2001). Lev Gumilev: his pretensions as founder of ethnology and his Eurasian theories. *Inner Asia*, 3(1), 1–18.

Solovyev, E. (2004). Geopolitics in Russia – Science or vocation? *Communist and Post-Communist Studies*, 37(1). 85–96.

Supreme Eurasian Economic Council Meeting: Minsk. (2013, 24 October). The President of the Russian Federation. Retrieved from http://eng.kremlin.ru/news/6169.

Toynbee, A. J. (1957). *A study of history.* New York, NY: Oxford University Press.

Tsygankov, A. (2014, 24 June). Putin is not a nationalist. *The Moscow Times.* Retrieved from http://www.themoscowtimes.com/opinion/article/putin-is-not-a-nationalist/502466.html.

Urban, M. (1998). Remythologising the Russian state. *Europe-Asia Studies*, 50(6), 969–992.

Utechin, S. V. (1964). *Russian political thought: A concise history.* New York, NY: Praeger.

van der Pijl, K. (1998). *Transnational classes and international relations.* London; New York, NY: Routledge.

Vinokurov, E., & Libman, A. (2012). *Eurasian integration: Challenges of transcontinental regionalism*. Basingstoke, UK: Palgrave Macmillan.

Yefremenko, D. (2010, 15 October). Forced or desired modernity? Russia's chances in the Post-American world. Russia in Global Affairs. Retrieved from http://eng.globaffairs.ru/number/Forced-or-Desired-Modernity-14996.

Yesdauletova, A., & Yesdauletov, A. (2014). The Eurasian Union: Dynamics and difficulties of the post-Soviet integration. *Trames*, 18(1), 3–17.

6 Aleksandr Dugin's Eurasianism

Co-opting or co-opted in Russia's Putin-era civilisational project?

1 Introduction

The purpose of this chapter is to locate Aleksandr Dugin's Eurasianism within the structures of embedded civilisationalism. The latter denotes the extent to which official Russia's Putin-era attempts at consolidating Russia's presence in Eurasia have involved the selective appeal to a civilisational logic by incorporating themes and motifs from a wide array of Russian thinkers. An active producer of concepts, theories and ideas pertaining to Eurasianism, Dugin has moved from a more marginal position in Russian intellectual circles in the 1990s to one in which he is a highly visible figure commenting on Russia's contemporary geopolitical situation. Attracting significant attention in Western academic circles due to his prolific contributions and perceptions of his extremism, Dugin has entrenched himself more firmly in 'official Russia's' structures and networks since the end of the 1990s.

Seeking to develop nothing less than a post-Soviet Eurasian *weltanschauung* predicated on geopolitical identity, mysticism, conservatism and a host of other philosophical tributaries, Dugin's persona and intellectual project remains hard to square with the parameters of the Putin-era 'state project' of Eurasian integration. Dugin, presumably no lover of capitalism due to its association with 'Atlanticism', nonetheless largely writes the economy out of the geopolitical divide between the Eurasian and the Atlanticist worlds, preferring instead to emphasise essentialist and irreconcilable differences between cultures and civilisations that manifest themselves in geopolitical practices. Dugin's work constitutes a multifaceted critique of American unilateralism and liberal political philosophy that results in the geopoliticisation of political values and conduct: the manner by which potentially discrete phenomena are re-coded according to their perceived or desired geopolitical significance.

In this chapter, I will examine the contours of Dugin's trajectory and how the public intellectual contributes to Putin's embedded civilisationalism, which I consider as a 'material' and 'ideational' project for Eurasian political and economic integration under executive leadership which remains open to a multifaceted 'discursive' rationale. Such an examination necessitates that we locate Dugin as an organic intellectual of Russian statism and consider the extent to which he does or does not contribute to Putin's Eurasian project. While popular commentary in the West increasingly views Dugin as the Kremlin's official ideologue on geopolitical matters, we must ask 'who is co-opting whom' in the relationship between Dugin and official Russia. Moreover, we must examine the 'polysemic' quality of Dugin's thinking – the manner in which it can be applied flexibly to a host of disparate geopolitical and geoeconomic phenomena in order to produce an appearance of coherence, consistency and historical stability.

2 Dugin, historicism and polysemic Eurasianism

Eurasianism is a multifaceted, polysemic and overdetermined phenomenon, as demonstrated in the previous chapter. In the present chapter I suggest that Dugin's primary significance to contemporary Russian domestic and foreign affairs comes by way of his propensity to read and code world affairs through the prism of Eurasianism. Dugin's work is a case study in the polysemic nature of theoretical paradigms and their application to political practice and discrete events. For Dugin, the generic distinction between Eurasianism and Atlanticism is applicable to any situation: he mobilises a zero sum geopolitical logic to code civil disputes, cultural contestation, religious fractures and wide- scale regional conflicts with equal force. Moreover, Dugin's Eurasianist thinking uncomfortably relies upon the logic of great power contestation while seeking to move beyond it through emphasising cultural, civilisational and ideological affinities that obviate modern symmetries between nation and state. Hence, Dugin's thinking is performed for three purposes. The first is to uphold conventional balancing postulates of modern international relations, placing Russia alongside other dissatisfied non-Western states in a concerted effort to challenge American unilateralism. The second is a post-modern one in which he recodes cultures, political spectrums, religions, civilisations, and tactical alliances in the context of a Eurasianist/Atlanticist divide whose connection to Russia as a territorially demarcated entity may not be always readily apparent. The third is to emphasise the essentialist nature of the *longue duree* of civilisations and the extent to which it conditions contemporary political culture and practice. As important as Dugin's actual thinking is the extent to which it does or does not represent Kremlin strategising and the extent to which it is embedded in larger structures of knowledge production, a matter that will be taken up in this chapter.

Dugin is at once a prolific commentator on contemporary Russian foreign policy and Russia's geopolitical situation and deeply steeped in new Right and esoteric philosophies. Unquestionably, amongst that of all contemporary Eurasianist thinkers, the work of Dugin, a publicist, strategist and thinker of myriad interests, has attracted the most attention in the West. Western approaches to the study and analysis of Dugin and his philosophy range from trivialising and dismissive on the one hand, whereby his academic credentials and claims to being the latest manifestation in a series of Russian philosophical traditions are disputed (see Clowes, 2011) to alarmist (see Clover, 1999) on the other. In short, Dugin has been received by Western scholarship largely as an intellectual charlatan who overstates his own importance to one who is to some degree embedded within Russian social and political power structures, up to and including being the Kremlin's unofficial spokesperson and forecaster. While deeming Dugin a Kremlin spokesperson strikes one as an overstatement, a study of Dugin's trajectory is a study in how ideas of the staunchly anti-systemic elements in post-Soviet society initially arrayed against the Western-leaning tendencies of Yeltsin have become selectively de-radicalised and incorporated into state discourse. Nonetheless, Dugin must be thought as simply part of a much larger, complicated and inconsistent process of discursive and material differentiation of Russia from the West in the post-Soviet era.

A brief biography of Dugin[1] serves as a useful indicator of the broad range of political affiliations he has pursued over the past 30 plus years. In 1988 he joined *Pamiat'*, a nationalist organisation of the *perestroika* era. He quit the following year, allegedly due to its monarchism and anti-Semitism. In 1990–1991 he founded the institutions *Arktogaia Association*, the group most responsible for establishing and supporting Russian contact with thinkers in the Western European New Right movement, and *The Center for Meta-Strategic Studies*. Dugin, through Arktogaia and *Den'*, was instrumental in the radicalisation of Russian nationalism in the early 1990s (Mathyl, 2002). Furthermore, Dugin and the entire Arktogaia group, in cooperation with the Western European Right, served as the source for the ideology of the National Bolshevik Party (NBP). With such influences, the NBP deliberately sought to create and foster a nationalist youth counter culture with itself at the centre. Arktogaia withdrew from the party following a dispute between Dugin and NBP founder Eduard Limonov in 1998. Arktogaia's precursor was the 'metaphysical underground' Yuzhinskiy Circle, a group of dissidents founded in the 1960s around the Russian poet and writer Yuri Mamleyev. Dugin joined the circle in 1980, long after Mamleyev had emigrated to the United States, a time in which the mystical writer Yevgeniy Golovin was introducing occult and Integral Traditionalist, Conservative Revolutionary and Fascist works into the group. The group also included Geidar Dzhemal', the Islamic traditionalist (Shekhovstov, 2008).

Dugin has been viewed as simply one amongst many 'metaphysical radicals' to emerge in Russia in the 1990s: thinkers who are allegedly conditioned by Russia's 'disruptive and catastrophic' historical dynamics to conduct continual metaphysical speculation in the attempt to create entire social orders. With such a prioritisation of radicalism and totalising thinking, the seemingly incompatible Marxist, nationalist and religious doctrines in post-Soviet Russian are easily synthesised (Epstein, 1996). In the 1990s, Dugin also drew closer to the CPRF and became a prolific contributor to *Den'*, the Russian nationalist periodical (subsequently renamed *Zavtra*). In 1993–1994 he became the ideologist for the NBP (leaving in 1998). In 1995 Dugin ran in national Duma elections in a suburban constituency outside of Saint Petersburg, receiving less than 1 per cent of the vote. 1997 saw the publication of his widely influential *The Foundation of Geopolitics: Russia's Geopolitical Future*, which he appears to have written with the help of General Igor' Rodionov, Minister of Defence of Russia in 1996–1997. In 1999 he became Adviser to the Duma Spokesman, Communist Gennady Seleznev. On April 21, 2001, he founded the *Evraziia* movement, the purpose of which being to formulate a new Russian idea. Of the movement, Dugin stated: 'Our aim is not to achieve power, nor to fight for power, but to fight for influence on it. Those are different things' (Laruelle, 2008, p. 111).

From the Analytical Department of the Movement Eurasia on evrazia.org[2] we find that the Eurasianists openly embrace a pursuit of ideocracy. The movement's political platform is written as such:

> Wealth and prosperity, a strong state and an efficient economy, a powerful army and the development of production must be instruments for the achievement of high ideals. The sense of the state and of the nation [which were previously discussed: the uniqueness of Russian Slav-Orthodox civilization expanded to include Eurasian elements; state in the form of Empire] can be conferred only through the existence of a 'leading idea.' That political regime, which supposes the establishment of a 'leading idea' as a supreme value, was called by the eurasists [sic] as'[sic] 'ideocracy' from the Greek 'idea' and 'kratos', power. Russia is always thought of as the Sacred Rus', as a power (derzhava) fulfilling its own peculiar historical mission. The eurasist [sic] world-view must also be the national idea of the forthcoming Russia, its 'leading idea.'

On 30 May 2002, *Evraziia* was transformed into a political party, described by Dugin as having a 'radical centrist' orientation. According to Sedgwick (2004), 'This new position… was centrist in that it endorsed President Putin as a patriot who appeared committed to the restoration of Russian power and receptive to the idea of Russia as a Eurasian power. It was radical in that Dugin's Neo-Eurasianism was central to the Eurasia movement, and in that the liberal elements in Putin's political program were tolerated rather than endorsed' (p. 234). In 2003, Dugin both flirted with the leftist (albeit Kremlin supported) party *Rodina* and had his fallout with them, as he claims to have held disdain for the monarchist tendencies of leaders Dmitry Rogozin and Natalia Narochnitskaia. In November 2003, *Evraziia* was transformed from a political party into the 'International Eurasianist Movement', an NGO seeking to become an international think tank influencing governments in Russia, Turkey, Kazakhstan (see also Laruelle, 2009). Dugin displayed an initial enthusiasm for Putin, but has allegedly become disappointed with him due to the presence of liberal figures in Putin's entourage.

Dugin has been prolific in a wide range of media, as well. He has been, at various times, an editor of the journals *Elementi, Milyi Angel, Evraziiskoe obozrenie, Evraziiskoe vtorzhenie*. He wrote and presented weekly one-hour radio broadcasts *Finis Mundi* in 1997, prohibited after commenting favourably on Boris Savinkov, an early twentieth-century terrorist. In 1998 he participated in creating 'New University', at which he subsequently lectured, whose curricula include Traditionalist and occultist teachings. In 2005, Dugin began anchoring *Landmarks*, a weekly broadcast on geopolitics on the Orthodox television channel *Spas* (savior).

A succinct, though now incomplete, history of the 'neo-eurasist' ideology appeared on the 'Analytical department of the Movement Eurasia'[3] on Dugin's evrazi.org website. It was, if nothing else, a fairly clear indication of the movement's self-identification and self-understanding. The movement portrays itself as an inheritor of the Eurasianist legacy but adapted to contemporary purposes through the incorporation of, among other things, traditionalism, the origins of sacredness, 'the search for the symbolic paradigms of the space-time matrix' (the study of ruins, mythology), Western geopolitics, a conservative interpretation and incorporation of the new left, and third way economics through the prism of autarchy of the 'great spaces'. Its history is distilled neatly into five stages, the contents of which reveal a wide range of positions and influences. The first stage (1985–1990) has Dugin involved with the conservative-patriotic, as well as monarchist, forces and highlights the influence of traditionalism on Eurasianist thinking. The second stage (1991–1993) has a reconsideration of the Soviet period from the perspective of national-bolshevism and left-wing Eurasianism, the rising popularity of Eurasianism amongst the patriotic opposition and intellectuals, as well as various interpretations of Eurasianism on the part of authors and thinkers. The third stage (1994–1998) has the development of neo-Eurasian 'orthodoxy' – an increasingly anti-Western, anti-liberal, anti-globalist position, in what are considered Dugin's main works, the creation of Arktogaia's website, a proliferation of publications, and a referencing of Eurasianism in the programmes of the CPRF, LDPR and NDR (New Democratic Russia). The fourth stage (1998–2001) involves a shift to the centrist position, which may be understood as closer affiliation with the government position (especially under Putin), support for Yevgeni Primakov as prime minister, a distancing from opposition stances and increased media presence. The fifth stage (2001–2002) contained the foundation of the Pan-Russian Political Social Movement EURASIA and the declaration of full support for Putin and the process of transforming the movement into a party.

Recently, Dugin has become both more internationalised and embedded in different structures of academic and popular knowledge production in Russia. In 2009, Dugin founded and became the chair of the *International Eurasian Movement.* From 2008 to the present, he has been a professor at Moscow State University (MGU) and manager of the Center for Conservative Studies within the Faculty of Sociology at MGU. From 2009 to the present he has been head of the faculty of Sociology of International Relations at MGU. From March 2012 to the present he has been Member of the Council of

Experts, which advises the chairman of the State Duma, Sergei Naryshkin (Laug, 2013).

Dugin's history is interesting not merely as artefact but as an indication of the broad circles that he has been a part of and the vacillations in his ideology, influences and tactics. Dugin's biography reveals a wide array of intellectual and political influences on the thinker. With such an eclectic mix of influences and various shifting positions from flirting with monarchist, fascist and communist standpoints, to a more politically astute 'radical centrist' position, to a figure embedded in more widely popular and mainstream knowledge structures, how is it possible to categorise Dugin's contribution to Eurasianism?

It is potentially misleading to think of Dugin as a direct intellectual descendent of original Eurasianists, given the extent to which he is influenced by multiple strands of thinking. For one, he is influenced by European Integral Traditionalism. Integral Traditionalism is a line of religious thinking originating with French-born Muslim Rene Guenon and Anglo-Ceylonese metaphysician Ananda Coomaraswamy, which rejects modernity outright in favour of a distant past during which the 'perennial wisdom' of spiritual truths was revealed during a transcendental unity of all religions. Whether Dugin's traditionalism is earnest or opportunistic is a source of debate (see Shekhovstov & Umland, 2009; Shekhovstov, 2008; Sedgwick, 2004). Guenon and Evola's Traditionalism holds that the pre-modern person had access to a spiritual experience that has since been clouded by modern institutions. The New Right's political philosophy is an extension of this thinking, consisting primarily of an aesthetic critique of modernity. In Russia, the political positions of its various supporters and ideologues have a propensity to vary considerably (see Sokolov, 2009).

Furthermore, Dugin is influenced by 'conspirology', or the study of the secret histories behind global political conflicts. Dugin's adherence to conspirology has him offering a secret history of the Soviet Union wherein a Eurasianist order opposes an Atlanticist order. The occult war between them culminated in the August 1991 putsch (Laruelle, 2008, p. 120).

Dugin is also evidently influenced by Western geopoliticians Halford Mackinder,[4] the statist geopolitician *par excellence*, who married geographical knowledge to the augmentation of state power (see Kearns, 2010) and Karl Haushofer.[5] Strains of geographical determinism found in Dugin, as well as his representing a perennial conflict between land- and sea-based powers, owe much to Mackinder. Dugin has adopted and adapted for Russian purposes Mackinder's general theory of geographical causality, wherein historical development is largely immune from human activity. Mackinder (1904) suggested that his time saw the end of the expansion of Western European maritime powers (the Columbian age) and a newfound ability of Russia to organise and defend its Eurasian territory. Russia constituted the Pivot Area of world politics:

> that vast area of Euro-Asia which is inaccessible to ships, but in antiquity lay open to the horse-riding nomads, and is to-day about to be covered

> with a network of railways? There have been and are here the conditions of a mobility of military and economic power of a far-reaching and yet limited character. Russia replaces the Mongol Empire. Her pressure on Finland, on Scandinavia, on Poland, on Turkey, on Persia, on India, and on China, replaces the centrifugal raids of the steppemen. In the world at large she occupies the central strategical position held by Germany in Europe. She can strike on all sides and be struck from all sides, save the north. The full development of her modern railway mobility is merely a matter of time. *Nor is it likely that any possible social revolution will alter her essential relations to the great geo-graphical limits of her existence.* Wisely recognizing the fundamental limits of her power, her rulers have parted with Alaska; for it is as much a law of policy for Russia to own nothing overseas as for Britain to be supreme on the ocean.
>
> (pp. 434–436)

Later, in his 1943 work, Mackinder offers the following definition of the Heartland, deemed the area by which the geopolitical future of humanity would be decided: 'The Heartland is the northern part and the interior of Euro-Asia. It extends from the Arctic coast down to the central deserts and has as its western limits the broad isthmus between the Baltic and Black Seas' (p. 597). The Heartland approximates the territory of the USSR, with the exception of 'Lenaland', a vast forested area in Eastern Russia which is centred on the Lena river and lies East of the Yenisei River (pp. 597–599). He writes primarily with the intention of detailing how to subdue Germany with an Atlantic coalition of Britain, France and the United States and a Heartland Soviet Union, while warning of the vast power and defensive capabilities of the USSR: 'All things considered, the conclusion is unavoidable that if the Soviet Union emerges from this war as conqueror of Germany, she must rank as the greatest land Power on the globe. Moreover, she will be the power in the strategically strongest defensive position. The Heartland is the greatest natural fortress on earth. For the first time in history it is manned by a garrison sufficient both in number and quality' (p. 601).

Dugin is also influenced by Weimar-era German thinkers of the 'conservative revolution' (Carl Schmitt, Ernst Junger, Arthur Moeller van den Bruck) and the francophone New Right (Alain de Benoist, Jean Thiriart, Robert Stauckers). Dugin has penned openly fascist works. Indeed, one need not look further than the title in one important case. In 'Fascism: Borderless and Red' Dugin (2006) emphasises socialist aspects in his version of fascism. He suggests that fascism is not national capitalism, and that any association of national capitalism with fascism resulted from an unfortunate historical necessity to accommodate national capital. Fascism for Dugin is a heroic, idealistic and revolutionary nationalism, the combination of 'right wing' cultural – political factors ('traditionalism, faithfulness to the soil, roots, national ethics') with 'left-wing' economic principles ('social justice, limitation to the market forces, deliverances from 'credit slavery', prohibition of stock market speculation, monopolies and trusts, [and] primacy of honest work' [pp. 508–509]). Russians are historically suited to a socialist orientation and are, according to Dugin, 'longing for freshness, for modernity, for unfeigned romanticism, for living participation in some great cause' (p. 509). Dugin's flirting with fascism and the Weimer Right (Luks, 2009) has led critics to suggest that he is more fascist than Eurasianist (Umland, 2007, 2009a, 2009b; Shekhovstov, 2008). Conversely, his eclectic intellectual pursuits render his commitment to a more robust fascism dubious (Gregor, 2006a, 2006b). For present purposes, his speculation on geopolitics receives the most attention, as they are a significant part of a wider tendency in post-Soviet Russia of contemplating the geopolitical basis of world politics.

3 Eurasianism and common-sense geopolitics

Conceived of as a broad intellectual movement, Eurasianism may be understood as a series of attempts to establish an integrated ideological doctrine. In this line of thinking, divisions within the movement are primarily manifested as various schools of thought competing with one another for readership and significance. Eurasianism as intellectual movement is comprised of three trends: that inspired by Gumilyov, which includes Dugin; that created by Edouard Bagramov, former member of the Communist Party of the Soviet Union's (CPSU's) Central Committee and creator of the journal *Eurasia, Peoples, Cultures and Religions* (*Evraziya, Narody, Kultury, Religii*), whose mandate was to promote cultural alliance and ethnic fusion between Slavs and Turkic people; and finally, a plethora of smaller movements and publications, including *Literary Eurasia* (*Literaturnaya Evrazia)* (Laruelle, 2004, p. 118). In such a presentation, Eurasianism is primarily that which occurs in the sphere of academic and literary production and there is little mention of the contemporary political significance of the movement (see also Laruelle, 2008).[6] One might also emphasise the extent to which Eurasianism has filtered into cultural production in Russia, as Eurasia has become a 'productive discursive literary space' (Filimonova, 2015) and a component of a new imperial literature that in various ways celebrates Russia's emboldened international conduct (Noordenbos, 2011).

There are grounds for rejecting the notion that any mere mention of Eurasia or a pragmatic orientation towards Eastern Russia or Asia constitutes a Eurasianist position or the wholesale adoption of certain radical Eurasianist philosophical and normative tenets (see Laruelle, 2007 for such scepticism). Nonetheless, when conceived of as a broader interest towards geopolitics, Eurasianism encompasses a great deal more territory. Eurasianism's position within the post-Soviet Russian discussion on geopolitics and geo-identity leads to a certain amount of confusion: while not all geopolitical discussions involve self-identified Eurasianists, Eurasianism has been used flexibly to describe a wide array of Russian statist and anti-Western positions. These positions express degrees of dissatisfaction with Russia's post-Cold War international position and exhibit healthy amounts of scepticism towards, if not outright condemnation of, Russia's wholesale adoption of Western norms and its integration into Western-led liberal democratic institutions. Eurasianism is therefore a polysemic concept that signifies both the comprehensive/philosophical and geopolitical/geostrategic arguments about Russia's position in contemporary world order.

In its most generic usage, Eurasianism signifies a commitment to continental orientation in foreign policy, a turn away from the West and a Russia that serves an integrative if not hegemonic function on the Eurasian continent. More comprehensive articulations of Eurasianism emphasise the civilisational distinctiveness of Russia and a moral imperative to resist unipolar Western, or primarily American, world order (see Chapters 4 and 5). However, while a rise in the interest of geopolitical themes and education in post-Soviet Russia is well documented, one should not overstate the extent to which this conceives of geopolitics in the intuitive, anti-scientific and essentialist manner of Dugin.[7] Hence, it is possible to see the manner in which official Russia selectively deploys the language of Eurasianism to capture a real scepticism towards a wholesale embrace of the West and to appeal to recalcitrant elements of Russian society without embracing Duginism *as such*. A lack of philosophical comprehensiveness and flair for eschatological speculation does not render certain expressions of Eurasianism meaningless. Rather, that Eurasianism as a concept has such considerable appeal is testament to its success as a galvanising ideological force and means of expressing Russia's position in the contemporary global political economy for a diverse range of thinkers, political actors and writers in the popular press. A turn to Duginesque Eurasianism's place within geopolitical debates is therefore warranted. Both Eurasianism and the broader Russian geopolitical protest against Russia's post-Cold War international position serve as a common sense about global affairs that is selectively appealed to by the Putin regime.

Dugin's primary work, *Foundations of Geopolitics* (*Osnovy geopolitiki*),[8] was allegedly written with the assistance of General Nikolai Klokotov of the General Staff Academy, suggesting that his ideas on geopolitics found a receptive audience in Russian military circles (Dunlop, 2004, p. 43). For Dugin, geopolitics is both an objective science in the narrow sense – geophysical realities determine the course of politics – and a more encompassing 'synthetic' discipline, which incorporates geography, history, demography, theology, ecology and the occult. It is a metadiscipline, a system of disciplines, an all-encompassing *weltanshaunng* according to which all natural and human phenomena are to be interpreted. Most of all, it is a means to restore the grandeur of Russia as hegemon of the Eurasian space.

Dugin's geopolitical worldview is predicated on a fundamental division between land-based, continental powers (tellurocracies) and sea-based powers (thalassocracies). There is irreconcilable conflict between the land and sea-based powers, between the Heartland and the World Island. Dugin's work is essentialising in the extreme, ascribing particular and oppositional qualities to land and water powers (Ingram, 2001).[9] Previous global conflicts to which Russia was a part, once stripped of historical vacillations of ideology, are at their core examples of this conflict.

According to Dugin, Russia's mission is to lead the continental powers against the sea-based powers. How it is to do this is not entirely clear, however. There are two separate and somewhat contradictory tendencies comprising Dugin's Eurasian New World Order. The first is the interaction and association of four 'geoeconomic belts' or 'zones': macro-regions formed through the consolidation of Big Spaces (*bol'shie prostranstva* – a Russian translation of the German *Grossraum*), whereby the larger spaces are hegemonic over the smaller. Equality and mutual recognition amongst the four geoeconomic belts – Euro-Africa, Asia-Pacific, America and Eurasia – are combined with an alliance of the three macro-regions against the United States. This concern with American hegemony is the second tendency, a tendency which trumps all other concerns (see Shlapentokh, 2001; 2007a; 2007b). Dugin's geopolitics is fundamentally oriented towards assembling a series of alliances and 'axes' to resist American unipolar hegemony. A Euro-Asian Empire from Dublin to Vladivostok would be realised through a series of axes: Paris–Berlin–Moscow, Tehran–Moscow and Tokyo–Moscow (see Bassin, 2008; Dunlop, 2001, pp. 108–115; Laruelle, 2008, pp. 115–120). In its most extreme variant, the parameters of Eurasia are ultimately decided by whether a country, irrespective of geographic location, adopts an anti-American (and therefore pro-Eurasian) stance: 'To the extent that any country or region of the globe is consciously oriented against American hegemonic designs, then as far as [Dugin] is concerned, it is de facto already a part of Eurasia' (Bassin, 2008, p. 293).

The logic of Dugin's anti-American Eurasian empire is well-captured in the following selection from *Evraziiskii vzgliad:*

> In such a broad understanding, Eurasianism takes on a new and unprecedented significance. Now it is not only a sort of national idea for a new postcommunist Russia (as intended by the movement's founding fathers...) but also a broad program of universal planetary significance, which goes far beyond the boundaries of Russia and the Eurasian continent itself. *In the same way that the concept of 'Americanism can today be applied to geographical regions located far beyond the limits of the north American continent, so 'Eurasianism' indicates a special civilizational, cultural, philosophical, and strategic choice, which can be made by any member of the human race, regardless of what national and spiritual culture they may belong to.*
>
> (quoted in Bassin, 2008, p. 294)

In addition to the geographical component of Eurasianism, a group may be said to be Eurasianist simply by virtue of its disposition towards Atlanticism. Religions are interpreted based on the extent to which they fit into a particular conception of the Eurasianism–Atlanticism binary. *Evraziia* has depicted traditional Islam, Sufism, Shi'ism and Orthodox Christianity as 'spontaneously Eurasian', while Catholicism, Protestantism and 'U.S. sponsored radical Islamism' as representative of Atlanticism (Laruelle, 2008, p. 118). As Kopanski (2013) suggests, Dugin's understanding of Islam is entirely derived from a Eurasian prism. Lukyanov (2013) suggests that Dugin has branded Mustafa Kemal Ataturk as a true Eurasianist, whereas Turkish Prime Minister Recep Tayyip Erdogan masks his Atlanticist orientation with Islamic rhetoric. Lukyanov quotes Dugin as stating: 'Sooner or later Moscow has to master the geopolitical ABCs and take action according to our fundamental long-term and objective national interests. Thus, we should support a people's uprising in Turkey. Don't take it personally, Mr. Erdogan, what goes around, comes around.'

The geographical parameters of the classical conception of Eurasia roughly equate to those of imperial Russia. Dugin's Eurasia is more ambiguous, varying according to perceived geopolitical necessity. That is, the borders of Eurasia are predicated on a number of scenarios envisioned by Dugin as possibilities for constructing a counter-hegemonic project against the United States. In his geopolitical vision is found a contrast to original Eurasianists. Dugin and other contemporary Eurasianists claim to be heirs to the intellectual tradition established by the classical Eurasianists. However, these similarities may be mostly superficial, including the view of Russia (or Russia-Eurasia) as a single cohesive civilisation on the Eurasian landmass, formed after centuries of cultural interactions; a fundamental incommensurability with the West; a divergence from narrow ethnic Russian nationalism – Eurasian identity consists of both an 'upper' consolidated portion as well as 'lower' ethnic-national ones; and that the two came to fruition in times of profound geopolitical upheaval (Bassin, 2008).

Its tenuous relationship to original Eurasianism notwithstanding, contemporary Eurasianism is significant within post-Soviet Russia as both a polarising and galvanising force. It is polarising insofar as its adherents articulate an ideological position as irreconcilably distinct from Westernism/ Atlanticism. It is not unreasonable to consider the main ideological divide in Russian geopolitical orientation since the middle of perestroika to be between Westernisers and Eurasianists. The former, broadly speaking, are inclined to highlight the universal validity of pluralist-democratic and liberal economic norms. The latter stress a unique continental identity for Russia that is simultaneously neither East nor West but which straddles both, exhibiting elements of cultural and civilisational particularity (see O'Loughlin, 2001).

Eurasianism may be thought of as galvanising insofar as it constitutes a pole around which seemingly disparate and potentially antagonistic political forces gather: in a general sense, it developed significantly in the early 1990s and enjoyed popular usage as an ideology capable of uniting a diverse range of anti-liberal and anti-democratic elements, including monarchist, Communist, nationalist and fascist forces seeking a restoration of the Soviet empire (Mathyl, 2002, p. 68). Indeed, the prominence of Dugin is a testament to the widely perceived need for a particularly Russian geo-identity among such a disparate group of anti-liberal forces. Such an affinity between Russian conservatives and communists is less startling to Russian commentators, however and not confined to the political landscape of the 1990s alone. Rabotiazhev and Solov'ev (2008) write that 'As far back as the nineteenth century, a certain spiritual kinship existed between Russian socialists and conservatives, based on their idealization of communal forms of social life and their rejection of Western liberal bourgeois civilization'. Both socialist Aleksandr Herzen and romantic conservative Konstantin Leont'ev alike despised the Western bourgeoisie; both Slavophiles and Populists believed in the messianic role of Russia (p. 29).

Such affinities were evident between Russian conservatives and communists in the 1990s. After becoming the common ideological glue for various 'red-brown' groups – the increasingly nationalistic Communists and various extreme right wing groups in the early to mid-1990s – and a means for anti-regime forces to express broadly anti-liberal and anti-democratic sentiments, Eurasianism has since come to signify a broader Russian rejection of a world order ensured by American unilateralism and liberal-democratic institutions. Hence, Eurasianism as geopolitical speculation signifies a series of disparate positions, not all of which have strong affinities with the more elaborate Eurasianist doctrine of the likes of Dugin, Gumilyov, or Panarin.

Geopolitical thinking was fashionable amongst the anti-Yeltsin opposition in the early to mid-1990s, among them LDPR leader Vladimir Zhirinovsky and CPRF leader Gennady Zyuganov. Zhirinovsky's most clearly formulated geopolitical treatise is to be found in his *Last Thrust to the South* (*Poslednii brosok na iug*), written in 1993.[10] For Zhirinovsky, the sphere south of Russia has been the country's main source of problems throughout history and requires Russian hegemony and pacification. He advocates that Russia annex the territory of the former Soviet Union as well as Afghanistan, Iran and Turkey in order to strengthen its Southern border, pacify troublesome nationalities of the regime, obtain access to warm seas and restore Russian great power status. Not only will Russia do its part in its own neighborhood, but in fact a new world order will exist wherein the civilised northern states (Russia, the European Union, the USA and Japan) will rule as great empires over the south (see Umland, 2008; Dunlop, 1994; Kipp, 1994). This conception of northern expansion to the south is inspired by the German geopolitician Karl Haushofer (Thom, 1994).

Zhirinovsky's LDPR echoed Duginesque geopolitical themes in the 1990s, advocating an authoritarian, centralised, expansionist state in which federalism is discarded and inclusion is defined by Russian ethnicity. World order is constituted by multiple civilisations; this, and not American hegemony, is the more appropriate form to safeguard the 'white' civilisation. A more specific reading derived from the Last Thrust to the South has northern states (one of which is Russia) dominate the southern states; in fact, this does not really fall short of formal incorporation into empire. The Russian neo-imperial state is at first protectionist at home, creating competitive sectors and the necessary infrastructure to marshal the economy's transition to a more market-based model (Kipp, 1994).

Likewise, the CPRF became increasingly preoccupied with geopolitics during the 1990s. Re-oriented towards geopolitics, national security and national interests by Aleksei Podberezkin, head of the national-patriotic think tank Spiritual Heritage, and under the domination of the 'superpower-patriotic' wing, the party espoused a Eurasianist understanding of world politics (without explicitly calling it such), wherein the world is viewed through the Duginesque (and Mackinderesque) prism of intractable conflict between maritime and continental powers.[11] Russia must align with other Eurasian powers in order to defend its national interests against the unilateral hegemony of the United States. The party came to express certain affinities with Russian conservatives through a focus on reconstituting the Soviet Union and viewing the divide in Russian politics in the 1990s through the prism of patriotic statists and anti-patriotic Westernisers. Under Zyuganov, they borrowed from nineteenth-century conservative thinkers such as the pan-Slavist Danilevsky, K.N. Leont'ev, as well as Ivan Il'in and Pyotr Savitsky (Rabotiazhev & Solov'ev, 2008). As Russia's most viable and enduring party of the 1990s, the CPRF therefore vacillated between an anti-systemic revisionist voice and a legitimate parliamentary force (Flikke, 1999).[12]

Zyuganov has been noted for subordinating Marxist terminology to the imperatives of patriotism and national development. He advocates a Russian renewal based on the heroism of the Russian people based on their timeless qualities of strict adherences to moral precepts, collectivism and selfless labour. This is to take place under a strong state – in fact, a 'majestic and powerful state'. Russia is infused with the historical responsibility of resisting the West and its immorality and materialism and charged with the responsibility of ensuring a balanced world order (see Gregor, 1998; Lester, 1997). In 1994 Zyuganov stated:

> By unifying the 'red' ideal of social justice, which is in its own way the earthly substantiation of a 'heavenly truth,' namely that 'all are equal before God,' with the 'white' ideal of nationally conceived statehood, understood as the form of existence of the centuries-old holy ideas of the people, Russia will obtain, at last, the long craved-for social consensus of all strata and classes as well as restore supreme state power, bequeathed to it by tens of generations of ancestors, acquired through their suffering and courage, and sanctified by the grief of the heroic history of the fatherland!
>
> (quoted in Vujacic, 1996, p. 147)

While the LDPR and CPRF echoed Eurasianist themes, Eurasianists cannot take sole responsibility for geopolitical speculation in Russia. Eurasianism is part of a broader Russian debate on geopolitics that emerged in the 1990s.

While critics have noted Dugin's propensity to reinscribe Russia's past in Eurasianist terms (see Senderov, 2009, p. 37), it should be noted that Dugin's propensity to re-interpret the Cold War as a primarily geopolitical rather than ideological struggle is not without precedent. Hauner (1990), for example examines the 'Soviet Eurasian Empire' in the context of Mackinder and Haushofer's theories and the so-called 'Heartland Debate', a debate with certain traction within the Soviet Union. In 1990, Igor Malashenko (1990: 46; quoted in Kerr, 1995) of the CPSU International Department stated:

> The confrontation of the continental power which controls the heart of Europe, and the coalition opposing it, is by no means confined, geopolitically, to a contest between East and West, socialism and capitalism (or 'totalitarianism' and 'liberal democracy' in Western parlance), as it has quite often been made out over the last few decades, but is an element of genuinely global politics. Properly speaking, the very terms 'East' and 'West' also reflect in a way, if inadequately, the fact that it is not only ideological rivalry or even a clash of social-political systems but also a de-ideologised geopolitical confrontation.

Deemed inappropriate during the Soviet period due to its association with thinkers deemed connected with Nazi and fascist thought (Kolossov & Turovsky, 2001), speculating on geopolitics became fashionable in Russian intellectual and political circles after the fall of the Soviet Union. As Solovyev (2004) notes, however, this has not always taken the form of rigorous scholarly practice and may therefore be considered more of a vocational than scientific pursuit.[13] Nonetheless, a wide array of Russian politicians and thinkers became preoccupied with geopolitics during the 1990s, including conceiving of Russia's national security in terms of geopolitical language and methodologies (Erickson, 1999). Official discourse in the late 1990s was replete with references to geopolitics and reflected some degree of geopolitical realism, of which Yevgeni Primakov was representative (Wohlforth, 2006, pp. 269–270). Whether viewing world affairs through a prism of geopolitical antagonisms comprises a new common sense in Russia is debatable: Russian citizens have not simply accepted these official accounts. Rather, they hold a complex mix of geopolitical affiliations as determined by a number of demographic indicators, exhibiting a range of geopolitical orientations and affinity towards areas of the former Soviet Union, Westernising orientations, Slavic Union with Belarus and Ukraine, and more aggressive visions of the restoration of Soviet space under Russian leadership (O'Loughlin & Talbot, 2005). On the whole, however, they take little interest in the geopolitical writings of the post-Soviet period in Russia (O'Loughlin, 2001) and the receptiveness of Russians to simplified geopolitical storylines offered by Russian officials varies (O'Loughlin et al., 2004a; 2004b).

Geopolitical concepts developed in Russia may be considered as integral to various Russian understandings of world order in the decade following the

Soviet break-up. Accepting that Eurasianism's geopolitical orientations enable it to be classified alongside communists and patriots (Wohlforth, 2006), four currents of geopolitical thinking are discernible in the decade following the Soviet breakup: 1) Eurasianism; 2) Westernism; 3) a moderate nationalist-isolationist position predicated on Russian Orthodoxy, Slavic Union and withdrawal from the Caucuses and Central Asia; and 4) a pragmatic academic school of geostrategy, which incorporates elements of the three: an understanding of Russia's geographical position between Russia and Asia, as well as its civilisational characteristics; the importance of mutually beneficial relations with the West; and pragmatism (Kolossov & Turovsky, 2001). Post-Soviet Russia has also witnessed the emergence of a new field called ethno-geopolitics, or *etnogeopolitika*, which 'argues that ethnicity – in all its various manifestations – represents the most fundamental force driving the political life of the 21st century. This is understood as universal principle, operating with equal intensity on the arenas of regional, national and international politics.' According to ethno-geopoliticians, ethnicity is entirely objective. Humans belong to invariable *etnosy* – ethnic units which are comprised of shared ethnic characteristics, themselves predicated on biology and a form of socio-biology. An individual *etnos* has an 'organic attachment to its own native region or homeland, identified by ethno-geopoliticians variously as its *Lebensraum* (*zhiznennoye prostranstvo*), its "ethnic space" (*etnicheskoye prostranstvo*), or its "endemic field" (*endemicheskoye pole*). It is through the occupation of this space that the existence of the group is materialised, so to speak, and the bond between the two has an existential character' (Bassin, 2009, p. 133). Dugin is undoubtedly a self-conscious representation of Eurasianism aspiring to be its leading figure. His 'competitive advantage' towards this end is to be found in his willingness and ability to synthesise disparate schools, social and geographical locations, and political dispositions under its umbrella. In this process, world history and contemporary events are foregrounded in a Eurasianist prism.

4 Putin's brain or organic intellectual of Russian nationalism?

One might view Dugin's trajectory as one in which he has shifted from the fringes of Russian public opinion to a position that has him closer to the nerve centre of Russian political power. Umland, who consistently highlights Dugin's far right and fascist tendencies, suggested (2010) that Dugin has transformed 'from a lunatic fringe figure into a mainstream political publicist'. For many Western commentators, there exists a unity between Russian executive direction under Putin and Dugin's philosophical orientation. In an article titled 'The expansionist behind Putin', Robert Sibley (2014) suggests that behind Putin's March 2014 speech following the incorporation of Crimea into the Russian Federation were 'an unspoken geopolitical theory and unacknowledged ideas of …. Dugin'. Sibley quotes John Dunlop as referring to the impact of Dugin's 1997 *Foundations of Geopolitics*, Dugin's 'neo-fascist treatise' as follows: 'There has probably not been another book published in

Russia during the post-communist period which has exerted (such) an influence on Russian military, police and statist foreign policy elites.' Moreover, Rukhadze (2013) suggests that in predicting that the Georgian regions of Adjara, Javakheti and Samegrelo would follow Abkhazia and South Ossetia and attempt to succeed from Georgia, Dugin functioned as an 'unofficial Kremlin mouthpiece', which the Kremlin utilised to 'send warnings'. That Dugin is the Kremlin's spokesperson or chief ideologist would suggest a rather straightforward relationship between the two. Although he provides somewhat tenuous links between Dugin and the Ukrainian conflict of 2014, Shlapentokh (2014) is probably closer to the relationship between Dugin and the Kremlin when he suggests that Dugin's Eurasianism resonates more as ideology than Kremlin political *strategy* in official Russia's post-Crimean discourse.

Elsewhere I have suggested that Eurasianist discourse has been selectively absorbed by Putin for the purposes of articulating a more comprehensive 'state project' of Eurasian integration (Silvius, 2015). There is considerable discord between the 'material' parameters of Putin's Eurasian projects and the more esoteric orientation of Dugin. Deriving a reading of world history from the standpoint of a civilisation-infused reading of geopolitics, Dugin emphasises the 'semiotic' nature of cultural, civilisational and religious interaction while having little to say about the economic and political structures that threaten or sustain such action, even as his *strategic* concern is to counter the architects of American influence in the Eurasian periphery, most notably Zbigniew Brzezinski. Indeed, it is unclear how Dugin would interpret the institutional economic or political infrastructure of a custom union or similar products of contemporary regional capitalism through Heidegger, the philosophical wellspring for his *Fourth Political Theory* (Dugin, 2012a), Mackinder or integral conservatism.

Nonetheless, the philosophical framework that Dugin cultivated in the 1990s while a more marginal, albeit demonstrably ambitious, figure has continued to find new purchase in new geopolitical contexts, demonstrating the polysemic quality of his thinking. If in the 1990s Dugin's geopolitical theories were deployed to recode the Soviet–American cold war conflict as one between not capitalism and communism but Westernism/Atlanticism and the Eurasian heartland, in more recent times they have been utilised to articulate the parameters of contemporary events, if not anticipate them.[14] And while positing an unproblematically straightforward relationship between Dugin and Russian executive structures is misleading, Dugin's works are of social and political significance. In addition to solidifying his position at MGU, as mentioned above, it would appear as though Dugin is embedded in prominent social and political networks, with numerous prominent Russian and 'international' officials and public figures, having been part of Dugin's *International Eurasian Movement* (see Umland, 2009a; see also Kipp, 2012).[15] Indeed, Dugin's project is intended for non-Russian public consumption, as evidenced by the number of external organisations, personalities and movements that have been enlisted in Dugin's Eurasianist project. Moreover, Dugin has cultivated a robust social media presence, and his ideas are routinely circulated across various media by both Russian and non-Russian language sources.[16]

As I have demonstrated in other works, while the language and practices surrounding 'embedded civilisationalism' have been in development since Putin's first term as president, they have increased in frequency and significance in Putin's third term, during which time the creation of the Eurasian Economic Union and the incorporation of Crimea into the Russian Federation have been accompanied by Eurasian 'discursive frames' (see Silvius, 2014; 2015). Such practices have coincided with the cultivation of knowledge production structures whose respective mandates are to articulate contemporary world order by decentring American unilateralism and liberal internationalism. One such structure is the Valdai discussion group, which, in spite of being frequently understood to be a more Western leaning body, has incorporated strains of embedded civilisationalism in recent times (Silvius, 2015). While Umland (2013) might overstate the similarities of three 'rabidly anti-American discussion clubs' – The Anti-Orange Committee, the Isborsk Club and the Florian Geyer Club – it is true that such clubs vie with Valdai for the ability to articulate Russia's place in contemporary world order and do so from a more overtly nationalistic position.

Dugin is very much a part of this phenomenon, evidenced by his bending of his Eurasianism towards the terrain of multipolarity, a concept that corresponds with official Russia's contemporary geostrategy (see Chapters 4 and 5). Dugin's contribution to a discussion on multipolarity ultimately reveals the extent to which his Eurasianist project is overdetermined and polysemic in nature. It is at once pre-modern, in the sense that civilisations are cultural zones that reflect the *longue duree* of migration, interaction, and, in the case of Russia, consolidation under Mongol, imperial Russian, or Soviet rule; modern, in the sense that they conform to a logic whereby (large) nation states' interests are a reflection of material capabilities and dictated by balance of power considerations; and post-modern, in the sense that Eurasianism has become a political signifier and a *value* unhinged from geographical moorings and entered into opposition against liberal democratic sentiments in a series of discrete conflicts.

> Multipolarity is a very concrete project where Russia sets out more than an aggregate of its national interests in the future, more than its defining values and its uniqueness, it also proposes that the entire world rethink its attitude to the historical process and the processes unfolding in the realm of foreign policy. The proposed multipolarity is a worldview challenge in a sense.
>
> (Dugin, 2012b)

In other words, Dugin's Eurasianist philosophy exhibits considerable tension between the continued presence of national states, particularly powerful ones existing outside of the Western core, the networked quality of post-modern (alter) globalisation, and acculturation processes that are millennia in the making. Dugin's Eurasianism is both a rereading of post-modern geopolitics from a non-Western perspective that challenges the epistemic superiority of globalisation as a Western hegemonic project and an exercise in branding, whereby seemingly disparate phenomena become subordinate to, and explained by, a rereading of global history through a Eurasianist and multipolar prism.

When equated with multipolarity, Dugin's thinking exhibits a tension between the pre-modern, modern and post-modern. It is at once ensconced in a modern framework of territorial geopolitics, whereby states marshal geographic knowledge for serving their direct interests. Dugin states, 'I advocate strongly a multi-polar construction of the world. I think that the pretension of the United States to be the unique pole of the world … is completely wrong, immoral and unacceptable by the other great centers of powers' (in Stack, 2008).

Dugin embraces a post-modern framework in which states are but one category alongside a multiplicity of social actors networked under conditions of contemporary globalisation and aligned against American unilateralism. Dugin (2009) asserts: 'The Eurasian Idea on a global scale is a global revolutionary concept, called upon to be a new platform for mutual understanding and cooperation for a large conglomerate of different powers: states, nations, cultures, and religions that reject the Atlantic version of globalization.' Moreover, 'Eurasianism is the sum of the natural, artificial, objective, and subjective obstacles on the path of unipolar globalization; it offers a constructive, positive opposition to globalism instead of a simple negation' (Dugin, 2009). He continues:

> In the broad sense the Eurasian Idea and even the Eurasian concept do not strictly correspond to the geographical boundaries of the Eurasian continent. The Eurasian Idea is a global-scale strategy that acknowledges the objectivity of globalization and the termination of nation-states (*Etats-Nations*), but at the same time offers a different scenario of globalization, which entails no unipolar world or united global government. Instead, it offers several global zones (poles). The Eurasian Idea is an alternative or multipolar version of globalization, but globalization is the currently major fundamental world process that is deciding the main vector of modern history.

Finally, it exhibits a deep and immutable historicising, whereby cultural attributes obtain as the sediments of the *longue duree*. However, such thinking is put into the service of contemporary Russian geopolitics. For example, Dugin's essentialist reading of culture and civilisation posits civilisational rupture between Western Protestantism and Catholicism, on the one hand, and Eastern Orthodoxy, on the other. However, such a division may become less binding on the contemporary chessboard of global politics. Dugin suggests, for example, that in the case of Hungary, its premodern Eurasian identity ought to prevail in spite of its hegemonic Catholicism. He writes that Hungary is 'a Catholic country, non-Slavic, not Orthodox. None the less it was part of our once Hun-dominated Eurasia territories and it is an East European country, according to its identity. East Europeans are beginning to understand their identity. This does not mean that Europe should be split up, but it means that one should join the process of forming this civilizational niche' (Dugin, 2009).

Importantly, however, all may partake in the project of multipolarity to combat, simultaneously, global liberalism and American unilateralism. In terms of the former, multipolarity is the safeguarding of *values* through geopolitical imperative. He writes:

> We realize that the West is determined to press on us its own protocols in economics, politics, ideology, the system of values, the information system, its own ideas of gender and other things, while relying not on any specific nation to safeguard these liberal-democratic standards, but on the world community. This is not a state hegemony, as is the case in a unipolar world, but hegemony of an ideology of values. This is the hegemony of a liberal absolute ideology which is coming for the entire humankind.
>
> (Dugin, 2009)

While Dugin has long been a thinker with strong new right and conservative leanings, more recently he has redoubled his efforts to make such thinking synonymous with Russian state power and Putin's presidency. In a March 13, 2013 article that appeared in the *Financial Times*, Dugin asserted that the essence of Vladimir Putin was conservative. He states, 'For his first 12 years in power, Mr. Putin's conservatism was tempered by the need to appeal to an influential liberal elite. But with the desertion of this class to the ranks of anti-government protestors since 2011, he is finally making his true views know. This should not be seen as winding back the clock, however. Russia is in transition from the pure totalitarianism of the Soviet era; this conservative moment represents a rethinking of what comes at the end of the transition.' Such thinking has multipolarity as its geopolitical correlate. In the same article, he states, 'Liberals, to paraphrase Leo Tolstoy, are all alike; but conservatives are all conservative in their own way. While liberals insist on universal human rights and the pursuit of a globalised world, conservatives value national uniqueness, sovereignty and identity, defending their exceptionalism from a single, encroaching world order.' Hence, Dugin is appealing to conservative forces and proposing a symmetry between non-Western centres, national values, and a desire to resist American rule.

Nonetheless, Dugin is willing to downplay the cultivation of conservative forces when pragmatically enlisting anti-American forces in the project of multipolarity. In such thinking, Dugin's calculus is simple: support forces that are deemed to be Russian allies and combat those deemed to be American allies. Zero sum geopolitical logic, rather than that which is informed by a 'civilizational' substratum, prevails. Regarding South Ossetia and Abkhazia, Dugin adds: 'It is not the rule that from now on we will recognize all the separatist regions. Absolutely no. We will recognize those separatists' regions that would be geopolitically on our side – either on our side or on our friends' – and opposed to the US' (in Stack, 2008). And yet in the case of the 'Atlanticist' Baltics, Dugin also appears willing to concede 'civilizational' ground even if the end result is presumably a geopolitical loss for Russia. Responding to the question, *How does Russia view the development of friendly relations between the United States and former Soviet republics such as Ukraine and Georgia?*, Dugin responds: 'As a declaration of war. As a declaration of psychological, geopolitical, economic and open war.' He continues,

> We consider that all of the post-Soviet space – except the Baltic states – we are dealing with Eurasian civilization. Not with European, not with the West. And to try to get these spaces out of our control, or out of our dialogue, or out of our special relations with them, based on history – it was a kind of attack, a declaration of war. It is not, as Americans like to put it, a competition… . It was perceived to be not a competition but an act of aggression, as Napoleon or Hitler, and nothing else.
>
> (In Stack, 2008)

Hence, in Dugin, at times geopolitical calculations are separated from their civilisational essence; at times, they are one and the same.

Contrary to the suggestion of Clowes (2011), the most significant quality of Dugin's work is not to be found in its academic shortcomings, contrived etymologies, or inconsistencies. Such a suggestion isolates Dugin's academic persona at the expense of his 'organic' political location. Rather, Dugin's work is significant precisely because of its polysemic quality and the manner by which it can be adopted flexibly as the strategic calculus warrants. To a large extent Dugin's thinking is a function of geopolitical strategy and his desire to enfold a flexible network of forces into the Eurasianist camp. In so doing, he seeks to contribute to the rebranding of Russia's international identity to one understood on cultural and civilisational terrain, which constitutes a radical departure from the logic of Soviet internationalism.

5 Conclusion

What does Aleksandr Dugin's trajectory tell us about Putin's embedded civilisationalism? Dugin exhibits the propensity to emphasise essentialist and irreconcilable differences between cultures and civilizations and link them to the practices of geopolitics. His multifaceted critique of American unilateralism and liberal political philosophy results in the geopoliticisation of political values and conduct, which I have demonstrated as the manner by which potentially discrete phenomena are re-coded according to their perceived or desired geopolitical significance.

I have suggested that we locate Dugin as an organic intellectual of Russian statism and consider the extent to which he does or does not contribute to Putin's Eurasian project. It is certainly an overstatement to suggest that Dugin serves as the Kremlin's official ideologue on geopolitical matters. However, selectively utilised by Russian state structures, Dugin demonstrates the extent to which ideas that may have been considered esoteric, marginal and counter systemic in the early post-Soviet period have found a place in the broader Russian state-sanctioned Eurasian project. This project, which has powerful 'material' currents, nonetheless absorbs multifaceted discursive dimensions, of which Dugin is certainly a part. Moreover, to evaluate Dugin's geopolitical and civilisational musings according to their academic shortcomings or analytical inconsistencies misses Dugin's broader strategic significance, and, correspondingly, their value to official Russia. Highly polysemic in nature, Dugin's work demonstrates the extent to which ever greater criteria can be subordinated under a singular geopolitical, geoeconomic, or civilisational logic. In a similar manner, a host of disparate geopolitical and geoeconomic phenomena may be cited so as to develop the appearance of coherence, consistency and historical stability. In such a way does Dugin's project comfortably absorb competing historical and disciplinary logics.

Notes

1 The following is derived primarily from Laruelle (2008, pp. 107–144) except where otherwise noted. For a succinct political biography of Dugin, see also Dunlop (2001, pp. 92–106). For a helpful examination of Dugin's trajectory, see Sedgwick (2004). Sedgwick portrays Dugin's metamorphosis from Soviet dissident, to an infiltrator of reactionary organisation Pamiat, to cementing the 'red to brown' opposition with his Neo-Eurasian thinking, to finally a 'radical centrism': supporting Vladimir Putin and entering the political mainstream.
2 As of 26 February 2010.
3 On 26 February 2010.
4 See Bassin & Aksenov (2006) for a review of the influence of Mackinder in post-Soviet Russian thinking on geopolitics. See also Sloan (1999), in which the author assesses Mackinder's Heartland Theory in a broader attempt to understand the relationship between geography and international relations.
5 See Wolkersdorfer (1999) for a discourse analytic study of Haushofer's work, following the assertion that geopolitics ought to be viewed as a discursive and not geo-materialist phenomenon.
6 In this and other works, Laruelle presents a series of in-depth accounts of Eurasianism's leading figures. Schmidt (2009) charges that this comes at the expense of being able to determine the significance of Eurasianism as a political movement.
7 Mäkinen (2014) suggests that Russian geopolitical culture is more 'Western' than neo-Eurasian, insofar as geopolitical instruction at Russian universities downplays essentialist and reflectivist understandings of geopolitics in favour of positivist approaches.
8 For summaries of *Osnovy geopolitiki*, see Ingram (2001) and Dunlop (2004). For an evaluation of Dugin's work as 'geopolitical revolution' and paligenetic rebirth, see Shekhovtsov (2008).

9 Ingram (2001, p. 1035) lists these essential oppositions as follows. Belonging to continental land powers and maritime powers, respectively: Earth-Water; Land-Sea; Continent-Island; Tellurocracy-Thalassocracy; Heartland-World Island; Rome-Carthage; Russia/USSR-England/USA; Eurasianism-Atlanticism; Space-Time; East-West; North-South; Hero-Trader; Ideocracy-Democracy; Warrior/Socialist-Capitalist; Tradition-Modernity; Traditional Religion-Antichrist.

10 Umland (2008) maintains that Zhirinovsky's entry into federal politics in 1993 influenced a change in his foreign policy from revolutionary expansionism to restorationist expansionism, in line with certain dictates of political correctness.

11 See Bassin & Aksenov (2006) for a review of Zyuganov's *The Geography of Victory: Foundations of Russian Geopolitics*, which borrows extensively from Mackinder.

12 Hashim (1999) offers a democratic transitions analysis focusing on the anti-system quality of the CPRF and the corresponding argument that the party constituted a threat to the democratic consolidation of Russia in the late 1990s. In an investigation of Gennady Zyuganov's attempts to unite nationalist and communist forces from 1990 to the mid-1990s, Vujacic (1996) argues that in combining leftist ideas of social justice and the rightist idea of a strong state, the CPRF leader is best understood as being in the intellectual tradition of national socialists and other twentieth-century European thinkers of the extreme right, such as Charles Maurras and Enrico Corradini.

13 Solovyev (2008) suggests that Russian geopolitical analysis may be divided into two camps: traditionalists, for whom international political life remains a struggle for power and the control of resources, and revisionists, who seek other ways of understanding the organisation of global space. Among the traditionalists Solovyev counts Dugin and Panarin. Among the latter he counts K. Pleshakov, V.L. Tsymburskiy, K.E. Sorokin, K.S. Gadzhiev, V.A. Kolosov and D.N. Zamyatin.

14 Responding to the question, *If Ukraine were to move into NATO, what do you think the Russian reaction would be?* Dugin states:

I think that Russian reaction would be to support an uprising in eastern parts and Crimea and I could not exclude the entrance of armed force there, as in the Ossetian scenario.

But the difference is that half of the Ukrainian population is Russian, is directly Russian, and this half of the population regards itself as being oppressed by the values, by the language, by the geopolitical issues, completely against their will. So I don't think that, in this case, direct intervention of Russian armed force will be needed. I think on the eve of the entrance into NATO there will be public riots and the split of Ukraine into two parts (in Stack, 2008).

15 Kipp (2012) suggests that Russian Army Colonel-General and President of the Academy of Geopolitical Problems, Leonid Ivashov, a key proponent of Russian–Chinese strategic alliance, is an ally of Dugin.

16 As of 12 June 2015, Dugin's twitter account had produced over 10,000 tweets and has 23.5k followers.

References

Bassin, M. (2008). Eurasianism 'classical' and 'neo' : The lines of continuity. In T. Mochizuki (Ed.), *Beyond the empire: Images of Russia in the Eurasian cultural context* (pp. 279–294). Sappuro: Slavic Research Center.

Bassin, M. (2009). The emergence of ethno-geopolitics in post-Soviet Russia. *Eurasian Geography and Economics*, 50(2), 131–149.

Bassin, M., & Aksenov, K. (2006). Mackinder and the heartland theory in post-Soviet geopolitical discourse. *Geopolitics*, 11(1), 99–118.

Clover, C. (1999). Dreams of the Eurasian heartland. *Foreign Affairs*, 78(2), 9–13.

Clowes, E. W. (2011). *Russia on the edge: imagined geographies and post-Soviet identity.* Ithaca: Cornell University Press.

Dugin, A. (2006). Fascism – borderless and red. In R. Griffin, W. Loh & A. Umland (Eds.), *Fascism past and present, West and East* (pp. 505–510). Stuttgart: Ibidem; Verlag.

Dugin, A. (2009). The Eurasian idea. Counter-Currents Publishing. Retrieved from http://www.counter-currents.com/2013/11/the-eurasian-idea.

Dugin, A. (2012a). *The fourth political theory.* Arktos.

Dugin, A. (2012b). A multipolar world and Russian foreign policy. *International Affairs: Summary No:6, 2012*, 18. Retrieved from https://interaffairs.ru/virtualread/eng/contents58_6.pdf.

Dugin, A. (2013). The world needs to understand Putin. *Financial Times.* Retrieved from http://www.ft.com/cms/s/0/67fa00d2-874b-11e2-9dd7-00144feabdc0.html#axzz3bMUpmeHz.

Dunlop, J. (1994). Zhirinovsky's world. *Journal of Democracy*, 5(2), 27–32.

Dunlop, J. (2001). Aleksandr Dugin's 'neo-Eurasian' textbook and Dmitrii Trenin's ambivalent response. *Harvard Ukrainian Studies*, 25(1/2), 91–127.

Dunlop, J. (2004). Aleksandr Dugin's foundations of geopolitics. *Demokratizatsiya*, 12(1), 41–57.

Epstein, M. (1996). The phoenix of philosophy: On the meaning and significance of contemporary Russian thought. *Symposium: A Journal of Russian Thought*, 1, 35–74.

Erickson, J. (1999). 'Russia will not be trifled with': Geopolitical facts and fantasies. *Journal of Strategic Studies*, 22(2/3), 242–268.

Filiminova, T. (2015). Eurasia as discursive literary space at the millennium. In D. Lane (Ed.), *The Eurasian project and Europe: Regional discontinuities and geopolitics* (pp. 117–132). Basingstoke, UK: Palgrave Macmillan.

Flikke, G. (1999). Patriotic left-centrism: The zigzags of the Communist Party of the Russian Federation. *Europe-Asia Studies*, 51(2), 275–298.

Gregor, A. J. (1998). Fascism and the new Russian nationalism. *Communist and Post-Communist Studies*, 31(1), 1–15.

Gregor, A. J. (2006a). Andreas Umland: The 'fascism' of Aleksandr Dugin. In R. Griffin, W. Loh & A. Umland (Eds.), *Fascism past and present, west and east: An international debate on concepts and cases in the comparative study of the extreme right* (pp. 466–473). Stuttgart: Ibidem; Verlag.

Gregor, A. J. (2006b). Response to Dr. Andreas Umland. In R. Griffin, W. Loh & A. Umland (Eds.), *Fascism past and present, West and East: An international debate on concepts and cases in the comparative study of the extreme right* (pp. 481–485). Stuttgart: Ibidem; Verlag.

Hashim, S. M. (1999). KPRF ideology and its implications for democratization in Russia. *Communist and Post-Communist Studies*, 32(1), 77–89.

Hauner, M. (1990). *What is Asia to us? Russia's Asian heartland yesterday and today.* London: Unwin Hyman Ltd.

Ingram, A. (2001). Alexander Dugin: Geopolitics and neo-fascism in post-Soviet Russia. *Political Geography*, 20(8), 1029–1051.

Kearns, G. (2010). Geography, geopolitics and empire. *Transactions of the Institute of British Geographers*, 35(2), 187–203.

Kerr, D. (1995). The new Eurasianism: The rise of geopolitics in Russia's foreign policy. *Europe-Asia Studies*, 47(6), 977–988.

Kipp, J. (1994). The Zhirinovsky threat. *Foreign Affairs*, 73(3), 72–86.

Kipp, J. (2012, May 14). Whither Russia: Looking East and ready to embrace it. *Eurasia Daily Monitor* 9(91). Retrieved from http://www.jamestown.org/single/?tx_ttnews%5Btt_news%5D=39371&no_cache=1.

Kolossov, V., & Turovsky, R. (2001). Russian geopolitics at the fin-de-siecle. *Geopolitics*, 6(1), 141–164.

Kopanski, A. B. (2013). The Russian Neo-Eurasianism, the West and the reconstruction of Islamic civilization in Alexander Dugin's geopolitical doctrines. *World Journal of Islamic History and Civilization*, 3(3), 124–133.

Laruelle, M. (2004). The two faces of contemporary Eurasianism: An imperial version of Russian nationalism. *Nationalities Papers*, 32(1), 115–136.

Laruelle, M. (2007). The orient in Russian thought at the turn of the century. In D. Shlapentokh (Ed.), *Russia between East and West: Scholarly debates on Eurasianism* (pp. 9–37). Boston: Brill.

Laruelle, M. (2008). *Russian Eurasianism: An ideology of empire*. Washington: Woodrow Wilson Center Press.

Laruelle, M. (2009). (Neo-)Eurasianists and politics. *Russian Politics and Law*, 47(1), 90–101.

Laug, Christoph (2013). Prominent right-wing figures in Russia. *Russian Analytical Digest*, 135(5).

Lester, J. (1997). Overdosing on nationalism: Gennadii Zyuganov and the Communist Party of the Russian Federation. *New Left Review*, I(221), 34–53.

Luks, L. (2009). A 'third way' or back to the Third Reich? *Russian Politics and Law*, 47(1), 7–23.

Lukyanov, F. (2013, 17 June). Russia sees Turkey through its own lens. *Russia in Global Affairs*. Retrieved from http://eng.globalaffairs.ru/redcol/Russia-Sees-Turkey-Through-Its-Own-Lens-16021.

Mackinder, H. J. (1904). The geographical pivot of history. *The Geographical Journal*, 23(4), 421–437.

Mackinder, H. J. (1943). The round world and the winning of the peace. *Foreign Affairs*, 21(4), 595–605.

Mäkinen, S. (2014). Geopolitics teaching and worldviews: Making the future generation in Russia. *Geopolitics*, 19(1), 86–108.

Mathyl, M. (2002). The National-Bolshevik Party and Arctogaia: Two neo-fascist groupuscules in the post-Soviet political space. *Patterns of Prejudice*, 36(3), 62–76.

Noordenbos, B. (2011). Ironic imperialism: how Russian patriots are reclaiming postmodernism. *Studies in East European Thought*, 63(2), 147–158.

O'Loughlin, J. (2001). Geopolitical fantasies, national strategies and ordinary Russians in the post-communist era. *Geopolitics*, 6(3), 17–48.

O'Loughlin, J., O'Tuathail, G., & Kolossov, V. (2004a). A 'risky westward turn'? Putin's 9–11 script and ordinary Russians. *Europe-Asia Studies*, 56(1), 3–34.

O'Loughlin, J., O'Tuathail, G., & Kolossov, V. (2004b). Russian geopolitical storylines and public opinion in the wake of 9–11: A critical geopolitical analysis and national survey. *Communist and Post-Communist Studies*, 37(3), 281–318.

O'Loughlin, J., & Talbot, P. (2005). Where in the world is Russia? Geopolitical perceptions and preferences of ordinary Russians. *Eurasian Geography and Economics*, 46(1), 23–50.

Rabotiazhev, N. V., & Solov'ev, E. G. (2008). From Lenin to Danilevsky: The changing geopolitical views of the Communist Party of the Russian Federation. *Russian Politics and Law*, 46(3), 27–42.

Rukhadze, V. (2013, 23 September). Russia gradually expands its occupation zone in Georgia. *Eurasia Daily Monitor,* 10(168). Retrieved from http://www.jamestown.org/programs/edm/single/?tx_ttnews%5Btt_news%5D=41396&cHash=5326d9ef24097701ac5797f71de3da10.

Schmidt, M. (2009). History, not exegesis. *The Review of Politics,* 71(3), 526–529.

Sedgwick, M. (2004). *Against the modern world: Traditionalism and the secret intellectual history of the twentieth century.* New York: Oxford University Press.

Senderov, V. (2009). Neo-Eurasianism: Realities, dangers, prospects. *Russian Politics and Law,* 47(1), 24–46.

Shekhovtsov, A. (2008). The paligenetic thrust of Russian neo-Eurasianism: Ideas of rebirth in Aleksandr Dugin's worldview. *Totalitarian Movements and Political Religions.* 9(4), 491–506.

Shekhovtsov, A., & Umland, A. (2009). Is Aleksandr Dugin a traditionalist? Neo-Eurasianism and perennial philosophy. *The Russian Review,* 68(4), 662–678.

Shlapentokh, D. (2001). Russian nationalism today: The views of Alexander Dugin. *Contemporary Review,* 279(1626), 29–37.

Shlapentokh, D. (2007a). Dugin Eurasianism: A window on the minds of the Russian elite or an intellectual ploy? *Studies in Eastern European Thought*, 59(3), 215–236.

Shlapentokh, D. (2007b). Dugin, Eurasianism, and Central Asia. *Communist and Post-Communist Studies*, 40(2), 143–156.

Shlapentokh, D. V. (2014). Implementation of an ideological paradigm: Early Duginian Eurasianism and Russia's Post-Crimean discourse. *Contemporary Security Policy,* 35(3), 380–399.

Sibley, R. (2014, May 1). The expansionist behind Putin. *Ottawa Citizen*. Retrieved from http://www.ottawacitizen.com/news/expansionist+behind+Putin/9801689/story.html.

Silvius, R. (2014). The Russian State, Eurasianism, and civilisations in the contemporary global political economy. *Journal of Global Faultlines*, 2(1), 44–69.

Silvius, R. (2015). Eurasianism and Putin's 'embedded civilisationalism'. In D. Lane (Ed.), *The Eurasian project and Europe: Regional discontinuities and Geopolitics* (pp. 75–88). Basingstoke, UK: Palgrave Macmillan.

Silvius, R. (Forthcoming). The embedding of Russian state-sanctioned multipolarity in the Post-Soviet conjuncture. *Globalizations.*

Sloan, G. (1999). Sir Halford J. Mackinder: The heartland theory then and now. *Journal of Strategic Studies*, 22(2), 15–38.

Sokolov, M. (2009). New right-wing intellectuals in Russia: Strategies of legitimation. *Russian Politics and Law*, 47(1), 47–75.

Solovyev, E. (2004). Geopolitics in Russia – science or vocation? *Communist and Post-Communist Studies*, 37(1), 85–96.

Solovyev, E. (2008). Russian geopolitics in the context of globalization. In D. Blum (Ed.), *Russia and globalization: Identity, security and society in an era of change* (pp. 287–306). Washington: Woodrow Wilson Center Press.

Stack, M. (2008, September 4). Russian nationalist advocates Eurasian alliance against the U.S. *Los Angeles Times.* Retrieved from http://www.latimes.com/world/la-fgw-dugin4-2008sep04-story.html#page=1

Thom, F. (1994). Eurasianism: A new Russian foreign policy? *Uncaptive Minds*, 7(2), 65–77.

Umland, A. (2007). Alexander Dugin, the issue of post-Soviet fascism, and Russian political discourse today. *Russian Analytical Digest*, 14(7), 2–4.

Umland, A. (2008). Zhirinovsky's 'last thrust to the south' and the definition of fascism. *Russian Politics and Law*, 46(6), 31–46.

Umland, A. (2009a). Fascist tendencies in Russia's political establishment: The rise of the international Eurasian movement. *Russian Analytical Digest*, 60(9), 13–17.

Umland, A. (2009b). Pathological tendencies in Russian 'neo-Eurasianism'. *Russian Politics and Law*, 47(1), 76–89.

Umland, A. (2010). Aleksandr Dugin's transformation from a lunatic fringe figure into a mainstream political publicist, 1980–1998: A case study in the rise of late and post-Soviet Russian fascism. *Journal of Eurasian Studies*, 1(2), 144–152.

Umland, A. (2013). New extreme right-wing intellectual circles in Russia: The Anti-Orange Committee, the Izborsk Club and the Florian Geyer Club. *Russian Analytical Digest*, 135(5.8). 2–5.

Vujacic, V. (1996). Gennadiy Zyuganov and the 'third road'. *Post-Soviet Affairs*, 12(2), 118–154.

Wohlforth, W. (2006). Heartland dreams: Russian geopolitics and foreign policy. In W. Danspeckgruber (Ed.), *Perspectives on the Russian state in transition* (pp. 265–281). Princeton: Lichtenstein Institute on Self Determination.

Wolkersdorfer, G. (1999). Karl Haushofer and geopolitics – the history of a German mythos. *Geopolitics*, 4(3), 145–160.

7 The legacy of Vladislav Surkov

Regime-sanctioned culture in the service of national political economy

1 Introduction

Vladislav Surkov is at it again. Surkov, who has seen his prominence wane in recent years after being widely regarded as the Kremlin's *eminence grise* during Putin's first two presidential terms, has recently become front and centre in Russia's on-going contestation over Ukraine. Surkov was one of the first Russian officials targeted for sanctions by the American government after the 2014 Crimean dispute (US Embassy, 2014). He did not waste the opportunity to demonstrate his particular brand of cultural *bricolage.* Upon hearing of the American sanctions, Surkov stated, 'The only things that interest me in the U.S. are Tupac Shakur, Allen Ginsberg and Jackson Pollock. I don't need a visa to access their work. I lose nothing' (Pomerantsev, 2014b).

Such a statement demonstrates Surkov's ostensible regime function: providing readymade sound-bites on Russian culture and geopolitical posturing for Russian public consumption. However, alone such an utterance does not disclose the broader economic function Surkov plays, and has played, in Russian state capitalism. Indeed, while US sanctions might not prevent Surkov from enjoying the products of Shakur, Ginsberg and Pollock, they will prevent him from travelling to the United States and the Massachusetts Institute of Technology to learn about the commercialisation of scientific innovation, like he did prior to the Russian government's declaration of support for the Skolkovo Innovation Complex in 2010, a private–public partnership for which Surkov was the Russian government's point person prior to his public spat with a representative of the Russian Investigative Committee (Kramer, 2010; Dolinskiy, 2013).

Surkov's handling of the Skolkovo portfolio was but one of his economic legacies. While scholars have focused on Surkov's role in the formation of regime-sanctioned ideology, little attention has been paid to Surkov's broader economic function within Russia's state apparatus. As a self-declared public philosopher during the first decade of the 2000s, Surkov developed and propagated the Putin regime's official narrative of domestic and global affairs. My argument in this chapter is that in addition to preparing the 'political' elements of the 'Putin Project' – the consolidation of the domestic political apparatus and Russia's return to prominence in an emerging multipolar world order – for Russian public consumption, Surkov has also been instrumental in rendering Russian capitalism acceptable through the appeal to Russian cultural motifs. Indeed, Surkov should be viewed as a complex lynchpin in Russia's Putin-era 'state capital nexus' (van Apeldoorn & de Graaf, 2012b), rather than simply contributing to the Kremlin's attempts at attaining discursive hegemony.

Far from merely an exercise in conceptual gymnastics, Surkov's articulation of a 'post-post-Soviet' – the period encompassed by the Putin era – public political philosophy can be understood within the context of Russia's transition from state socialism and global superpower to state-guided capitalist power integrating into the capitalist – but multipolar – global political economy. As Surkov reworks themes and motifs associated with Russian culture and civilisation to serve regime imperatives of political economy, he may be considered one of the foremost institutionalised organic intellectuals[1] of the Russian state, advocating for the continued modernisation of the Russian political economy by appealing to the Russian public through the language of cultural particularity.

This chapter distances its assessment of the Putin regime from the terrain of cultural essentialism to a reading of culture and civilisation which emphasises the complicatedly co-developing semiotic and extra-semiotic dimensions of official Russia's stance on contemporary world order. It demonstrates how appeals to Russian uniqueness serve to legitimate Putin's political and economic projects – including that of economic modernisation (see Chapter 3) – and investigates how Surkov's thinking contributes to a regime-sanctioned challenge to American universalism by providing a framework for non-Western national development. Its format is as follows. Section 2 surveys recent thinking on ideas and culture in both political economy and Russian studies literature and argues that Surkov's and the Putin regime's selective appeal to Russian cultural traits is better understood not as exemplifying essential features of Russian political culture but as securing legitimacy for projects of political economy. This has at times entailed a negation of Russian exceptionalism and at other times its celebration. Section 3 investigates Surkov and the structure of Kremlin 'political technologies' in the context of Russia's rise. Section 4 demonstrates Surkov's recent trajectory with a focus on his role in managing the Skolkovo Innovation Complex. Section 5 serves as a conclusion.

2 Locating Surkov, Russian culture and Russia's identity debates

Assessments of Russian politics increasingly have demonstrated a propensity towards their own cultural, ideational and identity turn (Tsygankov, 2007; Morozov, 2008). Speculation on Russian political culture enjoyed a resurgence in post-Soviet Russia amongst Russian political scientists reacting against the economistic and universalistic tendencies of Soviet Marxist thought. Part of this resurgence is to be found in the Russian discipline of 'Culturology' (*kul'turologiia*), the proponents of which are inspired by nineteenth and early twentieth-century Russian thinkers for whom reflection on Russian history and culture was central. Critics of Russian Culturology suggest that Culturologists treat culture in a speculative and unscientific manner and, in the process, reinforce common-sense notions about Russian national characteristics and the related idea that Russia requires its own special path of development and a foreign policy that is independent of Western countries (Malinova, 2007). Moreover, Culturology, while purporting to be a scientific study of the general laws of cultural evolution and national spiritual culture, has figured prominently in Russia's post-Soviet education curricula as a means to valorise Russian culture and norms (Scherrer, 2013). Affinities exist between academic and official political understandings of Russian cultural difference in post-Soviet Russia.

Cultural essentialists suggest that Russia is incapable of existing in a form other than that of a great power and offer 'cultural explanations' of Russian foreign policy, whereby the decision making of Russian state representatives are predicated on invariant cultural traits (see Tsygankov, 2012). Such scholars suggest that after the brief interregnum of the Yeltsin years, during which Russia embraced the West, pluralist norms and free-market capitalism, the Putin era signified a return to the more recognisable features of the Russian mentality. This line of thinking deems a centralised and unaccountable political authority, the weakness or absence of rule of law and the institution of private property, and a great power mentality coloured by messianism as intrinsically Russian features derived from history, geography, culture and religion (Kuchins, 2009). Critics of Putin-era Russia such as Pipes (2004) argue that under Putin the Russian state has resumed its *inherently* imperialist and expansionist nature, satiating a complicit population that seeks security in greatness. For Legvold (2007), Russian *derzhavnost* – great power standing – resonates across the post-Soviet Russian political spectrum and constitutes a *syndrome* that dates back to 'the beginning' of Russia. Similarly, a commitment to achieving great power status is in fact a cultural archetype which shapes Russian perceptions of the country's role in the international sphere, irrespective of its own internal conditions. Geopolitical position, military capabilities, resources, intellectual and spiritual potential give a timeless quality to Russian great power status (E. Batalov in Shakleyina & Bogaturov, 2004, p. 49; Shlapentokh, 2001). Amongst some Eurasianists, Russia is believed to be predisposed to expansion with an 'historical genetic code for empire building' (Shlapentokh, 2007, p. 230). Such arguments proceed from the position that there is something inherent in the Russian national character inimical to the pursuit of democracy and associated norms and attitudes, with a pursuit of territorial expansion necessitating a centralised, if not autocratic, structure and cultural chauvinism.

According to proponents of constructivist and 'ideational' forms of analysis, Russia's international conduct has been predicated historically on its self-image as a great power (Hancock, 2007; Hopf, 2005). One variation on this theme holds that the idea of great power is central to Russia's understanding of itself vis-à-vis the West since the early nineteenth century. The early to middle years of Putin's first two presidential terms can be characterised as being influenced by a great-power normaliser identity, which consists of a concentration on state authority, cooperation with the West, and the projection of influence in the former Soviet region (Tsygankov, 2005; 2006; 2007). For constructivists, great power status is determined by prevailing international norms and recognition by other great powers. A liberal reading of this position holds that international institutions and new forms of governance are necessitated by the patterns of interdependence which result from globalising processes. These institutions socialise weaker states into the acceptance of such norms (Hurrell, 2006). Since the mid-nineteenth century, the Russian state has failed in achieving recognition as a great power from the 'civilised' powers due to its inability to adopt indirect rule as a rationality of governing. Putin's statist tendencies are coming at precisely such a time that Western Europe has abandoned norms of state sovereignty (Neumann, 2008). A similar view might contend that the Russian state's attempt to firmly demarcate a 'modern' political subjectivity by appealing to exclusive forms of nationalism in the midst of post-modern capitalism is anachronistic (Morozov, 2008). One line of constructivist thinking holds that after an initial overtly liberal period, Putin began to bring policy and ideology more in line with the Russian 'public political ideal', a notion that stresses the centrality of a powerful state possessing broad responsibilities in politics and economics, including owning major industrial sectors and raising national living standards (Lukin, 2009).

Cultural essentialist and constructivist positions on Russian culture, ideas and identity are largely silent on the material dimension of Russian economic practices. Political economy approaches that seek to understand social and political totalities according to semiotic factors – meanings shared by a particular social group and conditioned by shared cultural and historical experience – as well as extra-semiotic (social and material) factors without reducing meaning to either exclusively are well-equipped to assess the culture–state–capital nexus in contemporary political and economic projects (Jessop & Sum, 2001; Cox, 1986; 2002; Germain, 2011). Regime practices in Putin-era Russia suggest that neo-liberal economic practices, national cultural representations and appeals to nationalism are not antithetical (Harmes, 2012; Kangas, 2013).

To recapitulate, during the Putin era, Russian officials have produced a relatively coherent set of concepts about world order that functions as a form of regime-sanctioned, common-sense thinking about global affairs to rival liberal internationalism. Surkov has been central to this, contributing to a Russian public political philosophy that seeks to challenge American hegemony.[2] Throughout, we can see powerful ambiguities within Russian state and society whereby the hegemonic position of the United States as steward of global capitalism has been challenged in spite of the fact that the Russian political economy is increasingly capitalist and integrated within structures of the capitalist global political economy, albeit with considerable 'statist' overtones. Surkov has contributed to such common-sense thinking, cultivating a 'home grown' vernacular to express dissatisfaction with the fundamental premises of liberal internationalism and American hegemony. Surkov can be considered an 'organic intellectual' (Gramsci, 1971) and regime supporting political technologist (see Chapter 2). Both the Putin regime and Surkov selectively utilise Russian culture to circumscribe the field in which debate occurs and in which political life is to be comprehended. In so doing they display the trappings of Gramsci's notion of common sense, shaping and constraining perception through the appeal to a 'chaotic aggregate of disparate conceptions' (Gramsci, 1971, p. 422). The concepts associated with commonsensical thinking exhibit enough consistency to mould public political consciousness while bending commonly held suspicions about national and international political and social life to serve regime imperatives.

Hegemonic projects have at their base networked organic intellectuals, who perform ideological functions from embedded social positions (de Graaff & van Apeldoorn, 2011; van Apeldoorn & de Graaff, 2012a; 2012b). Hence, ideas associated with hegemonic projects are more than merely 'discursive' in nature: they come from organic (and public) intellectuals who have the capacity to mobilise material and human resources to suit their political and economic aims in a manner that is consistent with their class positions. When examining Putin-era, Kremlin-sanctioned discourse, it is insufficient to perform a frequency count of 'buzzwords' contained in speeches, press releases and the like (Godzimirski, 2008). We can proceed on the assumption that the project to which the buzzwords are referring and which they are insulating has concrete social and economic dimensions.

A deeper examination of the Russian state's management of state-directed capitalism, its facilitating of Russia's uneven entry into global capitalism, its corresponding efforts to attenuate profound social conflict beginning in the 1990s, and particular manifestations of the Russian 'state–capital nexus' can be found in Chapter 3 of this work. The present chapter takes as its point of departure that such a project necessitates a 'home grown' ideology. As a Kremlin-affiliated official and political technologist, Surkov has contributed to the larger historical project of further distancing Putin-era ideology from Soviet internationalism by representing multipolarity in the global political economy as taking place on material (state–state) and cultural (civilisation–civilisation) terrain and largely devoid of class inequality. Surkov is a self-styled public intellectual who sought to cement Russian society's transition to a market economy under the aegis of the Russian state by synthesising notions about Russian culture, if not civilisation, its 'sovereign' nature vis-à-vis the USA, and its 'alternative' development model. Surkov valorised the cultural parameters of Russia's historical development trajectory alongside bending the more speculative aspects of the Russian philosophical tradition to suit the more productive and utilitarian ends of state-directed capitalism. One of Surkov's primary regime functions was to steer talk of Russia's unique 'path' and culture from speculative excesses and to discursively link it with socially and economically productive conduct.

3 Vladislav Surkov, sovereign democracy, political technologies and Russia's rise

An examination of Surkov's trajectory demonstrates his deep ties to the structures of Russian capitalism and the Russian state. During the first decade of the 2000s, Surkov rose to prominence as the Kremlin's chief ideologist (OSC Media Aid, 2008). Surkov served in Russian military intelligence (Vitebskaya et al., 2006), held senior positions at both Menatep and Alfa Bank during the 1990s, and served as a Deputy Chief of Staff of the Presidential Executive Office from 1999 to 2011, becoming First Deputy in 2008 ('Vladislav Yureyvich Surkov', n.d.). In a 2005 survey of Russian political elites he was named as the second most powerful man in Russia ('Spiegel Interview with Kremlin Boss Vladislav Surkov', 2005). As the Kremlin's *eminence grise*, Surkov was active in numerous political circles and public fora as a promoter of the sanctity of the Russian state and advocate for the contemporary unity of the Russian nation. It is difficult to overstate Surkov's role in relaying Kremlin ideology to the Russian public during the Putin era (Tretyakov, 2006). He has also been referred to as 'the godfather of United Russia' (Radzikhovsky, 2006), having served as the Kremlin's watchdog over the party (Levchenko, 2007) and having argued that a hegemonic United Russia is necessary for Russian economic and political stability (Romanov, 2008; 'Transcript of Surkov Speech', 2009). Surkov's post-2011 trajectory is considered in the subsequent section.

In addition to his formal roles, Surkov harbours literary ambitions. He is widely credited with writing the fictional book *Almost Zero*. Officially penned in 2008 by 'Nathan Dubovitsky', Surkov's pseudonym, *Almost Zero* has been interpreted to be a key to the post-modern relativism, logical inconsistencies and cynicism with which Surkov treats the construction of official Kremlin ideology. For the likes of Pomerantsev (2014a), Surkov's world is one in which literary tropes, public relations strategies and national systems management bleed into one another. In the process, disparate political positions cohere and are co-opted into state strategy: conservatism and liberalism, ultra-nationalism and leftist sentiments, Orthodoxy and autocracy can be accommodated under the umbrella of the Kremlin.

Surkov published widely and allegedly had ambitions to become Russia's foremost contemporary public philosopher. He sought to make contemplation serve a productive purpose, by marrying philosophical themes with the developmental imperatives facing the contemporary Russian political economy. For example, while releasing a collection of essays entitled *Texts 97–07*, [3] Surkov admonished philosophers to turn their speculations towards useful ends (Samarina, 2008). Surkov performed his philosophical functions as one with deep ties to official Russia, incorporating and synthesising disparate ideas into polysemic concepts for the purposes of dominating discursive space. Malashenko (2008) detects both a more moderate, reformist and modernising dimension and a neofundamentalist, anti-democratic apology for isolationism and tsarism in Surkov's work. Surkov's ambiguity is further evident in the wide array of criticisms and accolades granted to him by Russian public figures and intellectuals.[4]

Sovereign democracy, arguably Surkov's most enduring contribution to the Russian, if not the global, political lexicon, is a polysemic concept that incorporates a number of ideas frequently associated with Russia's rise and return to 'great power' status, including multipolarity and civilisational difference. Its basic premise is that only a handful of powerful states are truly sovereign and that hegemonic states 'manage' weaker ones. It serves as critical commentary on Western liberal universalism, seeking, in turn, to universalise the sovereign right of all states to choose national development systems and not be subject to interference by other states or Western cultural hegemony. It pilfers from Eurasianism – a body of work insisting upon Russia's essential geo-cultural difference – while sanitising it for the Putin regime's purpose of legitimating Russia's political system on the basis of Russian cultural attributes. Consistent with the Putin regime's speculation on the contemporary basis for Russian great power, sovereign democracy admonishes Russians to marshal intellectual, productive, moral and creative powers in the service of Russian national development initiatives. Sovereign democracy represents an attempt to foster productive civic solidarity under a consolidated Russian state apparatus (see also Okara, 2007).

One may note a longer post-Soviet Russian debate on sovereignty (Sakwa, 2012). However, sovereign democracy acquired particular significance during Putin's first two presidential administrations. Surkov's first article on sovereign democracy, titled 'Sovereignty is a Political Synonym for Competitiveness', appeared first on United Russia's official site in February 2006. While Surkov is widely credited with the term, it was first used by Vitaly Tretyakov (Belousov, 2012), emerging as an 'orange technology' used by the Kremlin to conceptualise the 2004–2005 Orange Revolution in Ukraine and critique geopolitical maneuvering by liberal, mature capitalist democracies on Russia's periphery. As such, it is a central technology in the Kremlin's 'preventive counter-revolution' strategy of the mid-2000s (Krastev, 2007), by which it sought to insulate itself and allied regimes on its periphery from the encroachment of regimes with geostrategic and geo-economic ties to the West.

Sovereign democracy was an integral part of Putin's ambitious 'symbolic policy' of reconstructing Russia's national identity (Malinova, 2013), reflecting the Kremlin's desire to 'democratise' democracy – relativising the criteria to be considered as constituting democracy so as to weaken the West's monopoly on the term (Sakwa, 2012; Averre, 2007). A discourse theory analysis might demonstrate that sovereign democracy was integral to the 'discursive stabilisation' of Russian politics under Putin, displaying hegemonic ('the expansion of a discourse in an attempt to domesticate more and more signifiers') and populist qualities (pinning 'the people against an institutional system, which is unable or unwilling to satisfy demands' while uniting demands under one name). Russia as a sovereign democracy is sovereign insofar as its particular traits 'exempt it from international comparison or judgement' (Casula, 2013, p. 6; see also Hayoz, 2009). Analysing sovereign democracy as a securitising discourse (Hudson, 2009) and from a broadly post-structural position (Casula & Perovic, 2009) can demonstrate how the term is part of the Kremlin's attempt to dominate discursive space. Constructivist analysis highlights the extent to which both sovereignty and democracy are culturally, socially and historically determined and emphasised the Russian concepts' relative difference from their Western cognates (Ziegler, 2012). However, both positions have little to say about sovereign democracy's relationship to economic practice in the person of Surkov.

Some argue that as an organising concept sovereign democracy reached its apex during Putin's first two presidencies and is now largely obsolete (Belousov, 2012; Casula, 2013). However, the term has seeped deeply into the Russian vernacular and remains a descriptor used by Russian commentators. Valery Fyodorov, the Director General of the Russian Public Opinion Research Center (VCIOM) suggested in 2013 that sovereign democracy resonates with a majority of Russians insofar as it is preferred to monarchic or Soviet ideologies and it captures that Russian democracy 'is different and … will always differ from its Western analogue'. In the foreword to Surkov's *Texts, 1997–2010*, Gleb Pavlovsky, a prominent political technologist, wrote that the emergence of Surkov irritated Russia's foes, as it demonstrated the Kremlin's newly found 'discursive activity'. Pavlovksy suggested that the use of Surkov's term positively by US Vice President Joe Biden in 2010 signified the extent to which sovereign democracy had become common parlance in *global* political discourse (in Surkov, 2011, pp. 3–4).

One may situate Surkov amongst a wider web of Kremlin-friendly political technologists who were responsible for mobilising concepts for then contemporary political and economic debates. Such individuals include Pavlovsky, long-time adviser to the president, President of the think tank 'The Foundation for Effective Politics' and former host of NTV's programme *Real Politics*; Konstantin Ernst, director of the Russian television channel *Pervyi* (Channel One); Sergei Markov, Kremlin-associated political analyst and director of the Moscow-based Institute of Political Studies; Konstantin Kostin and Aleksei Chesnakov, assistants to Surkov; and Valery Fadeyev, editor-in-chief of *Ekspert*, a weekly magazine aimed at Russia's upper middle class (see Sharafutdinova, 2012). Indeed, the article 'Nationalization of the Future', arguably Surkov's most elaborate treatment of sovereign democracy, was first published in *Ekspert*. Surkov's publicly espoused ideas emerged as part of an ideological strategy conceived by Kremlin-friendly political technologists, one component of which involved an inner series of loyalists – journalists, experts, academics and politicians – who 'explain the basic propaganda postulates'.[5] Another component is an outer circle whose members then relayed the idea of sovereign democracy to a variety of public contexts (Belousov, 2012). The end result is that sovereign democracy has become unleashed into the virtual sphere. By the end of 2009, Russian search engine

Yandex had two million citations for sovereign democracy; Google had one million (Belousov, 2012, p. 63).

Through his writings and speeches, Surkov provides a Russian critique of liberal universalism, American unipolarity and polyarchic regime change, seeking to sanctify Russia's place within a global political order of sovereign powers. He mobilises Russian cultural content for the purposes of national development and appeals to Russian cultural particularity to restore civic pride and insulate the Putin regime against allegations of authoritarianism. Surkov weds well understood concepts in Russian cultural, literary and intellectual production to the restoration of Russian sovereignty, Russia's purportedly unique democratic character, and the need for civic responsibility in the construction of a modern great Russia that is competitive in the capitalist global political economy. More than an apologist for authoritarianism, Surkov performs a pedagogical role: admonishing the Russian citizenry to participate actively in Russian political and economic life and abstain from pursuing the easy riches of resource rents or state patrimony. In short, Surkov foregrounds political economy and aspirations for Russian national development in his conversations about Russian culture.

Surkov legitimated Russia's post-Soviet turn to state guided capitalism and sought to defuse any strident calls from the Russian public for Soviet-style economic management. This must be understood as part of prominent political technologists' attempts to articulate Russian 'great power modernisation' – a comprehensive attempt on the part of the Russian state to resist Russia's marginalisation in the global political economy and its becoming a resource appendage of advanced economies. The 'knowledge-based economy' envisioned in 'Concept 2020' – the Russian government's most exhaustive formulation of its modernisation strategy – would be enabled by developing Russian human capital and technology, attracting foreign capital, promoting entrepreneurial activity, and increasing Russian foreign direct investment (FDI) abroad (see Chapter 3). The Russian state would play a coordinating role while attenuating social conflict and raising living standards. Surkov has frequently echoed the call for the development of Russia's human potential and its modernisation pursuits ('Surkov Calls for Russia's Intellectual Development', 2006), envisioning state-directed modernisation as a national development programme that can insulate Russia against self-enriching oligarchs, who prevent Russia's development (Ilyichev, 2006; Samarina, 2007). Notably, Surkov's initial contribution to the modernisation debate predates Concept 2020 and the presidency of Dmitry Medvedev, which is associated with a tilt towards liberal modernising discourse and practice. During a talk at the Russian State Humanities University, an institution renowned for producing Russian liberals, Surkov declared himself a 'beginning liberal' (Ilyichev, 2007). To the extent that Surkov may be declared a liberal, it is a highly conditional form of liberalism that subordinates concepts to the peculiar needs of a sovereign Russia seeking to overcome the 'anti-system' political practices evidenced by various strata of Russian society in the 1990s.

Surkov's article 'Sovereignty: The Political Synonym for Competitiveness' originated as a 2006 address to United Russia's Center for Party Studies and Personnel Training. It is an extended meditation on the dangers of oligarchic rule, Russia's 1990s economic collapse and the need for technological and economic modernisation. But Surkov is not nostalgic for the Soviet Union. In critiquing Russia's oligarchs of the 1990s and laying out a programme for the creation of a just, democratic and competitive society, Surkov suggests that 'social justice does not require yet another redistribution of property (why add one injustice to another?) – it needs the honest payment of taxes' (Surkov, 2011, p. 99). Somewhat paradoxically, perhaps, one international component of sovereignty for Surkov is Russia's integration in global systems on a competitive basis. He writes:

> Sovereignty is not Fortress Russia… We're not going and locking up our huts and drinking vodka from morning until night, with the door bolted shut and not even an idea what our neighbors look like. No! Sovereignty is openness, it's an entryway into the world, it's participation in this open battle. I'd say that sovereignty is the political synonym for competitiveness.
> (in Surkov, 2011, p. 103)

Central to the notion of sovereign democracy is the idea that Russia retains the ability to conduct its own internal affairs and develop a political system while remaining free from external influence. This is in contradistinction to the 1990s, when, according to Surkov and defenders of the sovereign democracy idea, Russia was considered incapable of making its own sovereign decisions due to Western interference. In Surkov's estimation, any semblance of independence enjoyed by Russians during this period was mitigated by the fact that most were incapable of fully exercising their freedom (Zakatnova, 2006a). It is in this context that Russian reforms gave democracy pejorative connotations for many Russians as the concept was associated with reckless free market reforms and deemed detrimental to sovereignty and national well-being. According to Andrey Isayev, a prominent United Russia member, the utility of the term sovereign democracy is to be found in its serving as a corrective to the notion of democracy evident in Russia during the 1990s during its time of 'national humiliation' (in Samarina & Varshavchik, 2006). According to Surkov, all objections to Russia's purported drift from democracy in suppressing 'colour revolutions' on its periphery have malicious intent behind them, including securing Russia's resources (Yevgrafova, 2006). Surkov draws from an unlikely source – Che Guevara – to demonstrate the need for both political sovereignty and economic independence in the contemporary world order (Zakatnova, 2006b). Sovereign democracy constitutes 'a liberalization of international relations and a de-monopolization of the global economy. That, of course, annoys the planet's strongmen and monopolists' (Surkov, 2011, pp. 60–61). If sovereign democracy includes the promise of sovereignty from moral suasion, interference and belligerence on the part of Western capitalist democracies, it also calls for the expression of Russian popular sovereignty and seeks to legitimate the activities of the Russian state on this basis.

For Surkov, sovereign democracy is not simply characterised as freedom from external interference, as it necessitates civic engagement in political, social and economic processes. This is predicated on a civic-oriented interpretation of a rehabilitated Russian national cultural legacy. Sovereign democracy is designed as a tempered defence of unaccountable statism, insofar as the state exists as a manifestation of the collective will of the Russian nation. According to Surkov, Russia exhibits the formal trappings of a democracy (parties, a free media, elections) but lacks a populace that has a fully developed civic orientation (Zakatnova, 2006a). A consolidated and centralised Russian state served the necessary historic task of preserving Russian sovereignty against oligarchical self-enrichment but will remain legitimate in the future only insofar as it facilitates Russia's transition to the next stage of social, political and economic development (Surkov, 2008). Surkov has elaborated on the precise nation-building components needed to prevent an over-reliance on the state as the arbiter of the political good, distributor of economic resources and primary agent of development.

A sovereign democracy is animated through the creation of a national symbolic order. For Surkov, it is of paramount importance that Russians adopt their own ideology and system of meanings. The first step in Surkov's cultural programme is valorising Russian culture and suggesting that contemporary efforts to construct democracy and capitalism in Russia are necessarily constrained, if not determined, by cultural factors. According to Surkov (2006, p. 11), democracy 'is viable to the extent that it is natural – that is, national. Our democracy is viable if it does not reject Russian political culture but is part of it, developing not in defiance but together with it'. It is not simply democracy, but all political practices which must adapt to Russian conditions in order to survive. The reforms of Peter the Great, Paul I, Bolsheviks and the 1990s democratic reformers 'succeeded only insofar as they were perceived as native to Russia, as acceptable to Russian culture. Anything incompatible with the life of our culture or harmful to its foundation was painfully rejected' (Surkov, 2006, p. 18).

Culture determines the nature of political practice itself as well as the success which political initiatives are likely to experience. Surkov appropriates features of Eurasianist discourse through suggesting that though cultures interact and adapt according to the interactions of the societies that carry them, they are naturalistic phenomena with inborn limitations. Russian political culture therefore manifests several 'archetypical and ineradicable properties'. Quoting Russian intellectuals Ivan Il'in, Nikolai Berdyaev and Nikolai Trubetskoy, Surkov contrasts holistic 'Russian cultural consciousness' with the 'mechanistic, reductionist consciousness' of the West, concluding that cultural consciousness has a 'geopolitical subtext' (Surkov, 2006, p. 11).

According to Surkov, this propensity to holism is manifested in Russians' desire for wholeness – political, territorial and spiritual – through the centralisation of power. They adhere to a form of political idealism, whereby the ideal goal must be retained in order to animate social activity and a secular form of messianism – seeking a role for Russia in global affairs – is required to animate national political life. Finally, Russians support 'the personification of political institutions', whereby charismatic personality dominates (Surkov, 2006, pp. 12–14). Surkov seamlessly upholds the essential aspects of Russian culture while suggesting that these are not incompatible with regime imperatives. He writes

> culture is fate. God commanded us to be ethnic Russians [*russkie*] as well as citizens of Russia [*rossiiane*]. Such we shall remain. We will take the problems into account and exploit the advantages of our national character and our political culture to create a competitive economy and a viable democracy.
>
> (2006, p. 18)

For Surkov, Russian idealism is reflected in the propensity of Russians to seek easy solutions and engage in speculative excess. The following extended quote from Surkov (2006, p. 17) captures this notion.

> One acquaintance of mine says, 'What you can't do in two weeks, you can never do.' That's very much our way of thinking: everything, at once, here and now; two weeks, five hundred days, communism in 1980. If it doesn't work out, the idealist gets angry and falls prey to depression and to the cynicism of disillusionment. The Petrine reforms, the reveries of February 1917, Bolshevik megaprojects, perestroika [fall into this category], as do the liberal reforms, dreams of the marvelous Kitezh[6] of Russian capitalism. All are conducted in haste, bedazzled by an idea, in extraordinary irritation with viscous reality; in despairing certainty of the approaching collapse of the old world (the monarchy, bourgeois democracy, the Soviet regime) with its tedium, violence, poverty, and injustice; in naive hope of a splendid new life in which everyone will lie down for a well-deserved rest (earned through suffering) – leaving all work and all worry to the almighty doctrine, the world revolution, universal human values, the invisible hand of the market, and other magical spells. Such is the simple eschatology…
>
> Do it quickly, give us the soonest possible relief, so that we can return to contemplative torpidity.

Sovereign democracy is offered as that which corresponds most accurately with Russian political culture and what is required to guide the Russian nation to the next stage of development in spite of these limitations. One of Surkov's principal works, 'Russian political culture: the view from Utopia', begins as a treatise on national political culture and ends with a call to move Russia up the scale on the international division of labour. It does so by appealing to two notions. First, the international place of a nation is decided by cultural superiority, which serves as the condition for a series of epiphenomena. Second, Russia's cultural potential and its historic accomplishments are currently denigrated due to the country's inability to marshal its intellectual and human resources for the sake of economic output (Surkov, 2006, p. 23). Russia must harness cultural resources in order to successfully realise a transition to the post-industrial society and 'become the white-collar workers in the worldwide division of labour and occupy an important place in the global hierarchy' by pursuing idealistic goals pragmatically, acknowledging culture, science and education as crucial elements in the production process, supporting knowledge workers and attracting foreign experts (Surkov, 2006, pp. 25–26). In *Nationalization of the Future*, Surkov states, 'We are obliged to build the foundation of an innovative culture, a system for generating unique knowledge, since knowledge is power and the capital for the preservation of the people... We are obliged to convert out natural resources economy into an intellectual one in order to lay a path for Russia forward, into the future, toward the community of creative nations that sets the course of history' (Surkov, 2011, p. 71). After accepting a deterministic reading of Russian culture, Surkov then performs the second step to his cultural programme: correcting aspects of Russia's cultural tendencies that inhibit a globally competitive economy, industriousness, productivity and political systems building. While Russian political authority must reflect certain inborn characteristics of Russian culture, so too must it acknowledge the shortcomings of Russian culture when faced with the imperative of national development.

4 Sovereign democracy realised? Skolkovo, Volodin and beyond

The manner by which Surkov foregrounds discussions of national economic development in his musings on Russian culture suggests that his roles were charged with 'material' content even during the high water mark of sovereign democracy. Surkov's trajectory during Medvedev's presidency further substantiates the notion that he served important economic functions for the regime. At the end of 2009, Medvedev charged Surkov with heading a working group for building 'an autonomous complex for the development of research' – that which would eventually become the Skolkovo Innovation Complex. 'Skolkovo' is interesting precisely because it was designed as a state of exception within the Russian economy a ('territorially autonomous complex'), but whose scientific innovations could be scaled up to the level of the national economy for the purposes of creating a national innovation sector and 'moving [Russia] to the next stage of civilization'. Surkov stated that contrary to the closed science cities and academic towns of the Soviet Union, 'the new complex will have a social environment that is as open, international and, if you will, cosmopolitan as possible' (Glikin & Kostenko, 2010).

With tax and other incentives, Skolkovo was provided to harness 'cosmopolitan', internationally mobile, creative capital and 'domestic' Russian capital. Skolkovo therefore represents a particular instance of Russian state modernisation efforts. Part of Surkov's task in heading the working group was to render the 'transnational' aspects of the project acceptable to more skeptical elements of the Russian public. When asked why three foreign nationals were included in the initial Skolkovo working group, Surkov stated: 'We are doing it to show that it's all right and perfectly patriotic… We need to get the best people here, and whether they are ours or not is unimportant' (Glikin & Kostenko, 2010). Surkov insisted that a consolidated state mechanism was indispensable as an instrument for modernisation in the context of Skolkovo, suggesting that 'spontaneous modernization is a cultural phenomenon, and it was achieved only in Anglo-Saxon countries' (ibid.). Skolkovo represents a component of Russia's national development strategy that is predicated on inducing private investment by mobilising state resources and offering an attractive investment climate. Furthermore, it serves as an example of the Putin-era propensity of embedding a particular brand of market civilisation in Russia through appealing to a series of nationalist discourses (Kangas, 2013).

State funding for the innovation complex was approved upon a visit by then Kremlin officials, including Surkov, to the Massachusetts Institute of Technology in 2010 (Kramer, 2010). While Surkov administered the disbursement of state funds for the project, prominent businessman Viktor Vekselberg has directed the project from its beginning. Vekselberg is not a disinterested public steward of Russia's national economic modernisation, but one with broad international and domestic private economic interests. In the 1990s he started the holding company SUAL, which in 2007 merged with Rusal, a Russian aluminum maker and mining company Glencore to create UC Rusal, the world's largest aluminum producer. With a documented personal wealth of $17.5 Billion, Vekselberg is listed as the 51st wealthiest person in the world and third wealthiest in Russia by Forbes magazine. Since Skolkovo started in 2010, three of his companies received grants from the Skolkovo Fund ('Viktor Vekselberg," 2014). The 'statist' element of Skolkovo therefore must be put into perspective. The Skolkovo Innovation Complex and adjacent Skolkovo business school are joint efforts on the part of the Russian state and Russian private capital, suggesting a state–capital nexus not dissimilar from comparable private–public partnerships elsewhere in the world.

Surkov's Skolkovo legacy is tarnished. Surkov had an open conflict with the Russian Investigative Committee [IC] concerning a corruption probe into Skolkovo. Vladimir Markin, spokesman for the Russian Investigative Committee condemned Surkov for the remarks the latter made at the London School of Economics on May 1, 2013, during which time Surkov chastised the IC for its ongoing investigations into Skolkovo. Surkov resigned as deputy prime minister and government chief of staff on May 7, 2013 and was replaced as government chief of staff by Sergei Prikhodko, a purported Medvedev loyalist and 'trusty technocrat' (Earle, 2013). Surkov himself suggested that he tendered his resignation two weeks before on April 26, whereas Kremlin spokesman Dmitry Peskov told journalists that Surkov resigned on May 7 following

Putin publicly admonishing the government for its failure to implement his decrees ('Surkov's last stand', 2013; Weaver and Clover, 2013). Some analysts conclude that Surkov's ousting and alleged problems with the IC signify that *siloviki* hard-liners have gained ground over liberal figures such as Surkov in their place within the Kremlin and the Russian government ('Target: Surkov', 2013; Grushetsky, 2013).

The developments that occurred in May 2013 have their origins in December 2011, during which time Putin removed Surkov as the Kremlin's first deputy chief of staff and after which he was given the position of deputy prime minister in Medvedev's cabinet in a move widely considered a demotion. In the process, however, he was given responsibility for the state's modernisation strategy, a file which he had been not unfamiliar with in past years, as demonstrated above. Vyacheslav Volodin, purportedly a long-time rival of Surkov's, replaced Surkov as the Kremlin's first deputy chief of staff. Volodin is a long time Kremlin and United Russia loyalist. Having served in the Duma as a representative of the Fatherland All-Russia faction, in 2003 he was elected deputy Duma speaker and the first deputy head of United Russia's faction. In 2005 Volodin was elected general council of United Russia's secretary of the presidium. In 2007, under Chairman Gryzlov, Volodin was elected deputy chairman of United Russia. In October, 2010, Volodin was appointed deputy prime minister and chief of staff of the government's Executive Office ('Vyacheslav Volodin', n.d.).

For some, the shift from Surkov to Volodin represents the regime's dissatisfaction with Surkov's managerial style in light of the late 2011 anti-regime protests at Bolotnaya Square and Sahkarov Prospekt. Surkov had overseen the reduction of parties in the Russian Duma to seven, promoted regime-friendly opposition parties and mobilised various strata of Russian society towards expressing dissatisfaction with perceived anti-Russian biases. Surkov utilised PR techniques like having the youth group *Nashi* ('our own') harass the British ambassador, picket outside of the Estonian Embassy and burn books authored by Vladimir Sorokin, a frequent critic of the Putin regime. For some, Volodin represents a turn from the more symbolic PR gestures of Surkov to employing the full legal, administrative and coercive capacity of the Russian state ('Surkov's Departure as Paradigm Shift', 2013; Kolesnikov, 2013; Bovt, 2013).

In Volodin's opinion, anti-regime protestors in 2011 were not representative of the broader Russian population, but rather constituted the 'mink coats' of Russian society. Reflected in this notion is the idea commonly espoused by Putin in his third presidential term: protest, political economy and matters of the state have been decidedly couched in 'values' ('Meeting of the Valdai International Discussion Club', 2013). For domestic matters, gone is the playful post-modern cultural *bricolage* of Surkov. Volodin is for Putin a 'new weapon, effective if somewhat primitive, like a Kalashnikov' (Kolesnikov, 2012) and representative of a shift witnessed during Putin's third presidential term whereby the Putin regime has consolidated a support base around

Russian traditionalism and conservatism, elevated values and morality within official discourse and rejected the 'modern' West (Vasilyev, 2013). However, such thinking does not displace the challenges faced by Russian capitalism in the post-Soviet period.

5 Conclusion

While Surkov has seen his star fade in recent years, he remains a significant member of Russia's political elite. In September 2013 he was appointed a presidential aide for social and economic relations with Abkhazia and Ossetia, an appointment that was surprising given Surkov's then recent fall (Ryzhkov, 2013). In May 2014 Surkov mediated between now recently resigned Abkhaz President Alexander Ankvab and members of the opposition following protests against Ankvab during which protesters set on the presidential administration building in Sukhumi (Nechepurenko, 2014). Such a post does not fully explain the scope of Surkov's contemporary mandate, however. Alexei Makarkin, deputy head of the Center for Political Technologies, speculated in September 2013 that Surkov might handle Russia's relations with Ukraine (Sukhov, 2013). Indeed, during Russia's current conflict with Ukraine, Surkov can be seen being up to familiar tactics. In addition to being one of the first Russians hit with US sanctions, he has published under a pseudonym ('Nathan Dubovitsky') in the online journal *Russian Pioneer*, warning of the advent of a 'non-linear war' in Crimea (Dubovitsky, 2014; see also Pomerantsev, 2014b).

Speculations abound as to Surkov's precise role in the contemporary Ukraine crisis. His present role is probably best described as assistant to president Vladimir Putin on foreign affairs (Pomerantsev, 2014a). He is widely regarded in Western media as Putin's 'point man' in Ukraine (see, for example, Quinn-judge, 2015; 'Kremlin's Former Chief Ideologue to Participate in Minsk Talks', 2015; Walker, 2015), if not the source of more damning, if imprecise, indictments: serving as a 'guiding hand behind Russia's invasion of Ukraine and annexation of Crimea, inspiring the feverish media campaigns that have delivered near-universal support for those moves' (Khrushcheva, 2015) and directing 'foreign sniper groups' during the Maidan protests ('Poroshenko says evidence shows Kremlin aide Surkov directed snipers in Kiev', 2015). Moreover, he has been credited with managing the public image of separatist leaders in Eastern Ukraine (Pomerantsev, 2014c). He is reported to have taken part in ceasefire negotiations between Russia, Ukraine, Germany and France in Minsk, Belarus in February 2015 ('Poroshenko says evidence shows Kremlin aide Surkov directed snipers in Kiev', 2015; 'Kremlin's Former Chief Ideologue to Participate in Minsk Talks', 2015).

Surkov's centrality in contemporary geopolitical hotspots should indicate his continued relevance to the Russian executive. Amid his expressions of fondness for American counter-cultural figures, as indicated in the introduction of this work, one should not lose sight of his larger contributions to Russian state-directed capitalism and post-American hegemonic multipolarity.

Surkov's legacy is as a once prominent and still relevant Russian state representative and self-declared public philosopher who has mobilised state-sanctioned representations of Russia and world order amid transitions to state-directed capitalism. Surkov was central in a mechanism that espoused the Kremlin line for Russian elite and public consumption, valorising a domestic and geopolitical identity that emphasised the cultural foundations of national political and economic systems while bending speculation on Russian cultural traits to utilitarian ends in line with state modernisation initiatives. Moving beyond cultural essentialist, ideational, or discursive analyses enables us to explore Surkov's broader economic function in Russian national political economy projects.

Along with political technologists Surkov has developed and activated novel concepts to express dissatisfaction with the advent of American influence into Russia's historical periphery and mythologised a powerful, sovereign state capable of resisting attempts at management by external forces and attenuating social conflict within Russia. He has sanctified the universal sovereign right of all states to choose their national development systems, which are derived from particular cultural systems, celebrating the cultural particularity of Russia while simultaneously attempting to redirect talk of Russian culture towards more productive and industrious ends. Finally, in appealing to the 'cultural' basis of political economy, Surkov has contributed to simplifying, if not obfuscating, the complex state–capital nexus facilitating, or impeding, Russian national development efforts toward modernisation.

Notes

1 I reject the distinction offered by Petras (1990) between organic and institutionalised intellectuals, with the former being reserved for grassroots intellectuals who serve a counterhegemonic function.
2 During periods of strong hegemonic leadership, 'concepts of control' – the world view of a particular hegemonic class, which is embedded to define the limits of the possible for society at large (van der Pijl, 1998, p. 51) – are prevalent and innocuous.
3 Evropa Publishing House later released Surkov's *Texts, 1997–2010*, an expanded version of the work.
4 See for example the broad range of responses from regime stalwarts and political technologists elicited by one of Surkov's programmatic articles, 'Russian Political Culture: The View from Utopia', in *Russian Politics and Law* (2006).
5 Belousov counts amongst them Sergei Ivanov, Yuri Luzhkov, Valentina Matvienko, Boris Gryzlov, Vitaly Tretyakov, Andranik Migranian, Dmitrii Orlov, Valery Fadeev, Sergei Glazyev, Vasili Ivanov, Mikhail Sokolov, Viacheslav Nikonov and Dmitrii Badovskii (p. 59).
6 Kitezh is a town in Russian folklore, mythical for having resisted a Mongol invasion by submerging into Svetloyar Lake.

References

Averre, D. (2007). Sovereign democracy and Russia's relations with the European Union. *Demokratizatsiya*, 15(2), 173–190.

Belousov, A. (2012). Political propaganda in contemporary Russia. *Russian Politics & Law* 50(3), 56–69.

Bilevskaya, E., & Aleksandra, S. (2008). United Russia to update party program. World News Connection.

Bodin, P., Hedlund, S., & Namli, E. (Eds.). (2012). *Power and legitimacy – Challenges from Russia*. London; New York: Routledge.

Bovt, G. (2013). After Surkov. *Current Digest of the Post-Soviet Press*, 65(19), 3–5.

Brown, A., & Whitefield, S. (Eds.). (2005). *Political culture and Post-Communism*. New York: Palgrave MacMillan.

Casula, P. (2013). Sovereign democracy, populism, and depoliticization in Russia. *Problems of Post-Communism*, 60(3), 3.

Casula, P., & Perovic, J. (Eds.). (2009). *Identities and politics during the Putin presidency: The foundations of Russia's stability.* Stuttgart: Ibidem-Verl Press.

Cox, R. (1986). Social forces, states and world orders: Beyond international relations theory. In R. Keohane (Ed.), *Neoliberalism and its critics* (pp. 255–300). New York: Columbia University Press.

Cox, R. (2002). *The political economy of a plural world: Critical reflections on power, morals and civilisation*. London: Routledge.

de Graaff, N., & van Apeldoorn, B. (2011). Varieties of US post-Cold War imperialism: Anatomy of a failed hegemonic project and the future of US geopolitics. *Critical Sociology*, 37(4), 403–427.

Dolinskiy, A. (2013). A complicated fate of Skolkovo. Retrieved from http://valdaiclub.com/economy/59500.html. Accessed 22 July 2014.

Dubovitsky, N. (2014, March 12). Bez Neba (Without the Sky). *Rus Pioneer.* Retrieved from www.ruspioner.ru/honest/m/single/4131. Accessed 22 July 2014.

Earle, J. (2013). Surkov replaced by trusty technocrat. *Current Digest of the Post-Soviet Press*, 65(2), 9.

Etkind, A., & Shcherbak, A. (2008). The double monopoly and its technologists: The Russian preemptive counterrevolution. *Demokratizatsiya*, 16(3), 229–239.

Fyodorov, V. (2013). Russian identity and the challenges of the time. Retrieved from http://valdaiclub.com/culture/61340.html. Accessed 22 July 2014.

Germain, R. (2011). New Marxism and the problem of subjectivity: Towards a critical and historical International Political Economy. In S. Shields, I. Bruff, & H. Macartney (Eds.), *Critical International Political Economy: Dialogue, debate and dissensus* (pp. 61–79). Basingstoke, UK: Palgrave Macmillan.

Glikin, M., & Kostenko, N. (2010). A miracle could happen. *Current Digest of the Post-Soviet Press*, 62(7), 9–11.

Godzimirski, J. (2008). Putin and Post-Soviet identity: Building blocks and buzzwords. *Problems of Post-Communism*, 55(5), 14–27.

Gramsci, A. (1971). *Selections from the prison notebooks.* London: Lawrence & Wishart.

Grushetsky, X. (2013). How to recruit an Agent without really trying and the demise of a puppet master. *Current Digest of the Post-Soviet Press*, 65(19), 2.

Hancock, K. (2007). Russia: Great power image versus economic reality. *Asian Perspectives*, 31(4), 71–98.

Harmes, A. (2012). The rise of neoliberal nationalism. *Review of International Political Economy*, 19(1), 59–86.

Hayoz, N. (2009). Russian "sovereign democracy": A powerful ideological discourse in a quasi-authoritarian regime. In P. Casula & J. Perovic (Eds.), *Identities and politics during the Putin presidency: The foundations of Russia's stability* (pp. 125–147). Stuttgart: Ibidem-Verlag.

Hopf, T. (2005). Identity, legitimacy, and the use of military force: Russia's great power identities and military intervention in Abkhazia. *Review of International Studies*, 31(s1), 225–243.

Hudson, V. (2009). Sovereign democracy as a discourse of Russian identity. In P. Casula & J. Perovic (Eds.), *Identities and politics during the Putin presidency: The foundations of Russia's stability* (pp. 189–210). Stuttgart: Ibidem-Verlag

Hurrell, A. (2006). Hegemony, liberalism and global order: What space for would-be great powers? *International Affairs*, 82(1), 1–19.

Ilyichev, G. (2006). This isn't some Philology club – Vladislav Surkov insists on continued discussion of the essence of sovereign democracy. *Current Digest of the Post-Soviet Press*, 58(38), 6–7.

Ilyichev, G. (2007). Evolution of Putin's aide Surkov's sovereign democracy principle viewed. World News Connection.

Jenson, J. (2010). Diffusing ideas for and after neoliberalism: The social investment perspective in Europe and Latin America. *Global Social Policy*, 10(1), 59–84.

Jessop, B., & Sum, N. (2001). Pre-disciplinary and post-disciplinary perspectives. *New Political Economy*, 6(1), 89–101.

Kangas, A. (2013). Market civilisation meets economic nationalism: the discourse of nation in Russia's modernisation. *Nations and Nationalism*, 19(3), 572–591.

Keohane, R., (Ed.). (1986). *Neorealism and its critics*. New York: Columbia University Press.

Kolesnikov, A. (2012). All the lone king's men. *Current Digest of the Post-Soviet Press*, 64(49), 3–7.

Kolesnikov, A. (2013). Surkov's last word. *Current Digest of the Post-Soviet Press*, 65(19), 3–5.

Konsepsiya dolgosrochnovo sotsial'no- ekonomicheskvo razvitiya Rossiyskoy federatsii na period do 2020 goda. (Concept of the Long-term Social and Economic Development of the Russian Federation for the Period until 2020). (2008). Retrieved from www.economy.gov.ru/wps/wcm/myconnect/economylib/mert/resources/3879cd804ab8615ab426fc4234375027/kdr_171108.doc. Accessed 20 November 2008.

Krastev, I. (2007, 17 November). Russia as the 'other Europe'. *Russia in Global Affairs*. Retrieved from http://eng.globalaffairs.ru/number/n_9779.

Kramer, A. E. (2010, 10 April). Innovation, by order of the Kremlin. *The New Times*. Retrieved from www.nytimes.com/2010/04/11/business/global/11russia.html.

Kremlin's former chief ideologue to participate in Minsk talks. (2015, 10 February). *The Moscow Times*. Retrieved from http://www.themoscowtimes.com/article/515687.html.

Khrushcheva, N. (2015, 23 June). Behind the Kremlin's theatre of fear, an agitprop master. *The Globe and Mail*. Retrieved from http://www.theglobeandmail.com/globe-debate/behind-the-kremlins-theatre-of-fear-an-agitprop-master/article25065866.

Kuchins, A. (2009). Why Russia is So Russian. *Current History*, 108(720).

Lane, D. (2008). From chaotic to state-led capitalism. *New Political Economy*, 13(2), 177–184.

Lane, D. (2013). *The capitalist transformation of state socialism: The making and breaking of state socialist society, and what followed*. New York: Routledge.

Legvold, R. (2007) Russian foreign policy during periods of great state transformation. In R. Legvold (Ed.), *Russian foreign policy in the twenty-first century and the shadow of the past*. (pp. 77–143). New York: Columbia University Press.

Levchenko, A. (2007, 12 November). Surkov holds confidential meeting with United Russia deputies. World News Connection.

Lukin, A. (2009). Russia's new authoritarianism and the post-Soviet political ideal. *Post-Soviet Affairs*, 25(1), 66–92.

Meeting of the Valdai International Discussion Club. (2013, 19 September). President of the Russian Federation: Novgorod. Retrieved from http://eng.kremlin.ru/news/6007.

Malashenko, A. (2008). From Suslov to Surkov. *Russian Politics and Law*, 46(5), 67.

Malinova, O. (2007). 'Political culture' in Russian scholarly and public discourse. *Russian Politics and Law*, 45(3), 31.

Malinova, O. (2013). Russia and 'the West' in the 2000s: Redefining Russian identity in official political discourse. In R. Taras (Ed.), *Russia's identity in international relations: Images, perceptions, misperceptions* (pp. 73–90). London; New York: Routledge.

Morozov, V. (2008). Sovereignty and democracy in contemporary Russia: A modern subject faces the post-modern world. *Journal of International Relations and Development*, 11(2), 152–180.

Motalev, A. (2008, June 3). Russia: Surkov sees establishment of four party system as 'natural,' desirable. World News Connection.

Nechepurenko, I. (2014, May 28). Moscow steps in as arbiter in Abkhaz conflict. *The Moscow Times*. Retrieved from www.themoscowtimes.com/news/article/moscow-steps-in-as-arbiter-in-abkhaz-conflict/501098.html.

Neumann, I. (2008). Russia's standing as a Great Power, 1494–1815. In T. Hopf (Ed.), *Russia's European Choice* (pp. 13–34). New York: Palgrave MacMillan.

Okara, A. (2007, August 8). Sovereign democracy: A new Russian idea or a PR project? *Russia in Global Affairs*, 2. Retrieved from http://eng.globalaffairs.ru/number/n_9123.

OSC Media Aid: Russia – profile of Surkov. (2008, 8 August). World News Connection.

Perovic, J., & Casula, P. (2009). The stabilisation of Russia during the Putin presidency. In P. Casula & J Perovic (Eds.), *Identities and politics during the Putin presidency* (pp. 19–30). Stuttgart: Ibidem-Verlag.

Petras, J. (1990). The metamorphosis of Latin America's intellectuals. *Latin American Perspectives*, 17(2), 102–112.

Pipes, R. (2004). Flight from freedom: What Russians think and want. *Foreign Affairs*, 83(3), 9–15.

Pomerantsev, P. (2014a, 7 November). The hidden author of Putinism. *The Atlantic*. Retrieved from http://www.theatlantic.com/international/archive/2014/11/hidden-author-putinism-russia-vladislav-surkov/382489. Accessed on 23 July 2014.

Pomerantsev, P. (2014b, 5 May). How Putin is reinventing warfare. *Foreign Policy*. Retrieved from www.foreignpolicy.com/articles/2014/05/05/how_putin_is_reinventing_warfare.

Pomerantsev, P. (2014c, 11 December). Russia's ideology: There is no truth. *The New York Times*. Retrieved from http://www.nytimes.com/2014/12/12/opinion/russias-ideology-there-is-no-truth.html.

Poroshenko says evidence shows Kremlin aide Surkov directed snipers in Kiev. (2015, 20 February). *Reuters*. Retrieved from http://www.reuters.com/article/2015/02/20/us-ukraine-crisis-surkov-idUSKBN0LO1B620150220.

Quinn-judge, P. (2015, 27 July). Rebel infighting bringing chaos to East Ukraine. *The Moscow Times*. Retrieved from http://www.themoscowtimes.com/opinion/article/rebel-infighting-bringing-chaos-to-east-ukraine/526305.html.

Radzikhovsky, L. (2006). Russia: commentary views Kremlin ideologist Surkov's 'sovereign bureaucracy' idea. World News Co*nnection.*

RFERL. (2013, 15 May). Surkov's last stand. RFERL. Retrieved from www.rferl.org/content/surkovs-last-stand/24987291.html. Accessed 11 October 2013.

RFERL. (2013, 23 May). Target: Surkov. RFERL. Retrieved from www.rferl.org/content/target-surkov/24995478.html. Accessed 11 October 2013.

Romanov, I. (2008). Vladislav Surkov joins in United Russia debate on what constitutes an elite. World News Connection.

Rossiya 2020: Glavniye Zadachi Razivitiya Ctrany ('Russia 2020: Main Objectives for the Country'). (2008). Moscow: Evropa Publishing.

Ryzhkov, V. (2013, 8 October). Same old Kremlin, same old Surkov. *The Moscow Times.* Retrieved from www.themoscowtimes.com/opinion/article/same-old-kremlin-same-old-surkov/487354.html. Accessed 26 June 2014.

Russia's Putin plans to bring back grey cardinal, newspaper says. (2013). Reuters. Retrieved from http://www.reuters.com/article/2013/08/20/us-russia-surkov-idUSBRE97J06B20130820. Accessed 11 October 2013.

Sakwa, R. (2008). Russian political culture through the eyes of Vladislav Surkov: Guest editor's introduction. *Russian Politics and Law*, 46(5), 3–7.

Sakwa, R. (2012). Sovereignty and democracy: Constructions and contradictions in Russia and beyond. *Region: Regional Studies of Russia, Eastern Europe, and Central Asia*, 1(1), 3–27.

Samarina, A. (2007). Vladislav Surkov textbook offers new 'development model' for Russia. World News Connection.

Samarina, A. (2008, April 30). 'Strategy-2020' roundtable welcomes pragmatic approach of Kremlin aide Vladislav Surkov. World News Connection.

Samarina, A., Moshkin, M., Romanov, I. & Kostenko, N. (2006). Sovereign democracy in danger. *Current Digest of the Post-Soviet Press*, 58(47), 7.

Samarina, A., & Varshavchik, S (2006, September 3). Russia: Surkov explains 'sovereign democracy' at roundtable, others comment. World News Connection.

Scherrer, J. (2013). The 'cultural/civilisational Turn' in post-Soviet identity duilding. In P. Bodin, S. Hedlund, & E. Namli (Eds.), *Power and legitimacy: Challenges from Russia* (pp. 152–168). Routledge: Contemporary Russia and Eastern Europe Series.

Shakleyina, T., & Bogaturov, A. (2004). The Russian realist school of international relations. *Communist and Post Communist Studies*, 37(1), 37–51.

Sharafutdinova, G. (2012). The limits of the matrix. *Problems of Post-Communism*, 59(3), 17–30.

Shlapentokh, D. (2001). Russian nationalism today: The views of Alexander Dugin. *Contemporary Review*, 279(1626), 29–37.

Shlapentokh, D. (2007). Dugin Eurasianism: A window on the minds of the Russian elite or an intellectual ploy? *Studies in Eastern European Thought*, 59(3), 215–236.

Shields, S., Bruff, I., & Macartney, H. (Eds.). (2011). *Critical International Political Economy: dialogue and dissensus.* New York, NY: Palgrave Macmillan.

Spiegel interview with Kremlin boss Vladislav Surkov: The West doesn't have to love us. (2005). Retrieved from www.spiegel.de/international/spiegel/0,1518,361236,00.html. Accessed 25 November 2010.

Stepashin, S. (2008). Do we have to seal the retort? *Russian Politics and Law*, 46(5), 41.

Sukhov, O. (2013). Surkov return may signal softer Kremlin side. *Current Digest of the Post-Soviet Press*, 65(39), 14.

Surkov calls for Russia's intellectual development. (2006, 14 August). World News Connection.

Surkov condemns revolutions. (2007, 13 March). World News Connection.

Surkov's departure as paradigm shift. (2013). *Current Digest of the Post-Soviet Press*, 65(19), 3–5.

Surkov, V. (2006). Russian political culture: The view from utopia. *Russian Politics and Law*, 46(5), 10–26.

Surkov, V. (2011). *Texts 1997–2010*. Moscow: Publishing House Europe.

Taras, R. (2012). *Russia's identity in international relations: Images, perceptions, misperceptions*. London; New York: Routledge.

Transcript of Surkov speech to strategy 2020 forum. (2009). Retrieved 25 November 2010, from http://www.acg.ru/english/news2.phtml?m=4389.

Tretyakov, V. (2006, March 22). Putin chief strategist Surkov's statement on Russia's official ideology viewed. World News Connection.

Tsygankov, A. (2005). Vladimir Putin's vision of Russia as a normal great power. *Post-Soviet Affairs*, 21(2), 132–158.

Tsygankov, A. (2006). If not by tanks, then by banks? The role of soft power in Putin's foreign policy. *Europe-Asia Studies*, 58(7), 1079–1099.

Tsygankov, A. (2007). Finding a civilisational idea: 'West,' 'Eurasia' and 'Euro-East' in Russia's foreign policy. *Geopolitics*, 12(3), 375–399.

Tsygankov, A. (2012). Assessing cultural and regime-based explanations of Russia's foreign policy. 'Authoritarian at heart and expansionist by habit'? *Europe-Asia Studies*, 64(4), 695–713.

US Embassy. (March 17, 2014). FACT SHEET: Ukraine-related sanctions. Retrieved from http://london.usembassy.gov/europe176.html. Accessed on 21 June 2014.

van Apeldoorn, B., & de Graaff, N. (2012a). Corporate elite networks and US post-Cold War grand strategies from Clinton to Obama. *European Journal of International Relations*, 1–27.

van Apeldoorn, B., & de Graaff, N. (2012b). The limits of open door imperialism and the US state–capital nexus. *Globalizations*, 9(4): 593–608.

van der Pijl, K. (1998). *Transnational classes and international relations*. London; New York: Routledge.

Vasilyev, I. (2013). Against all but him. *Current Digest of the Post-Soviet Press*, 65(31), 12–13.

Vekelberg, Viktor. (2014). *Forbes*. Retrieved from http://www.forbes.com/profile/viktor-vekselberg. Accessed on 23 July 2014.

Vitebskaya, T., Livotkin, D., & Politov, Y. (2006, 14 November). Moscow daily views Kozak's, Surkov's Draft in GRU Spetsnaz. World News Connection.

Vladislav, Yureyvich Surkov. (n.d.) *Kremlin.ru*. Retrieved from http://archive.Kremlin.ru/eng/subj/22172.shtml# . Accessed 25 November 2010.

Vyacheslav, Volodin. (n.d.) *The Moscow Times*. Retrieved from www.themoscowtimes.com/people/article/vyacheslav-volodin/437827.html. Accessed 18 July 2014.

Walker, S. (2015). Escalation of fighting in east Ukraine leaves ceasefire teetering on the brink. *The Guardian*. Retrieved from http://www.theguardian.com/world/2015/jun/04/escalation-fighting-east-ukraine-leaves-ceasefire-tatters-russian-forces. Accessed 14 December 2015.

Weaver, C. & Clover, C. (2013). Political backlash blamed for woes at Russia's 'Silicon Valley.' *Financial Times*. Retrieved from www.ft.com/cms/s/0/a9d3bd90-c157-11e2-. Accessed July 22, 2014.

Yevgrafova, N. (2006, 22 December). Commentary challenges 'facts' presented in WSJ article on Putin aide Surkov. World News Connection.

Zakatnova, A. (2006a, 13 September). Putin staff deputy head questioned on sovereign democracy, xenophobia. World News Connection.

Zakatnova, A. (2006b, 17 July). Russia: national business forum views economics of sovereign democracy. World News Connection.

Ziegler, C. (2012). Conceptualizing sovereignty in Russian foreign policy: Realist and constructivist perspectives. *International Politics*, 49(4), 400–417.

8 Conclusion

The material and ideational bases of geopolitical and geocultural difference remain underexplored in critical international political economy. That they are dependent on capitalist relations of production is but one part of the story. It is my assertion that during the Putin era, we have witnessed the development or prolongation of powerful fault lines between the Russian state and the liberal unipolarity of the United States. The former has challenged the latter in spite of the fact that the Russian political economy is increasingly capitalist and integrated within structures of the capitalist global and/or regional political economy. In cultivating a rival vernacular to express dissatisfaction with the fundamental premises of liberal internationalism, Russian officials demonstrate that liberal capitalist 'concepts of control' have not become fully engrained amongst the Russian elite or society as a whole. This contributes to a tendency in which the Russian state remains set on articulating its *samobytnost'* or uniqueness. I view this phenomenon in the contours of a broad historical question: what are the various compatibilities and contradictions in Russia's prolonged integration into a capitalist global political economy after the fall of the Soviet Union? It is unsurprising that imperial nostalgia and ideas about Russian cultural or civilisational particularity that largely predate the contemporary period should resonate in the present age in spite of the fact that Russia's economy increasingly operates on market principles. Nonetheless, a political economy analysis must insist that such ideas are never entirely independent of the imperatives of political economy. Hence, we have seen these ideas reformulated and rearticulated by the Putin regime in order to foster legitimacy in Russian society and support national development imperatives.

In this work, I explored the material and ideational limits to liberal democratic universalism through the example of the Putin-era Russian state and its alternative understandings of world order. The Russian 'case' is significant to contemporary studies of world order, as the Russian state resists a strong version of the American hegemonic neo-liberal imperative and challenges the geographical spread of the Western bloc – i.e. through active stances against NATO expansion to Ukraine and Georgia. Russia's integration into the contemporary global political economy is one that involves considerable state direction and an unwillingness to wholeheartedly accept liberal-democratic precepts. Correspondingly, the Russian state has simultaneously rejected Western triumphalism by appealing to 'homegrown' ideas and cultural frames and seemingly felt compelled to demonstrate that it meets the criteria of a democratic polity in international society. State-produced Russian alternative understandings of world order are inflected with three qualities: 1) a defence of state power, loosely conceived; 2) a demonstration of the Russian state's ambiguous relationship with global capitalism, whereby a strong version of liberal democratic norms and unfettered markets are criticised as components of American hegemony; and 3) ideas and cultural frames which sanctify Russian national/civilisational values and practices. Such alternative understandings constitute a form of common-sense thinking about global affairs for the Putin regime that is comprised of a series of polysemic ideas that challenge American liberal democratic triumphalism while granting the Russian state sufficient latitude to determine its internal form of government. Nonetheless, such thinking also represents a considerable departure from the comprehensive counter-hegemonic, counter-systemic position of the Soviet Union.

State-sanctioned Russian alternative understandings of world order are comprised of intersubjectively held, or produced, ideas and beliefs that have accompanied political consolidation and socio-economic transition under Putin. Throughout this work I have used a critical historicist approach to accentuate how representations of intersubjectivity have been fostered amid the prolonged 'transitional' Russian political economy. Russian state officials and political technologists have produced a proliferation of concepts about world order that contribute to a desired common-sense thinking about global affairs that rivals liberal internationalism. That such concepts cohere into stable understandings of world order is not due to some straightforward calculation of 'power', a given typology of 'state society complex', or any unproblematic deductive understanding of world order. In recycling, conveying and producing ideas about world order, the Russian state engages in acts of persuasion, attempting to convince the Russian citizenry and the external world of the veracity of such concepts.

My point of departure for this work is to problematise any simplified correspondence between the semiotic and extra-semiotic in contingent and complex historical transitions. While a 'classical' historical materialist approach might be more concerned about the place of social forces in the process of production, I have focused my approach to understand the 'pedagogical' role of the Russian state as producer of concepts and ideas about world order. We can conceive of the Russian state as having an authoritative, bureaucratic, and coercive role in administering the Russian economic base and also articulating a palpable and palatable vision of national political and economic life. In addition to its role of organising the Russian economy along statist and capitalist principles, the Russian state, exemplified by the Putin regime, develops concepts and ideas that seek to render these moves intelligible according to longer Russian intellectual and cultural legacies and acceptable according to the dictates of common sense.

In focusing on the cultural and ideational aspects of state-sanctioned Russian alternative understandings of world order, I have sought to avoid viewing Russia's post-Soviet incorporation into the capitalist global political economy as merely the extension of capitalist relations from the core into a previously outlying space. To augment materialist conceptions of world order and global capitalism, I have demonstrated how the Putin regime developed and utilised notions of culture – understood as purported tendencies, shared intersubjective meanings, and familiar frames derived from Russian historical experience – as a means of rendering political decisions intelligible and acceptable. To some, this might signal an unwarranted degree of instrumentalism, whereby culture is the handmaiden of political authority and exploited to realise political and economic objectives. The ideas that animate our collective political and economic life may in fact go all the way down, as constructivists argue; however, this portrayal is incomplete. In their coercive and consensual roles, states employ ideas to serve a number of strategic objectives, one of which being to constantly create and recreate social legitimacy. In the context of late twentieth-century and early twenty-first-century encounters with capitalist globality, any reassertion of national or civilisational autonomy by those deemed historically on the semi-periphery or periphery enjoys a certain amount of political and social traction. Emerging from the communist period, Russian state actors have been active in producing norms and ideas about Russia's domestic and international life, drawing on particular Russian traditions, which are then packaged and repackaged to suit present objectives. While I argue that Russian cultural content infuses alternative Russian understandings of world order in the contemporary age, I reject a deterministic reading of culture which holds that Putin somehow exemplifies a quintessentially Russian form of political practice.

With this work, I have sought to contribute to debates about world order through an analysis of the ideological limits of liberal internationalism in Putin-era Russia, which demonstrates to us the failure of an easy transmission of the ideas associated with a Western-inspired liberal democracy. This is partly due to the historical association of liberal democracy with state implosion and social disorder in the 1990s in Russia. It is partly due to geopolitical concerns. Regardless of liberalism's normative connotations, it is clear that the tradition represents something more than benign ideas insofar as it is implicated in geopolitical and geoeconomic imperatives. Components of the world order articulated by the 'official' Russia reflect a perceived need to offer a vision of Russia in the world which captures Russia's reputed uniqueness and reflects a wealthier, more assertive and 'sovereign' Russia than was evident in the immediate post-Soviet period. It is a state that is more and more capable of challenging the march of the American-led Western bloc to the East while nonetheless adapting to the exigencies of a capitalist global political economy. In Russia, the uncontested adoption of Western liberal ideology deemed to correspond with American liberal hegemony did not occur as those seeking Russian polyarchy may have liked: the Putin regime has developed – tacitly and explicitly – a particularly Russian 'filter' to shape understandings of global political life and Russia's place within it. In addition to reflecting material conflicts surrounding economic competition and military threats, Russian understandings of world order display a thoroughly intersubjective or ideational component, whereby global political life is translated through shared understandings of moral appropriateness, legitimacy, and manageability. Such understandings are not mere cultural archetypes consistently and perennially manifested in political practice; rather, they are animated and re-directed to articulate regime imperatives and enlist social, political, and economic forces, at 'home' and 'abroad' that are at most hostile and at least lukewarm towards American stewardship. Indeed, for all of the ideational variance of the longer Putin era, the emerging constant is the capacity to generate cynicism towards American global systems management and governance according to multiple lines of argumentation.

I attempted here to offer an empirical and theoretical demonstration of broad material parameters of Russia's post-communist transition, its position in world order, including its resurgence under Putin and limits to this resurgence, as well as Putin's consolidation of authority. The building of a market economy in Russia has been accompanied by 'political variables' pertaining to social cohesion and state capacity. The Russian case suggests that state capitalism is not entirely incompatible with broad market imperatives, if we take state capitalism to mean providing the environment in which market mechanisms take root in some form. In the Putin era, the consolidation of market society has been coupled with state contributions to a normative order which, while inviting a celebration of geocultural difference, act within a paradigm for social, economic, and political management that is far more 'capital-friendly' than that witnessed in the counterhegemonic project of the Soviet Union. Russian officials have rejected many of the precepts of contemporary world order seeking to replace American, liberal-democratic ideas with those derived from Russian history and philosophy, especially those which emphasise autonomy, sovereignty, and Russia's inherent right to determine national development priorities and practices. Nonetheless, one should critically scrutinise the extent to which such priorities fundamentally challenge the capitalist organisation of the Russian economy.

The major concepts around which the substantive chapters develop – Eurasianism, multipolarity, civilisationalism, and sovereign democracy – are treated ambiguously within the discourse of academics and Russian officials alike. Insofar as they are animated by any political imperative, they contribute to a form of common sense cultivated by Russian officials and are frequently presented in a manner in which their meaning is taken for granted but never fully articulated. These concepts are buried in the text of official Russian state documents and feature prominently in press releases and sound bites offered by Russian officials. Taken together, they comprise a flexible vision of world order in line with Russian aspirations for renewed significance and authority in global affairs. A demonstration of difference from 'Western', if not

'American' ways is but one aspect of this phenomenon, and such an articulation of difference constitutes a decisive wedge by which culture and civilisation are rendered geopolitical and geoeconomic affairs.

While the concepts I have chosen are ambiguous and contested, I have imposed a certain unity on them for analytical purposes. They follow from my intention to demonstrate their polysemic quality, in that they offer some degree of coherence for analytical purposes while allowing for numerous common-sense interpretations. Eurasianism and multipolarity have been considered in this work as broad expressions of Russia's geopolitical protest against American hegemony and unipolarity. The Putin regime has activated classical and contemporary Eurasianism's deep reservations about the moral, ethical, and cultural legitimacy of Western and American hegemony. Multipolarity has been treated in this work broadly as the Russian alternative to American unipolarity and a system comprised of multiple authoritative decision-making centres. This is consistent with the Putin regime's general treatment of the notion. However, multipolarity also exhibits a wide array of objective and subjective, existing and potential qualities. Of all of the central concepts, sovereign democracy has proven to be the most ambiguous. While also reflecting national development imperatives, sovereign democracy has been treated by Surkov and the Putin regime as a synthesis of multiple concepts: a master signifier for articulating Russia's right to autonomy in global affairs; a way of valorising the cultural basis of national political practices; and a way of redirecting Russia's purported cultural tendencies to more productive and industrious ends.

I have demonstrated how certain Russian thinkers have perceived Russia's civilisational difference from the West, beginning with the 'classic' Eurasianism of the 1920s to the contemporary age. While Eurasianism constitutes a comprehensive, philosophical, cultural, social and, at times, religious doctrine on geographical difference, it resonates in different ways in the post-communist period. On the one hand, it remains a key concept for expressing Russia's civilisational difference with the West and signals the country's unwillingness or inability to seamlessly integrate into an American-led world order. In contemporary parlance, Eurasianism also signifies a commitment to a continental orientation in foreign policy, a turn away from the West and a Russia that serves an integrative if not hegemonic function on the Eurasian continent. While Putin cannot be considered a Eurasianist in the robust meaning of the word, the civilisational thinking of Eurasianists continues to colour Russian state discourse and provides Russian officials with a readymade discourse to valorise Russian difference and express dissatisfaction with Western liberal triumphalism. Eurasianism resonates in contemporary Russian state thinking insofar as geopolitical difference remains portrayed as a matter of cultural and moral concern.

I have also sought to spell out Russia's self-assessed geopolitical position within world order through a theoretical and empirical demonstration of the concept of multipolarity. Multipolarity is a concept whose significance in academic literature and in Russian state discourse is well established. The

Putin regime has attempted to construct a multipolar world order and sought to redefine world order in multipolar terms. The significance of multipolarity lies in its emergence as a new form of common-sense thinking to rival liberal internationalism. The Russian state's treatment of the term reflects its ambiguous status: multipolarity is purported to reflect both an objective state of affairs resulting from the global redistribution of wealth away from the capitalist core and a project that the Russian state would like to implement through its actions and constant advocacy.

Multipolarity has been accorded great significance by Russian politicians, Russian scholars, and Western scholars alike. In this work, I have emphasised that multipolarity is less interesting as an abstract or measurable concept and more interesting as that which has been utilised by Russian officials to somehow capture or exemplify a desired conception of world order. Geopolitics may have at its basis material calculations of power and influence, but such ideas are conveyed with a sense of moral purpose and in a form that is palatable to a wider audience, as the usage of the concept of multipolarity demonstrates. Advocating for a democratic multipolarity enables Russian officials to embed a common-sense thinking about global affairs and the natural state of affairs that is to succeed American unipolarity. It is at once an emerging, objective condition, a moral imperative, and a project to be implemented to ensure global security and governability. The cultural correlate to a multipolar world – that is, that which a multipolar world order protects and sanctifies – is the notion of cultural and civilisational diversity. In a manner similar to past and present Eurasianist scholars, the Russian state expresses geopolitical concerns through the language of civilisation, morality, and culture.

A multipolar, if not multicivilisational, world order is the external condition that serves as a correlate to Russia's pursuit of sovereign democracy and sovereign development. Multipolarity may be considered as the international principle foregrounded by the Russian state so as to preserve the integrity of the sovereign democracy paradigm on a global level. Furthermore, for the Russian state, sovereign democracy represents a need to pursue and speak about a multipolar world order in which sovereign states need not follow the dictates of the American hegemon, instead pursuing their own purportedly culturally and historically appropriate model of development.

It may appear to some that for a work that acknowledges the significance of a broadly conceived historical materialist scholarship, this book lacks a robust and consistent Marxist lexicon. There are good reasons for this. I have conceived of this work not as Marxist but offering a Coxian-inspired critical historicist orientation. I have sought to develop a strand in the Coxian tradition that is more overtly concerned with intersubjective ideas and civilisations. While I would refrain from calling my approach historical idealism (Germain, 2007), I nonetheless acknowledge that human consciousness is not reducible to material, economic bases but instead intertwined with material structures in complex, sometimes contradictory, and historically contingent ways. Focusing on ideas that have direct 'world order significance' has precluded me from probing deeper into the relationship between Russian state and society. Furthermore, such a focus has precluded me from exploring further the role of social forces in Russian society and what I assume to be their complex and contradictory relations with the Russian state. While I engage with neo-Gramscian scholarship here, I depart from a full deployment of the neo-Gramscian understanding of state as political plus civil society. I have referred to the Russian state largely as political authority, headed by the president and comprised of those supportive of his declared vision of Russia in world order. The move is done out of methodological necessity amid a circumscribed problem field. For the sake of this work, I am primarily curious about the role that the Russian state has played as a socialising force, and how it has sought to manufacture stability and consent in a period of profound social, economic, and political transformations. Full treatment of the idea of 'state–society complex' would have necessitated an exploration, in greater detail, of the relationships between this Russian political state and the vast complex of civil society institutions, economic elites, the Russian Orthodox Church, think tanks, technocratic experts, bureaucratic fractions, and the media, but such a project is more ambitious than the present one.

I have provided what is to my mind only a broad sketch of the material parameters of the Russian political economy's position within the contemporary global political economy. I have portrayed Russian statism partly as a defensive response to prevent Russia from occupying an inferior position within the international division of labour. Consistent with its strategy of multipolarity, Russia will likely continue to politicise the BRICS framework as a means to press for greater inclusion in global political decision and mute criticism of its internal political order (Roberts, 2010). This depiction, however, does not do full justice to the role of foreign capital in Russia, the place of Russian capital internationally, or the complex relationship between Russian capitalists and state officials (on the latter point, see Dzarasov, 2013). An investigation into national and international bases of accumulation for 'Russian' capital is needed to augment the line of inquiry undertaken in this work. Furthermore, an extended analysis of the contradictions within Russia's modernisation debate from 2009 to the present would be a useful undertaking. Extending all of these lines of inquiry would be helpful to further elaborate on Russia's material position in world order and the contradictions within the Russian social formation. Such an analysis would complement and possibly challenge prevailing interpretations on 'official' Russia's position in foreign policy matters.

Ultimately, this work has been animated by the epistemological question about how one might study that of which one is not a part. Meaning and significance are not transparently transmitted to one standing outside of linguistic, political, and historical boundaries. A related question might be, 'What is culture?' I acknowledge that in this work, culture is analysed largely from an instrumentalist perspective, as that which is mobilised by various political and economic forces in the context of larger geopolitical and geoeconomic projects. This is a methodological choice as opposed to a strong ontological statement. Indeed, culture is constituted by material and symbolic practices, but it encompasses an emotive and existential dimension not readily disclosed to academic study. Standing outside of the historical processes on which we comment, and incapable of living corresponding 'culture' as such, we are largely confined to the analysis of representations, as they provide an accessible meta-political reality and content that structures and mediates our understanding of historically and geographically distant processes.

In such an environment, the task for the critical scholar of IPE is to acknowledge the veracity of cultural difference in the context of the limits of intelligibility. To do so means to avoid the latent, but still seductive, trap of colonial mentalities, whereby undesirable (geo)political outcomes are ascribed to archetypical behaviour that deviates from prescribed international norms. The danger remains, however, that the acknowledgement of difference then becomes ossified, irreconcilable, and prone to an intractable geopoliticisation whereby difference is enlisted in the service of territorial exclusivity. An additional task for the critical scholar here may be to resist the geopolitisation of one's own thought: the temptation of both presuming a geopolitical basis for cultural conduct and amplifying cultural difference to the level of geopolitical significance.

The 'case' of Putin-era Russia is challenging to apprehend, precisely because post-Soviet Russia has been painted into a discursive and ethical corner by actors and structures associated with a world order that still bares the imprint of American global stewardship, if not unilateralism, neo-liberal capitalist norms, and corresponding polyarchic practices. In such an environment, that Russian exceptionalism and difference has been willingly cultivated by Russian officials and political technologists should not surprise us. Such difference has been articulated at the level of the cultural and civilisational as precisely the time in which capitalist practices, if of a 'statist' nature at times, have been entrenched in the country.

As I have stressed in this book, an astute historicism emphasises that the ideational and material practices associated with capitalist consolidation need not directly coincide, and they certainly will not manifest in a manner representative of historical Anglo-American experiences and corresponding scholarship and 'problem solving'. In the context of geopolitical and geoeconomic competition, such economic practices may appear as 'developmental' or 'appropriating' in nature; regardless, the (semi)peripheral state becomes an object which, by its material or symbolic actions, resists the straightforward adoption of capitalist norms whilst nonetheless being implicated in transnational capitalist practices.

Finally, in this work, I have focused on a handful of world order concepts generated in Russia that have a degree of purchase with a non-(nationally) Russian audience. It is not a book about Russian nationalism for the sake of Russian consumption, and, hence, I have avoided many debates and much scholarship associated with the notion. The work is about that which sustains

Russian-centred regional or larger international projects beyond a specifically national base. Concepts of control deployed by those with aspirations to global hegemony must appeal to a broader audience with an articulated general interest. So too must those emanating from Russia, and Russian state organs have to offer something beyond naked self-interest when articulating a vision for broader national, regional or international consumption, to enlist allies, and counter American 'semiotic' and 'extra-semiotic' practices. For some time, I have suspected that having long abandoned Soviet-style counterhegemonic practices and socio-economic offerings, the greatest soft-power at the disposal of an increasingly capitalist Russia is to be found in distarticulating the political, popular and scholarly claims of the American project. Having completed this book, I agree with this assessment.

References

Dzarasov, R. (2013). *The conundrum of Russian capitalism: The post-Soviet economy in the world system*. London: Pluto Pr.

Germain, R. (2007). 'Critical' political economy, historical materialism and Adam Morton. *Politics*, 27(2), 127–131.

Roberts, C. (2010). Russia's BRICs diplomacy: Rising outsider with dreams of an insider. *Polity*, 42(1), 38–73.

Appendix

Table A.1 Russian GDP growth (percentage)

	1999	*2000*	*2001*	*2002*	*2003*	*2004*
Volume	6.4	10.0	5.1	4.7	7.3	7.2
Per Capita	6.7	10.5	5.5	5.2	7.8	7.6
	2005	*2006*	*2007*	*2008*	*2009*	
Volume	6.4	8.2	8.5	5.2	-7.8	
Per Capita	6.8	8.5	8.7	5.3	-7.8	
	2010	*2011*	*2012*	*2013*	*2014*	
Volume	4.5	4.3	3.4	1.3	0.6	
Per Capita	4.5	4.2	3.2	1.1	-1.1	

'Volume' source: http://stats.oecd.org/Index.aspx?DatasetCode=SNA_Table1#.
'Per capita' source: http://data.worldbank.org/indicator/NY.GDP.PCAP.KD.ZG?page=3 (accessed 11 November 2015).

Table A.2 Russian central government debt, as percentage of GDP

2001	*2002*	*2003*	*2004*	*2005*	*2006*	*2007*	*2008*	*2009*	*2010*	*2011*	*2012*
49.0	41.4	–	–	16.7	9.9	7.2	6.5	8.7	9.1	9.3	9.4

Source: http://data.worldbank.org/indicator/GC.DOD.TOTL.GD.ZS?page=1 (accessed 10 December 2015).

Table A.3 Russian current account surplus and reserves, in current US dollars (billions)

	2003	*2004*	*2005*	*2006*	*2007*	*2008*	*2009*	*2010*	*2011*	*2012*	*2013*	*2014*
Current Account Surplus	35.4	58.6	84.4	92.3	72.2	103.9	**50.4**	67.5	97.3	71.3	34.8	58.4
Reserves (Including gold)	78.4	126.3	182.3	303.7	478.8	426.3	**439.3**	479.2	497.4	537.8	509.7	386.2

'Current Account Surplus' source for 2003–2004: Derived from World Bank, 2008, p. 3; and for 2005–2014: http://data.worldbank.org/indicator/BN.CAB.XOKA.CD/countries?page=2 (accessed 10 December 2015).
'Reserves' source for 2003–2014: http://data.worldbank.org/indicator/FI.RES.TOTL.CD (accessed 10 December 2015).

Table A.4 Gross domestic product per capita, in current US Dollars, select years

Country	*1990*	*1999*	*2000*	*2008*	*2009*	*2010*	*2013*
Russia	3485 (Soviet Union)	1331	1772	11635	8563	10675	14487
United States of America	23954	34621	36450	48401	47002	48374	52630
China	316	870	955	3441	3801	4515	7594
Brazil	3087	3499	3766	8837	8603	11318	11613

Source: Derived from http://data.worldbank.org/indicator/NY.GDP.PCAP.CD (accessed 27 July 2015).

Table A.5 Gini Index (0 = perfect equality; 100 = perfect inequality); select years

Country	*1993*	*1998*	*1999*	*2003*	*2008*
Russia	48.4	N/A	37.4	38.3	34.1
United States of America	38.9 (in 1994)	N/A	40.2 (in 2000)	40.6 (in 2004)	41.6 (in 2007)
China	35.5	N/A	58.7	N/A	42.6
Brazil	60.1	59.6	59	58	54.4

Source: Derived from http://data.worldbank.org/indicator/SI.POV.GINI (accessed 27 July 2015).

Table A.6 Outward foreign direct investment, percentage of world total, select years

Country	*1994*	*1999*	*2004*	*2009*	*2013*
Russia	0.1	0.2	1.5	3.7	6.7
United States of America	25.5	19.2	32.1	24.6	24.0
China	0.70	0.2	0.6	4.8	7.2

Source: Derived from http://unctad.org/en/Pages/DIAE/FDI%20Statistics/FDI-Statistics.aspx (accessed 29 June 2015).

Table A.7 Inward foreign direct investment, percentage of world total, select years

Country	*1994*	*1999*	*2004*	*2009*	*2013*
Russia	0.3	0.4	2.1	3.0	5.5
United States of America	17.6	25.9	18.4	11.8	12.9
China	13.2	3.7	8.2	7.8	8.5

Source: Derived from http://unctad.org/en/Pages/DIAE/FDI%20Statistics/FDI-Statistics.aspx (accessed 29 June 2015).

Table A.8 Commodity structure of exports of the Russian Federation, percentage of total

	2000	*2008*	*2013*
Mineral products	53.8	69.8	71.6
Metals, precious stones, articles thereof	21.7	13.2	10.5
Food stuffs and agricultural raw materials	1.6	2.0	3.1
Wood, pulp and paper products	4.3	2.5	2.1
Chemical products, rubber	7.2	6.4	5.8
Machinery, equipment, transport means	8.8	4.9	5.4

Source: http://www.gks.ru/wps/wcm/connect/rosstat_main/rosstat/en/figures/activities/ (accessed 12 August 2015).

Table A.9 Ease of doing business rankings

	2005	*2006*	*2007*	*2008*	*2009*	*2010*	*2011*	*2012*	*2013*	*2014*
Russia	79	96	106	120	120	123	120	112	92	62
USA	3	3	3	3	4	5	4	4	4	7
China	91	93	83	83	89	79	91	91	96	90
Brazil	119	121	122	125	129	127	126	130	116	120

Source: www.doingbusiness.org (accessed 12 August 2015).

Table A.10 Number of people employed in the Russian economy by ownership type (measured by the thousands)

	1992	*2000*	*2005*	*2010*	*2013*
State, municipal	49660	24371	22499	21097	19221
Private	13887	29773	36178	39014	40684
Public and Religious Organizations	583	526	382	319	307
Mixed Russia	7580	8114	5202	3880	4020
Foreign, Joint Russian and Foreign	195	1730	2531	3227	3553

Source: http://www.gks.ru//bgd/regl/b14_12/IssWWW.exe/stg/d01/06-03.htm (accessed 10 December 2015).

Table A.11 Percentage of people employed in the Russian economy by ownership type

	1992	*2000*	*2005*	*2010*	*2013*
State, municipal	69.1	37.8	33.7	30.4	28.4
Private	19.3	46.1	54.1	58.6	60
Public and Religious Organizations	0.8	0.8	0.6	0.5	0.5
Mixed Russia	10.5	12.6	7.8	5.7	5.9
Foreign, Joint Russian and Foreign	0.3	2.7	3.8	4.8	5.2

Source: http://www.gks.ru//bgd/regl/b14_12/IssWWW.exe/stg/d01/06-03.htm (accessed 10 December 2015).

Index

Note: numbers in bold refer to tables

2000 National Security Concept 88
2007–2008 financial crisis 66, 82, 92
2008 Foreign Policy Concept of the Russian Federation 14–15, 91, 109–10
2008 Review of Foreign Policy of the Russian Federation 98
2013 Foreign Policy Concept of the Russian Federation 93, 109–10

Akayev, Askar 93n3
Amsterdam School 2
ASEAN (Association of Southeast Asian Nations) 90
'Atlanticism' 122–3, 131–2, 141

Belarus 112–13, 135
Beslan 64
Bolshevism 105, 118n1
BRIC(S) 15–6, 40, 67, 69, 80, 82, 86, 90, 93, 177
Brzezinski, Zbigniew 33, 137
bureaucracy 2, 52, 58–9
Bush, George W. 88

Caesarism 57, 63
Cambridge School of Historians 25
capitalism 22–3, 26, 32, 39–40, 43; *and* Russia 18, 34–7, 42, 45, 52–63, 68–9, 71–2, 83, 103, 111, 117, 149–52, 158–9, 172–4, 178; state-directed 17, 33, 37, 54, 149, 152
Carr, E. H. 25
China 26, 67, 86–7, 90, **181–2**; Bishkek Declaration 86; Chinese–Russian declarations 86–7; Russian–Chinese relations 82, 86–7; *see also* BRIC
civilisation 34, 36–7, 42, 84–6, 100–2, 105–9, 113, 117–8, 132–3
civilisationalism 2, 14–15, 30, 34, 53, 85–6, 90–1, 93, 100–5, 115, 117, 123, 136, 141–2, 172–3, 175, 178; 'embedded civilisationalism' 17, 101, 109–11, 116–17, 138
class 27–8, 30–2, 34, 36, 56–7, 60, 103, 106, 152; *see also* transnational capitalist class
Cold War 33, 135, 137; post-Cold War 33, 42, 100, 102, 117, 129–30
Collective Security Treaty Organisation (CSTO) 86, 90
common sense 13–16, 32–8, 45, 84, 130, 135, 152, 172, 174
Commonwealth of Independent States (CIS) 15, 113–14
Commonwealth of Independent States Free Trade Agreement (CISFTA) 113
comparativism 6, 55, 63
'Concept 2020' 69–71, 156
'concepts of control' 5, 8, 41, 103, 171, 179
configurative-ideographic case studies 6
'conservative revolution' 128
'conspirology' 127
constructivism 30, 36, 150–1, 155
Cox, Robert 10, 12–13, 21–4, 27–8, 38–43, 176
CPRF 124, 126, 133–4, 143n12
Crimea 136, 138, 148, 163
Critical Theory 23
Cultural Political Economy (CPE) 5, 21–2, 27, 29–32
culture 26–8, 34–5, 42, 44–5, 46n10, 83–4, 91, 100–11, 117–18, 149–52, 154, 158–60, 164, 172–8; difference 85–6, 105, 139, 141, 160; production

of 2–3, 7, 37–8, 114–15, 152, 156; *see also* Cultural Political Economy, Culturology
'Culturology' 149–50
Current Digest of the Russian Press 12
Customs Union (CU) 113

Danilevsky, Nikolai 105
derzhavnik 63
derzhavnost 150
'development state' model 56
Dobrolyubov, Nikolai 104
Dostoyevsky, Fyodor 104
'dual state' 62
Dubovitsky, Nathan 161, 163
Dugin, Aleksandr 17, 106, 108, 122–42; *see also* Eurasianism, multipolarity

ethnos 106–7; superethnos 107
Eurasian Economic Community (EurAsEC) 86, 113
Eurasian Economic Union (EEU) 5, 111, 113, 138
Eurasian Economic Union Treaty 85, 112
Eurasian Union (EaU) 85, 112–14, 116
Eurasianism 17, 26–7, 38, 70, 85–6, 100–18, 122–3, 125–7, 129–39, 142, 175; *and* Dugin 122–3, 125–7, 130–9, 141–2; 'International Eurasianist Movement' 125–6, 137; 'pragmatic Eurasianism' 85, 101, 108–9, 129
Evraziia 125, 131
extra-semiotic *see* semiotic

finance 60, 65–8; international 59, 70–1; neo-liberal 82; *see also* international financial institutions
Florovsky, Georgy Vasileyvich 104
foreign direct investment (FDI) 60, 63, 66–7, 156
Foundations of Geopolitics 130, 136

Gazprom 18n3, 66, 87
Geertz, Clifford 9
geoeconomic/geopolitical 5, 33, 45, 100, 108–9, 178; geoeconomic belts 131
Gini Coefficient 66, **181**
globalisation 33, 35–6, 40–2, 53, 56–7, 69, 72, 90–2, 93n1, 100–1, 103, 108–9, 139; 'globalisation debates' 81–3
Gogol, Nikolai 104
Gramsci 13, 15, 27, 33, 36, 47n18, 84, 152; neo-Gramscian 21, 23, 27, 30, 33, 35, 43, 57, 63; *see also* common sense
Gryzlov, Boris 64, 162
Gumilyov, Lev 104, 106–7, 110–11, 129

Haushofer, Karl 127, 133, 135
Hegemonic Stability Theory 37, 84, 87
hegemony 13, 22, 26, 35–6, 39, 41, 103, 152, 154; American 9, 13, 16, 33, 35, 37, 41–5, 53, 56, 87–8, 93, 101–3, 116–18, 131, 133–4, 152, 171–2, 175–6; *and* Gramsci 33, 35, 43, 57, 63; *and* Russia 34–5, 57–8, 63, 83, 101, 103, 106, 108, 111, 130, 133, 140, 173–5, 179
heuristic case studies 6
historical knowledge 24–5, 29; knowledge production 26, 114, 138
historical materialism 22–3, 25–6, 28, 40, 46n3, 172
historical structures 27–8, 32, 41
historicism 2, 6, 24–9, 32, 43, 81, 102, 123–4, 178; critical 6–7, 22, 24, 28; historicist IPE 6–7, 23–4
Hobbesian contender states 43, 45
Hu Jintao 87

international financial institutions (IFIs) 54, 57–8, 72, 87
International Political Economy (IPE) 2, 4–7, 23–4, 26, 32, 37, 81–4, 178; critical IPE 27, 38, 43–4; *see also* historicist IPE
International Relations (IR) 12, 15, 25, 80, 88, 90–2, 100, 110, 123
internationalisation 38–41, 72
intersubjectivity 2, 4–5, 21–2, 27–32, 36, 42–4, 102, 172–4
intrinsic case studies 6
Ivanov, Igor 88
Izborski Club 115

Karaganov, Sergei 114–15
Kazakhstan 112–13, 125
Kennan, George 33
Keohane, Robert 23
Khodorkovsky, Mikhail 58, 62, 66
Kozyrev, Andrei 86, 109
Kremlin 10, 15–17, 18n3, 34, 54, 62, 64, 115, 137, 153–5, 164; Kremlinology 10
Kyrgyzstan 112–13

Lancaster School of Political Economy 29
Lavrov, Sergei 35, 90–2, 114, 116–17
LDPR 126, 133–4
League of Arab States 90
liberal internationalism 2–3, 22, 38, 42, 82, 86, 102–3, 138, 151–2, 171–3
loans for shares programme 62
Lockean heartland 43, 45
Lukashenko, Aleksandr 85, 112
Lukin, Aleksandr 112
Lukoil 66

Mackinder, Halford 127–8, 135, 137
Marxism 23–4, 31, 46n3, 46n8, 124, 134, 149, 176
May Decrees 71
Medvedev, Dmitri 5, 18n3, 36, 69, 112, 156, 160
MERCOSUR 90
methodological nationalism 3
methodology 6, 9, 11, 177–8; *in* IPE scholarship 23–5
Mikhaylovsky, N.K. 105
Milosevic, Slobodan 86
Moldova 113
Mongol Golden Horde 110
Moscow State Institute of International Relations (MGIMO-University) 112
multipolar global political economy 21, 26–7, 37
multipolarity 37–8, 80–93, 108, 116–17, 174–7; *and* Dugin 138–40; *and* Lavrov 83, 90–2; *and* Primakov 83, 85–6, 91; *and* Putin 10, 65, 80, 83, 86–8, 90–2, 175; *and* Surkov 84, 152, 154
'Munich Speech' 91–2, 117

National Bolshevik Party (NBP) 124
NATO 41, 86, 171
Nazarbayev, Nursultan 85, 112, 114
neo-liberalism 33–4, 36, 41–2, 53, 56–8, 64, 81–2, 103, 151
neo-patrimonial state 61–2
nomenklatura system 58

Orange Revolution 93n3, 154
'organic intellectuals' 16, 33–4, 58, 122, 136, 142, 149, 152, n164
Organisation for Economic Co-operation and Development (OECD) 67

Panarin, Aleksandr 106–8
passionarnost' 106
pax Americana 13, 41
pax Britannica 13, 41
Peter the Great 105; reforms 105, 158
Pisarev, Dmitri 104
Pobedonostev, Constantine 104
'political technologists' 8, 34–5, 38, 84, 101–3, 109, 111, 117, 152, 155–6, 164, 172, 178
polyarchy 34, 37, 54, 56, 73n4, 102–3, 118, 173, 178
polysemicity 13–14, 32–5, 38, 45, 84, 90, 102, 153–4, 172, 175; *and* Eurasianism 123, 130, 141
positivism 6, 23–25, 29, 46n5, 142n7; post-positivism 23, 25
praxis 27
Primakov Doctrine 86
Primakov, Yevgeni 35, 69, 85–6, 91, 109, 114, 126, 135
Prince Nikolay Sergeevich Trubetskoy 104
Putin, Vladimir 5, 14, 35–7, 56–8, 61–72, 80, 86–92, 104, 110–17, 125, 137, 140, 151, 174; Putin era 1, 9, 14, 22, 26, 41, 53, 56–8, 61–72, 88, 92, 103, 117, 149–53, 161, 171–4, 178; regime 41, 45, 53–4, 62, 65, 68, 106, 108, 117, 152–6, 164, 171–6

Radio Free Europe and Radio Liberty 12
reflexivity 11, 24, 26, 47n18
reiderstvo 62
Republic of Tatarstan 110
Reserve Fund 65
Revealed Comparative Advantage (RCA) 67
Robinson, William 2, 39–40
Rodina 125
Rose Revolution 93n3
Rosneft 18n3, 66
Russia: economic modernisation 69–71, 113, 157, 161; Federation Council 64; foreign policy 8, 26, 69, 81–2, 85, 87–8, 109, 117, 130, 150, 175, 177; 'modernisation' 53–4, 70–1, 84, 156, 161, 164; Russian state 2, 8–9, 26–7, 34–8, 40–2, 52–7, 61–3, 100–3, 109–10, 114–15, 171–2, 177
Russian Orthodoxy 107–9, 113, 115, 136, 153
Russian Public Opinion Research Center (VCIOM) 155
Russian Studies 10, 12, 55, 149

Saakashvili, Mikhail 93n3
Sachs, Jeffrey 58
samobytnost' 1, 37, 171
Savitsky, Pyotr Nikolaevich 104
schools of democracy theory 55; 'consolidologist' 55; 'orthodox' 55; 'transitologist' 55
semiotic 1, 21–2, 27, 29–30, 35, 45, 101–2, 151, 172, 179
Shanghai Cooperation Organisation (SCO) 85–6, 112
Shevardnadze, Eduard 93n3
Skolkovo Innovation Complex 148–9, 160–1
Slavic 17, 27, 105, 108, 125, 129, 135–6
Slavophiles 104
social forces 9, 13, 22, 26, 39, 41–2; transnational 39, 42
Solovyev, Vladimir 104, 133, 135, 143n13
sovereignty 3, 15, 18, 34, 40–1, 53, 65, 85, 90, 117, 151; sovereign democracy 108, 154–60, 175–6
Soviet Union (USSR) 3, 30, 33, 44, 103, 111, 113, 126–9, 135–6, 160, 172, 174; transition from 34, 43, 52–61, 66–9, 71, 140, 171
stabilisation fund 65
state project 1, 4, 14, 26, 30–1, 35–7, 102, 122
state-society complex 13, 38–9, 42–4, 177
Surgutneftgaz 66
Surkov, Vladislav 17, 35, 84, 111, 114, 148–64, 175
Suvchinsky, Pyotr Petrovich 104
Syria 5

Tajikistan 112–13
transnational capitalist class (TCC) 40
transnationalisation 38–41, 60
Tulip Revolution 93n3
Tyumen Oil Company-British Petroleum (TNK-BP) 66

Ukraine: *and* competition between Russia and West 5, 87, 100, 141, 143n14; Crimean dispute 137, 149, 163; *and* Eurasian Union 112–13; *and* NATO 41, 171; Slavic Union 135
unipolarity 34–5, 37, 44, 82–6, 89, 91–2, 93n1, 117, 139, 175–6
United Russia 64, 113, 153–4, 157, 162

Valdai International Discussion Club 115, 138, 162
Vekselberg, Viktor 161
Volodin, Vyacheslav 162
Voronin, Vladimir 112

World Bank's 'Ease of Doing Business' rankings 69, 71, **182**
World News Connection 12
world order 4, 12–13, 102, 178; *in* critical IPE 23, 38, 41–3; Russian understandings *of* 1–4, 8, 35, 37–8, 44, 53, 80, 84–7, 92, 102–3, 106, 108, 131, 133–4, 138, 151, 157, 172–6; 'world order concepts' 18
World Trade Organisation (WTO) 65, 67–8, 81

Yanukovych, Viktor 93n3, 112
Yeltsin 54, 57–8, 61–2, 72, 86–8, 124, 133, 150
Yukos 58, 62
Yushchenko, Viktor 93n3

zapadnik 63
Zhirinovsky, Vladimir 133
Zyuganov, Gennady 133–4